BAUHAUS WEAVING THEORY

AF400655

BAUHAUS WEAVING THEORY

FROM FEMININE CRAFT TO MODE OF DESIGN

T'ai Smith

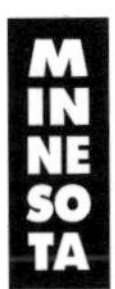

University of Minnesota Press

Minneapolis

London

Publication of this book has been aided by a grant from the Millard Meiss Publication Fund of the College Art Association. MM

An earlier version of chapter 3 was published as "Limits of the Tactile and the Optical: Bauhaus Fabric in the Frame of Photography," *Grey Room* 25 (Fall 2006): 6–31. An earlier version of chapter 4 was published as "Anonymous Textiles, Patented Domains: The Invention (and Death) of an Author," *Art Journal* 67, no. 2 (Summer 2008): 54–73.

Published by the University of Minnesota Press
111 Third Avenue South, Suite 290
Minneapolis, MN 55401–2520
http://www.upress.umn.edu

Library of Congress Cataloging-in-Publication Data
Smith, T'ai.
   Bauhaus weaving theory : from feminine craft to mode of design / T'ai Smith.
   Includes bibliographical references and index.
   ISBN 978-0-8166-8723-7 (hc) — ISBN 978-0-8166-8724-4 (pb)
   1. Textile design—Germany—History—20th century. 2. Weaving—Germany—History—20th century. 3. Women textile designers—Germany. 4. Bauhaus. 5. Modernism (Art). 6. Art and craft debate. I. Title.
   NK8998.B38S65 2014 746.0943—dc23
   2014028046

Printed in the United States of America on acid-free paper

The University of Minnesota is an equal-opportunity educator and employer.

30   29   28   27   26   25   24   23   10 9   8   7   6   5   4   3   2

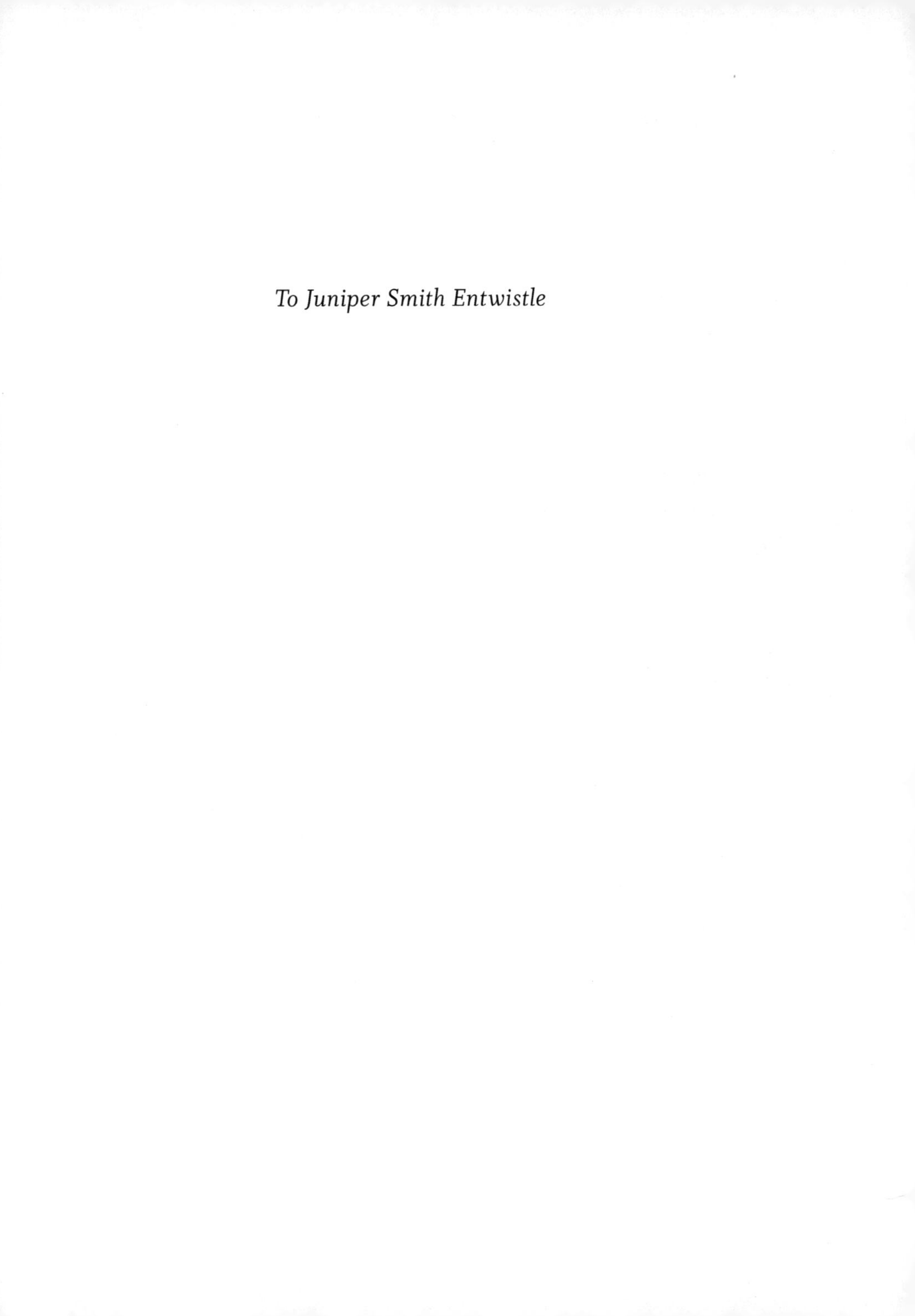

To Juniper Smith Entwistle

Just as it is possible to go from any place to any other, so also, starting from a defined and specialized field, can one arrive at a realization of ever-extending relationships. Thus tangential subjects come into view. The thoughts, however, can, I believe, be traced back to the event of a thread.

<hr>

—ANNI ALBERS, *ON WEAVING*

CONTENTS

ACKNOWLEDGMENTS

This book began as a doctoral dissertation, a project "discovered" one day serendipitously, in a university library, when I came across Anni Albers's book *On Designing* while doing research about her husband. I recall vividly the powerful effect her essays had on my thinking about media at the time—how the material practices and metaphorical associations she described forced a collision in my mind among several methods and fields. Indeed, it is because of that heterogeneity (the particular antidisciplinarity of textile thought) that I have required the help of so many people.

I never would have fully pursued the topic had I not had the encouragement of certain individuals. First, I thank Catherine Soussloff, who led the independent study course that helped me begin parsing through the mountain of Bauhaus literature and convinced me it wouldn't be so hard to learn German. I am ever grateful to Randall Halle, whose course on Marx and Marxism in graduate school and whose knowledge of the Weimar critical context were invaluable to my methodological approach. Douglas Crimp was the best doctoral supervisor one could ever ask for: a rigorous, theoretically astute reader who gave me the latitude to develop my thoughts independently. His generosity and brilliance were crucial in the most fundamental way.

There are also many, many others: professors, editors, and peers whose ideas and feedback at one point or another meaningfully shaped my approach to art and design history and theory: Benjamin Buchloh, Joan Snitzer, Janet Wolff, David Rodowick, Janet Catherine Berlow, Susanne von Falkenhausen, Judith Rodenbeck, Karen Beckman, Felicity Scott, Branden Joseph, Reinhold Martin, Glenn Adamson, Daniela Sandler, Norman Vorano. There are my dear friends in Berlin, who offered friendship and support over ten years: Ursula Tax, Axel Wieder, Rike Frank, Rita Bakacs, and Saskia Wendland. There are those whose camaraderie during my years in Baltimore meant the world to me: Kerr Houston, Jennie Hirsh, Monica Amor, Suzanne Garrigues, Joseph Basile, Jenny Carson, Judith Lidie, Susie Brandt, Piper Shepard, Annet Couwenberg, David East, Jan Stinchcomb, Dennis Farber. I thank my current colleagues at the University of British Columbia for their support, especially John O'Brian and Scott Watson. To my closest friend, Jaleh Mansoor, whose own work on abstraction, communization theory, and feminist Autonomia continues to inspire an expansiveness of thought, I prefer to say I look forward to many more years of collaboration. And to Graham Entwistle, for his undying patience, love, and support in the chaotic years of early parenthood (in which I turned the thesis into a proper book), the sincerest form of thank you would be inadequate. Finally, I am grateful to my parents, Bonnie Buhler Smith and Nico Smith, for their continuous inspiration.

This project was aided by several institutions and agencies in the form of scholarships and grants, without which my archival research and the production of this book would have been impossible: the DAAD (Deutscher Akademischer Austausch Dienst); the Susan B. Anthony Institute, University of Rochester; the Lucas Grant and the Stanley A. Rosen Grant, Maryland Institute College of Art; the University of British Columbia. The dissertation out of which this book came was awarded a Susan B. Anthony Dissertation Award. I am thankful to the Josef and Anni Albers Foundation and to the Bauhaus-Archiv in Berlin, in particular to former archivist Elke Eckert for incredible assistance and unlimited access to materials and documents during my research over several years. I wholeheartedly thank all of these sources for their support.

TEXTILES, TEXT, AND A MEDIUM-SPECIFIC CRAFT

> The structure of a fabric or its weave—that is, the fastening of its elements of threads to each other—is as much a determining factor in its function as is the choice of the raw material. In fact, the interrelation between the two, the subtle play between them in supporting, impeding, or modifying each other's characteristics, is the essence of weaving.
>
> —ANNI ALBERS, *ON WEAVING*

Anni Albers published her second book, *On Weaving*, in 1965. A well-respected German American weaver who taught from 1933 until 1949 at Black Mountain College and had developed popular fabric designs for Knoll, she was also a prolific writer. Like her former volume *On Designing*, which was initially published in 1959 and reprinted several times due to its popularity, *On Weaving* became at the outset a powerful voice of the midcentury textile design movement in the United States.[1] Professional and amateur weavers read her texts, finding in them a philosophy of their craft's "essence"— the "supporting, impeding, or modifying" tension between structure and material that described a fabric's dimensions. But Albers's books also participated in a wider discourse within modernism concerning medium specificity. Indeed, the former Bauhaus student learned much from her education at that school, where different workshops investigated the limits of specific materials—like thread, clay, or celluloid and light—and tools—like looms, pottery wheels, or cameras—to grasp and articulate the principal elements of each craft. Drawing on the language of her mentors and peers, she analyzed "basic" and "modified" textile structures, narrated the loom's technological history, and argued for a "tactile sensibility"—the activation of "a distinctive textile trait": the "tactile blueprint" or "latent perceptivity of *matiere*."[2] So with her 1965 book, Albers synthesized what could be described as the definitive treatise on weaving as a field of practice, a specific craft or medium that also, in so many tangential ways, could speak to other disciplines: to "those whose work in other fields encompasses textile problems."[3]

To understand how Albers's philosophy of weaving developed—how this craft came into a modernist language and also challenged its fundamentals—it is important to begin at the so-called beginning. The initial Bauhaus text, a 1919 brochure titled "Program of the State Bauhaus in Weimar," scripted by founder and director Walter Gropius, is well known for its attempt to establish the school's goal of art-craft "unity" in the aftermath of World War I. Here, Gropius envisions the school as a means toward the "unified work of art—the great structure" that is the built house. Yet among the bullet points of its final page concerning the "Range of Instruction," he also outlines areas of "craft training," distinct workshops. Applied arts intermingle with fine arts and theoretical instruction, suggesting that unity is a pedagogical matter of joining "practical and scientific areas of work."[4]

The pedagogical program sketched in this manifesto would, it should be said, prove less than stable.[5] As the workshops' identities and products shifted under the weight of economic pressures and the school's changing artistic and political allegiances, many of the initial crafts ("wood carvers, ceramic workers . . . lithographers") would be dropped over the course of the first several years, while new areas (furniture, advertising, and photography) would be added.[6] Significantly, only one mentioned area, weavers, was equipped with tools (several looms) shortly after the school opened in the city of Weimar and would continue to operate until the institution's doors finally closed in Berlin under pressure from Nazi forces. Weaving materialized in this context as a specific practice or craft—one dealing in a particular technology, material, and set of structures based on the interlocking of warp (vertical threads) and weft (horizontal threads). But perhaps more significant to this narrative is the fact that Bauhaus weavers began writing essays to develop parameters (and justifications) for their woven objects. Unlike most of their craft-workshop colleagues at the Bauhaus, the weavers were avid about the practice of writing; they were preoccupied with formulating (and reformulating) a theory of their craft's *Stoffgebiet* (material field) or *Gestaltungsgebiet* (formal field).

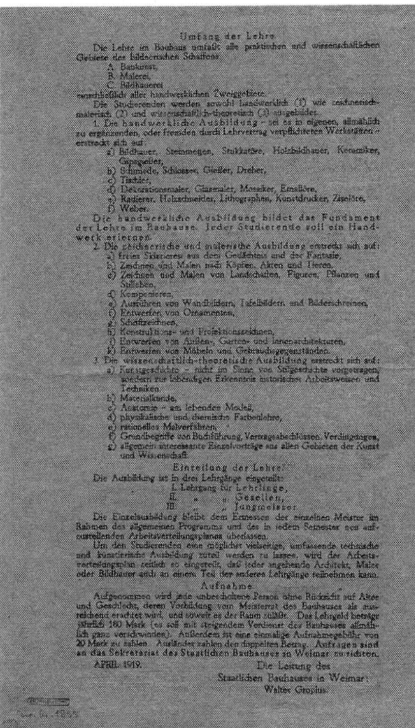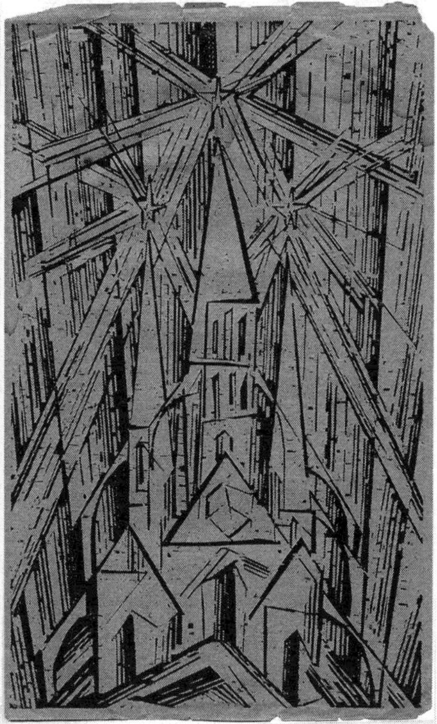

Walter Gropius, "Manifesto and Program of the State Bauhaus in Weimar," April 1919, with *Cathedral* by Lyonel Feininger (detail, pages 1 and 2). Photograph by Markus Hawlik. Bauhaus-Archiv Berlin. Copyright 2013 Artists Rights Society (ARS), New York / VG Bild-Kunst, Bonn.

Through texts that explored weaving's material elements, loom practice, and functional applications, a Bauhaus theory of weaving emerged. And against a backdrop of political and social upheaval in the Weimar Republic, weavers like Anni Albers, Gunta Stölzl, and Otti Berger harnessed at different moments (and to different ends) the rhetoric of expressionist painting, Neues Bauen architecture, and Neue Optik photography, often defying the categorical boundaries that defined modernism. What they accomplished was a profound step in the recognition of weaving as a specific craft—one that could be compared to, and differentiated from, other media.

To further sketch out the context of the workshop's theoretical project, it is important to turn to the year 1926, when during the initial full year of the Bauhaus's operation in Dessau the weaving workshop's technical master Gunta Stölzl published her first essay on the field, "Weaving at the Bauhaus."[7] Halfway through the life of the school, in reaction to the expressionist ideology that characterized its first several years, Stölzl sought to bring her workshop in line with Gropius's new directives, his new "Principles of Bauhaus Production."[8] Gropius had already abandoned the romanticism of the earliest years—the antitechnology stance that owned the school from 1919 to 1923—but by 1926 he was fully engaged in the functionalist paradigm and insisted that the workshops do the same.[9] So following the director's insistence that in order for design to "function correctly—a container, a chair, or a house—one must first of all study its nature," Stölzl declared in sync that "a woven piece is always a serviceable object, which is equally determined by its function as well as its means of production."[10]

In order to arrive at this relatively simple dictum—drawing on the functionalist paradigm introduced to design through architecture—the weaver first had to diagnose a troubling condition of the early, Weimar-period textiles. Stölzl pointed to the fact that so many wall hangings and carpets woven by the workshop's students (Hedwig Jungnik, Lore Leudesdorff, Ida Kerkovius, or herself) were based on "principles of pictorial images," or that they were, essentially, "picture[s] made of wool."[11] She had to dismiss the paradigm of one medium (painting) in order to accommodate the rhetoric of another (architecture). The problem was not, it seems, that the early works were formally experimental, but that unlike the later textiles there had been little investigation into weaving's means—the interactions of color and material, "the variety of possible interlacings"—or that "the characteristics of the material limit[ed] its usage." As pictures made of wool—concerned with applying Paul Klee–like motifs or Wassily Kandinsky–like abstract compositions—the early tapestries failed to provide an understanding of the "basic laws of [their] field of specialization."[12]

One might interpret Stölzl as saying that the workshop's earliest work was inadequate on two interrelated levels: on the one hand, weaving's specific strengths as a craft had been neither developed nor theorized; on the other, the early tapestries lacked the transcendental or emotive impetus of the expressionist paintings to which they were compared; the fabrics merely "started with image precepts." If evaluated against the "true" picture, painting, pictorial weaving inevitably appeared a weaker, ineffectual medium.

This book thus wrestles with the problem implicit in Stölzl's statement regarding the "picture made of wool": how, in other words, did the weavers come to terms with the specificity (and apparent inadequacies) of their field with respect to others (like painting or architecture), and how did they go about giving it a theoretical voice?

As it turns out, the 1926 text by Stölzl followed on the heels of another essay by student Anni Albers, titled "Bauhaus Weaving," which argued that weaving's processes, structures, and materials are best explored through direct experimentation on a loom.[13] In 1924, Albers's text functioned as a manifesto of sorts, arguing against modern methods of textile design, whereby the pattern draughtsman (*Zeichner*), due to the mechanization of cloth production, was too isolated from the material and practice. She thus contended that it was necessary to "begin again," to better integrate handwork at the loom with design.[14] What Albers's essay precipitated was a language for understanding how craft and design at the Bauhaus were always bound—one was dependent on the other.

Perhaps most remarkable about Albers's essay, published five years after the opening of the Bauhaus, is not just that it counts as *her* first text on the workshop's craft, but that it might also count as *the* first attempt to specify a modernist approach to weaving practice—one that embraces an "old" method of "handwork" in order to consider the fundamental elements of the weave, and to experiment and create new fabrics from within these constraints.[15]

Earlier and contemporaneous essays by other textile practitioners lack an attention to the means and the materials. The English Arts and Crafts movement leader William Morris, for instance, examines in his essay on "Textiles" (1893) the history of woven cloth and gives recommendations for the best way to design patterns (implicitly on paper) for tapestries and carpets.[16] Russian avant-garde artist Varvara Stepanova, alternatively, considers modern clothing's relationship to fabric design.[17] She declares in "From Clothing to Pattern and Fabric" (in 1929, several years after she and Liubov Popova started designing for a cotton-printing factory) that it "is time to move from designing a garment to designing the structure of the fabric," stressing the importance of beginning with a consideration of the cut of clothing in their drafting of geometric patterns.[18] Albers, by contrast, describes how Bauhaus weavers were attempting to renew a direct, manual contact with materials through work at the loom. In this text and others by Albers or her Bauhaus colleagues, we find a textual exploration of weaving's material elements, its technical practice, functional applications, and similarities to (or differences from) other media in order to determine what constitutes a specifically modern practice—one suited to creating various kinds of textiles for modern life. In other words, a modern theory of *weaving* does not emerge until the students of this Bauhaus workshop begin coming to grips with their craft's "basic conditions."

Reframing the History

The weaving workshop tended for many decades to be an afterthought in historical discussions of the institution.[19] This changed in the early 1990s when Sigrid Wortmann Weltge published *Bauhaus Textiles: Women Artists and the Weaving Workshop*.[20] Crucial in framing the history of the workshop and bringing the original work of the weavers to an English-speaking audience, Weltge's text documented the activities of the workshop and showed how the status of textiles at the school was largely problematic given the fact that it was associated with "women's work." Around this time, two monographs on its master, Gunta Stölzl, and one exhibition catalog on the workshop were also published in German.[21] Since then, Anja Baumhoff has investigated the problematic role of gender within the school's internal politics and craft–fine art hierarchy, providing significant research on the weaving workshop's position within school policies.[22] And Virginia Gardner Troy's monograph on Anni Albers has examined the interest of Bauhaus weavers (and modern German artists generally) in ancient textile artifacts and techniques from South America.[23]

From these authors much was learned and transmitted about the weaving workshop's history and its key players—one that may otherwise have been lost. Prior to the Bauhaus's opening in April, Helene Börner—the weaving workshop master at the Weimar applied arts school, directed by Henry van de Velde—signed a contract with Walter Gropius stipulating that the school could use her looms while providing her with free rent. Börner thereby became the de facto master of craft for the workshop until 1925, when the Weimar Bauhaus closed. Though a trained weaver, Börner's presence in the workshop seems not to have made much of an impact on the students. According to the recollections of Anni Albers, who joined the workshop in 1923, the students had little clear instruction in proper technique in these early years and so approached the medium through "amateurish" experimentation with techniques and materials and as pictorial compositions that resulted, predominantly, in wall hangings, carpets, and blankets.[24] In 1920, the Masters Council and Gropius decided to form a women's class for the school's female population, which was then tethered to the weaving workshop. Following Johannes Itten, painter Georg Muche became the workshop's master of form in 1921. By 1923, the year of the first Bauhaus exhibition, several among the students began to stand out. Among them were Gunta Stölzl and Benita Otte, who had together gone to Krefeld to be trained in the technique of dyeing the previous year. So when the school left Weimar in 1925, Stölzl, who had passed her journeyman's exam in 1922, became the workshop's master of craft and, then later, in 1927, the workshop's head (replacing Muche). Moving into its new Dessau home in 1926, the workshop purchased its own equipment and became increasingly sophisticated in its instruction, orienting classwork to the production of industrial prototypes for architectural textiles. After Hannes Meyer's resignation as director in 1930, with the appointment of Ludwig Mies van der Rohe, the weaving workshop became an extension of the interior design workshop and Lilly Reich was its head from 1931 until the school closed in 1933.

This narrative has gone a long way to understanding the weaving workshop's production, characters, and alliances. Little to none of the current scholarship, however, has critically analyzed how the weavers shaped their craft through text, or how their textual pursuits significantly engaged with thought on craft and media more generally. There has been no investigation of the ways that weaving, as it was theorized through the weavers' writing and practice, retextures the Bauhaus's discursive field. This is not to say that the weavers' writings, or the fact that they wrote, are unaddressed; Nicolas Fox Weber and Brenda Danilowitz have, for instance, commented extensively on the crucial role of writing in Anni Albers's practice.[25] But very little of the extant literature on the workshop provides a sustained view of the Bauhaus weavers' writings within the school's and Weimar Republic's theoretical landscape, or that of postwar discussions of media more generally. The present volume thus finds new value and significance in the work they did as writers.

If this reframing is important, it is because it raises (and begins to answer) several fundamental questions about the relationship of specific "crafts" to other fields nominated as "art" or "design." Most important, are the concepts of craft and medium isomorphic, or structurally distinct? How might a craft, like weaving, challenge modernist assumptions about specific media, like painting or photography? And to what degree are crafts and media reliant on theoretical, textual armatures to be specific? And related to these questions, the investigation opens onto an interdisciplinary terrain: how is a particular craft's *value* a function of social categories (of gender, or manual versus intellectual labor)? Does weaving's association with women require us to reconsider a general (neutral) understanding of craft practices, forms, and skills? Conversely, how are notions of gender and femininity complicated when confronted with the techniques, functions, and art historical or modern-industrial metaphors that are used to define textiles?

Bauhaus Weaving Theory thus draws on the recent surge of critical interest in the area of craft and textile studies, which has resulted in new perspectives on a domain traditionally denied a meaningful place in mainstream art history and art theory.[26] As today's e-textile designers increasingly become theoreticians of their field, needed now is a prehistory of those investigations of new media.[27] Textile designers after the Bauhaus continued to be technological and scientific researchers, but few scholarly studies have examined their critical import.[28] Through this book I hope that a study of the Bauhaus weaving workshop's craft will frame a stronger understanding of these and subsequent developments in textile design and fiber art.

Finally, and perhaps most important, the present work seeks to open up the debate over the related concepts of "craft" and "medium," and to consider how an application of theory to weaving might shed light on some of the assumptions of the art historical discipline.[29] In focusing on the weavers' texts about their objects and practice, *Bauhaus Weaving Theory* confronts a long-standing assumption in art history that the crafts are manual or technical, but never intellectual, arts.

A Specific Craft, a Specific Medium

The assumed binary between manual and intellectual practices has been addressed by a few authors in recent years.[30] Most notable among these is craft theorist and historian Glenn Adamson. Beginning the introduction to his book, *Thinking through Craft,* with a question that sums up craft's predicament, Adamson writes: "Thinking through . . . craft? Isn't craft something mastered in the hands, not in the mind? Something consisting of physical actions, rather than abstract ideas?"[31] And defying this expectation, Adamson looks at craft from a kind of meta-level, as a category, process, and "conceptual limit." Indeed, his book does just what the title sets out to do: *think through* the conflicted terrain that marks craft as a limit of modern art. This is important, for while the field of fine art has a longstanding connection to "concepts" or "intellectual labor" in Western culture dating back to the Renaissance (in treatises like Alberti's on architecture or Leonardo's on painting), craft's relationship to "theory" and "thinking" in that context has been a bit more tenuous.[32] Craft, it seems, is by definition not an "intellectual exercise."[33] Although the nineteenth century generated ideas on craft by John Ruskin and William Morris of the Arts and Crafts movement, attempts at generating a specific philosophy or theory of craft since modernism (the early twentieth century) have in most ways been marked by fits and starts. David Pye's writing on "workmanship" and skill is a notable exception, though his writing is obscure among mainstream art and design circles.[34]

A significant argument of Adamson's book is that while craft is certainly a category used to classify certain medium-specific practices (like glass blowing or ceramics), it needs most of all to be understood as a "a way of doing things"; it does not refer to a "defined practice but a way of thinking through practices of all kinds."[35] According to Adamson's account, the concept of craft is organized around "material experience" on the one hand, and "skill" on the other. Indeed skill, as he argues following Pye, may be "the most complete embodiment of craft as an active, relational concept rather than a fixed category."[36] (To put it another way, unlike this word *art,* the word *craft* can be used in a sentence as both a noun and a verb.) Thus, it applies to the sculptural work that Constantine Brancusi shapes out of stone as much as it applies to Peter Voulkos's work in clay—something connected to the history of ceramics, a so-called handicraft or decorative art with all of the assumptions about amateurism and skill that go with it. And as a process, craft is not just a distinct category but is the veritable "horizon" of (all) art—that which yields its possibilities yet disappears in the process. Citing Jacques Derrida's notion of the *parergon,* Adamson ultimately argues that craft must be understood as that which is "supplemental" to the "autonomous" (modern) work of art.[37] Craft is pervasive (everywhere in art and design), and yet mostly unrecognized. As the concepts of art come to the fore, the work's craft is that which recedes, or moves to the periphery, like a frame.[38]

It requires noting that Adamson's thought on craft while incredibly valuable to a discussion of weaving is less about an investigation of the specific thinking that arises within a particular craft than about the underlying "way of doing things" that permeates "practices of all kinds." This means that Craft, a general category like Art, is given conceptual clarity, but the specific knowledge and ideas generated by certain manual techniques and tools are less central to his argument. The differences between specific crafts and media are reduced, in some sense, to "process" writ large.

In the final count, the question remains whether "craft," as it is applied to weaving or carpentry, can be differentiated from "medium," as it is applied to painting or photography. Both concepts, when related to specific categories of practice, are used to describe the "properties," "materials," "techniques," and "skills" of various disciplines. If craft is not seen as the inverse (or supplement) of art, as Adamson determines, but is rather understood in relation to medium, then the questions organizing the art-craft field shift: are "medium" and "craft" symmetrical, or are these two categories structurally distinct? Or both?

Adamson might argue that the term *craft* is better understood not so much categorically from within the various disciplines or individual crafts but, rather, as the supplement or horizon of modern art. Or, as he says more recently, we need to understand the idea of craft historically, as that highly contested concept that was in some sense invented alongside design within and against the beginnings of industrialism.[39] While agreeing with these points wholeheartedly, I would nevertheless argue it is productive to consider more actively the structural parity of craft and medium (or the crafts and media) as they exist within modernist discourse in order to account for the crossover between the high and applied arts, or technical switches that happen, especially today, as the realms of craft and new media have begun to assemble. It is productive to exploit the similarities and differences between these terms in order to think through, for instance, Buckminster Fuller's comparison of Anni Albers's "woven fabric surfaces," with the "multi-dimensional . . . complexities" of "Earth's cities," as seen from "aeronautical altitudes."[40] (Spaceships, televisions, architecture, and Peruvian textiles similarly collide in Albers's writing.) And to think of a specific craft in Germany and America in the twentieth century it is necessary, I would argue, to understand how it plays out within the parallel discourses of "medium specificity" and media studies as they arose at the Bauhaus (in the writings of Wassily Kandinsky on painting and László Moholy-Nagy on photography) and were further developed in postwar America. Much is gained by looking at a certain genus of trees to gain a picture of the forest's health. Using a case study, like Bauhaus weaving theory, which harnessed various other discourses, provides a lens onto the specificity and permeability of individual crafts or media within modernism. In other words, understanding how one medium-specific craft came to be defined helps to grasp related parameters, the key questions and values, that defined others.

The emergence of a modernist, early-twentieth-century discourse concerning medium specificity finds precursors in the large number of texts that evolved in the wake of the Enlightenment.[41] Just as the idea of "art as such" was coming into being in the eighteenth-century field of aesthetics, a contradictory but also supportive discourse emerged that sought to distinguish the "unique nature of each art and the material medium in which it operated."[42] In 1766, Gotthold Ephraim Lessing's *Laocöon* attacked the idea that painting and poetry were "unified" as mimetic arts; instead, he argued for distinguishing them according to their different "means and signs," or the fact that one "employ[s] figures and colors in space" while the other "articulate[s] sounds in time."[43] A

Lessing-like argument extended into the nineteenth century, when critics like August Wilhelm Schlegel (in his *Philosophische Kunstlehre*) hoped to establish a "natural history of art" that explained "the very laws governing the stages of the unfolding of a process."[44] And then with Hegel came an articulation of the ways that different art forms are "distinctly fitted to manifest the ideas and attitudes of a particular age."[45]

The concern with defining the parameters of specific arts became most acute in the early twentieth century in essays by abstract painters like Kandinsky. Defending nonobjective form against what critics saw as its decorative nature, the artist would declare in 1914 that the "greatest dangers" facing painting include "ornamental form, the form belonging mainly to external beauty, which can be and as a rule is outwardly expressive and inwardly expressionless."[46] By this he meant to distance his practice in abstraction from a certain, general condition of "stylized form" across the applied arts—as found, for instance, in the Jugendstil or art nouveau movements. So while Kandinsky's notions of synesthesia were integral to his grasp of formal problems (Richard Wagner and Arnold Schoenberg inspired his notion of a form or color's inner *Klang*, or sound), that contradiction was also suspended in his ambition to capitalize on a certain image of pictorial practice as self-sufficient, internally motivated.[47] He would even insist that "every art has its own language and means appropriate to itself alone—the abstract inner sound of its elements. As far as this abstract, inner sound is concerned, none of these languages can be replaced by another."[48] Painting deals in color, music in sound, dance in movement. The analytical specificity of any artistic "language" or art (like painting) must be grasped completely before it can be resynthesized, for example, into a theatrical stage set or as the mural on a modern building.

The concept of medium specificity took several decades and a continental divide to become fully entrenched as a modernist dictum, but when Clement Greenberg insisted in 1960 that the task of modernism was to "eliminate . . . the effects borrowed from another art," such that "each art would be rendered 'pure,'" the critic could claim this process as the result of a teleological end game.[49] The insistence on specificity became a rigid doxa, and the contradictions of medium-specific investigations would come to a head: a positivist examination and promotion of painterly materials and technique (*techné* and matter) paradoxically established art's (Hegelian) Spirit or idea. The goal—somewhat as it was for Kandinsky in 1914—was to combat "Kitsch"—all mass and popular forms, like television, but also all things "decorative" and functional, like "craft."[50] So when "medium" took over from "the particular arts" as the lingua franca of the mid–twentieth century, it stressed the distinction held by Kant between art and handicraft, affirming that the process of each particular art was "free" and "purposive . . . in itself" (whereas the crafts were mere "work").[51] Kantian aesthetic autonomy was fully conflated with medium specificity; Greenberg's (rather positivist) "medium" could be "art" precisely because it was defined by clear material and practical parameters.[52]

Still, it must be noted that the concept of *medium* also bears a different history—as this term came into significant use in the Bauhaus context in the 1920s primarily through discussions of media like film and photography. When Moholy-Nagy brought his photographic and typographic practice to the Bauhaus in 1923, his texts on "optics" published in avant-garde journals like *i10* were among some of the initial attempts to capture the conditions of this instrument and its light-produced images, setting the stage for subsequent investigations of media that deployed distinctly modern apparatuses. That the Bauhaus weavers looked to architectural and then photographic theory for their initial theories of the craft is telling. A formal vocabulary borrowed from Paul Klee's and Kandinsky's ideas about the pictorial arts is certainly apparent in their writings, but more notable were the *Sachlichkeit* discourses of architecture and photography. Perhaps the student Otti Berger, who in 1929 related textiles to photography and architecture in her first essay on "Stoffe im Raum" (Fabrics in Space), recognized a potential that was otherwise unattainable (and outdated) in the academic arts.[53] It could even be said that media and crafts were determined by a similarly peripheral identity at that time.

It is with this background in mind that a productive ambivalence is witnessed throughout this book—about whether to call weaving a craft or a medium. The point of bringing the word *craft* into dialogue with *medium* is not meant to legitimate weaving practice as "art." (As Adamson reminds quite bluntly: "Anything can be taken for art, craft included, and that is all there is to say on the matter."[54]) Rather, an investigation of the weavers' theories, if framed by this relationship, has the radical capacity to shed light on each category's already hybrid nature—the fact that, even within early-twentieth-century modernism, a textual understanding of any practical field (be it weaving, painting, architecture, or photography) was always striated by the terms of other media, other crafts. Emphasizing the craft of weaving, nevertheless, bears a political weight, insofar as it becomes necessary to grant that *thinking* indeed emerges within manual practices, within labor. Perhaps craft and labor are not about turning off the brain but about reactivating different centers. As the weavers' writings and textiles show, ideas became manifest in their physical manipulation of the loom— either unwittingly or with a bit of savvy.

The Bauhaus provides the perfect setting in which to analyze the relationship between crafts and medium. For it is here, in the school's workshops and modernist curriculum, that the two areas came head to head, in dialogue and in juxtaposition. What the work and writing of the Bauhaus weaving workshop reveal is that no medium or craft, however specific, can be divorced from the network of other media—and the political landscape—in which they come alive, (re)produce, and reside. While specific crafts may bear specific, unique properties, structural features, and technical practices, the terms of their identities are always counted along these lines. It is in this space of parity that differences and values emerge.

Feminized

Important to understanding weaving's identity as a craft or medium at the Bauhaus is an investigation of its apparently feminine gender and the contradictions that this identity entailed. In a passage from her 1957 essay "The Pliable Plane: Textiles in Architecture," Anni Albers reflected on what she identified as the paradox of weaving's "feminine role" in modern culture:

It is interesting . . . to observe that in ancient myths from many parts of the world it was a goddess, a female deity, who brought the invention of weaving to mankind. When we realize that weaving is primarily a process of structural organization this thought is startling, for today thinking in terms of structure seems closer to the inclination of men than women.[55]

Even twenty-four years after leaving the Bauhaus and Berlin, Albers was never able to reconcile weaving's apparent femininity with her technical approach to and theoretical conception of her medium. While the craft has been historically designated as feminine, weaving's "process of structural organization" indicated to Albers that the mental faculties used to construct a woven textile (such as the complex mathematical determinations used in threading a loom for various structures) seemed "closer to the inclination of men than women."

Although Albers hoped to discard this association, annoyed over a lack of respect for her work in the hierarchy of the arts, her statement only affirms that a definition of weaving is entwined with the question of gender. Weltge and Baumhoff have pointed out that the gender politics of the Bauhaus firmly established the femininity of the weaving workshop, and that this identity has a history. During the first two years, before the workshops were fully established, no definitive gender was assigned to them, and a male student, Max Peiffer-Watenphul, participated in weaving activities.[56] But by 1921, the weaving workshop and the women's class were tied together. The women's class was set up by the weaver Stölzl, who claimed a desire to create a separate space for the many women entering the school, but also at the encouragement of Bauhaus director Walter Gropius. He wanted to segregate the female population from the other, "masculine" workshops, such as metalwork or furniture, which held more direct links to architecture; thus, a policy established what was and wasn't so-called women's work.

But if weaving's feminized identity was reinforced by policies, it was also, according to Weltge and Baumhoff, produced through statements about the nature of the craft: like the words of painter and Bauhaus master Oskar Schlemmer: "Where there is wool, there is a woman who weaves, if only to pass the time."[57] The very craft is, as Schlemmer's ditty indicates, a pastime, one accomplished with little mental concentration. And women weave, one is led to think, out of sheer habit. So when Georg Muche took over as form master of the weaving workshop in 1921, he made every attempt to disassociate himself from the weavers' work, putting his energy toward painting or his first architectural design, the Haus am Horn in Weimar (1922–23), and he swore never to "weave a single thread, tie a single knot, make a single textile design."[58] While it may be easy and amusing to dismiss the thoughts of these men, what their language shows is that gender not only pertained to the actual women weaving in the workshop; it also involved the way in which the textile craft was defined. It seems that the physical material of thread and the process of handling it might have, as Muche thought, threatened his status at the school, for weaving with its grounding in manual (not intellectual) abilities is intrinsically feminine. Weaving's femininity was not simply a matter of subjects but also of objects, practices, and semantics.[59]

Weaving occupied a feminized status at the Bauhaus institution in many ways, but perhaps primarily because its materials and practices were considered subordinate to the more fundamental practice of form and color theory (taught by painters like Johannes Itten or Kandinsky) or the functionalist logic of architecture. Especially early on, the Bauhaus masters mostly dismissed weaving as an applied art, whose secondary (or tertiary) position afforded it no intellectual dimension of its own. As a manual practice, weaving was seen merely to borrow or *apply* the formal and functional theories that painting or architecture developed.[60] So more than its connection to a female subject who weaves, weaving was feminized as a "linguistic absence" in the language of artistic media.[61] The fact that weaving could not reference a longer history of theoretical inquiry into its specificity—as found, for instance, regarding painting (from Leonardo to Kandinsky), or regarding architecture (from Vitruvius to Adolf Behne)—contributed to its feminine role.

Still, it is important to understand that the Bauhaus workshops, crafts, and artistic media do not correspond to a field of neat analogies between masculine and feminine. Even the discipline of painting was always on the verge of slipping into the (feminine) status of a merely decorative art, and architecture held tenuously to its rights to authorship.[62] Expressionist painters anxiously wrote essays denying any association of their work with ornamentation, and internal debates within the Werkbund and the Neues Bauen movement suggest that architects were often nervous about their discipline's status as an art.[63] Moreover, the metal workshop, presumably a domain of men, was led in its most productive years by a woman, Marianna Brandt; and while the pottery workshop's form master Gerhard Marcks rejected the intrusion of women into its ranks, it

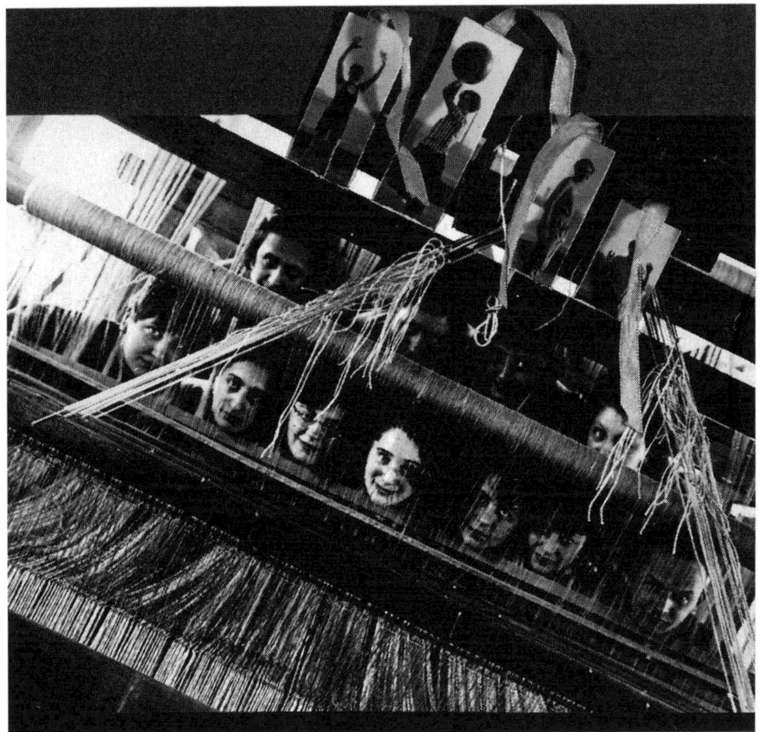

Students of the Bauhaus Weaving Workshop, collage for "9 jahre bauhaus. eine chronik," 1928. Upper row, from left: Lisbeth Östreicher, Gertrud Preiswerk, Helene Bergner, Grete Reichardt; lower row, from left: Lotte Beese, Anni Albers, Ljuba Monastirski, Rosa Bergner, Gunta Stölzl, Otti Berger, and workshop master Kurt Wanke. Bauhaus-Archiv Berlin.

was nevertheless a site where women were assigned. Ultimately we find that the term *feminine* weaves together multiple, often contradictory, associations.

Thus, a project on weaving at the Bauhaus must investigate the inconsistent signifieds attached to this singular, gendered signifier. Adolf Loos's infamous essay "Ornament and Crime," integral to modernist architectural thought in the early twentieth century, situates the applied arts and ornament in a homologous relationship to femininity and degeneracy.[64] But the discursive connections that gender weaving also sprout from a dual history of domestic (amateurish) production on the one hand and industrial (wage) labor on the other. While the Bauhaus tended at first to view weaving

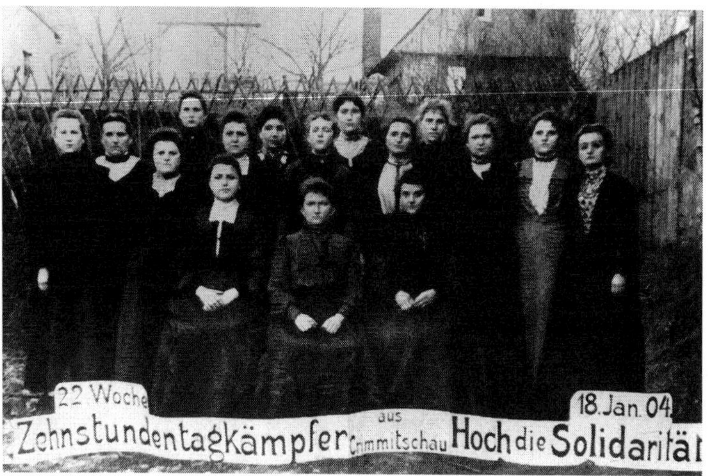

Women textile workers in Crimmitschau, Saxony, Germany, striking for a ten-hour working day in 1903–4. ullstein bild / The Granger Collection, New York.

practice as a gentle, domestic craft best suited to the female sex, in Germany at this moment the identification of textiles with industry involved the image of women toiling in factories, or striking for twenty-two weeks to achieve a ten-hour workday.[65] Karl Marx wrote of the new surplus of women who entered textile factories in the late nineteenth century once the deployment of "machinery dispense[d] with muscular power," allowing for the employment of "workers of slight muscular strength."[66] And so by the 1920s, the association of textiles, machines, labor, and women had become so pervasive in the popular imagination that these terms were inextricably bound.[67]

The terms and values of Weimar culture are, as design historian Frederic Schwartz has said, "not merely unstable; they could, in fact, turn into their opposites."[68] So, too, the role of gender within Weimar society and the Bauhaus institution was often marked by contradictions and turns that made the designation of weaving as feminine a complicated proposition. As I hope to show, the understanding of this medium as at once a handicraft, a product of mechanized labor subject to an apparatus, a sign for the problems of domesticity, and an anonymous entity reveal the extent to which the label *feminine* was never consistently applied with the same meaning or value. Neither *masculine* nor *feminine* are understood here as absolute qualifiers.

Why Writing?

It seems useful at this point to address a question subtending the discussion thus far. Before turning to the chapters to understand the complex avenues through which theoretical writing on weaving first emerged at the Bauhaus—that is, the *how*—it is important first of all to address the *why*: why was this discourse first initiated here and not, say, at other locations in Germany (that is, in Crimmitschau or Krefeld, which were major textile industry towns, or at Burg Giebichenstein, where former Bauhaus student Benita Otte taught between 1925 and 1933)?

Answering this first of all requires making some general arguments about the far-reaching importance of the school's theoretical program. The Bauhaus may ultimately have achieved mythic status because so many *Bauhäusler* emigrated to the United States and became leading figures in art and design education there (Josef and Anni Albers, Moholy-Nagy, Gropius, Marcel Breuer, and so on), but the school's reputation was crystallized even before this—precisely because Bauhaus artists were constantly engaged in debates within the classroom and then publicized those debates with the outside ("to expand its pedagogical range").[69] Most significant, there was the production of the *Bauhausbücher* series, which was edited by Gropius and Moholy-Nagy and ultimately yielded fourteen volumes, the authors of which included many of the most important figures in the international avant-garde.[70] As Adrian Sudhalter has pointed out, "Reaching a widespread international readership, the *Bauhausbücher* effectively promoted the school and its production-oriented position of the mid-1920s."[71] Indeed, as I will argue in chapter 2, there is a degree to which the weavers' early theorctical writings were initiated as part of what could be called a marketing campaign by the school in its drive to gain political recognition from the supporting state apparatus and from industrial clients. Discourse in the form of magazine articles, special issues, and books was an important part of the school's functional lifeblood, not just an abstract engagement with modernist ideas. Moreover, the Bauhaus was especially vexed politically in part because it was so vocal in its ideas and so good at broadcasting them; one might say it was caught in a kind of vicious circle: the more the institution felt it needed to back up its program with text, the more it was attacked, the more it needed to respond. (Other institutions in Germany at the time were not as visible and hence not as theoretically motivated, or perhaps they were less visible because they were not as motivated by political fallout at every turn.) And unlike most schools in Germany at this time, the Bauhaus had one particular "modernist titan"—Kandinsky—who was already a prolific writer on art when he came to the school to teach in 1920. Surely his complex ideas on the medium of painting in 1912, as I will discuss in chapter 1, inspired the weavers so enormously that they almost needed to respond through language.

Language and writing as much as painting were central to Kandinsky's practice as an artist, and his presence was especially important to the fostering of a discursive Bauhaus early on. Likewise, Gropius's "Manifesto and Program," which was meant as an advertising pamphlet to appeal to students, suggested at the outset that the school was as much a practical site as a space for quasi-philosophical explorations. The ideas expressed through texts by Moholy-Nagy and Klee only fortified this environment. And so the Bauhaus weavers were rather born from a theoretically charged matrix, where the articulation of ideas was as important as the practice. They had to secure their status at the school by way of text. It was not enough to do a practice, like weaving; they also had to establish the "basic laws" of their medium, in writing, for the workshop's products to be considered valid in the eyes of the school.

The Work of the Chapters

The chapters in this book do not provide a comprehensive survey of the Bauhaus weaving workshop and its products; rather, they consider the weavers' writings on their craft in the context of other media: painting, architecture, photography, and patents. Determined by a general chronology, each of the first three chapters examines a key moment in the workshop's evolving theory of its formal field set against the school's inconsistent political ambitions and the cultural and sociological debates of the time. These chapters will demonstrate how various competing discourses of the Bauhaus overlapped and clashed, and how they erupted in the writings of the weavers. Their essays are used as a lens onto several important dualities that defined media during the Weimar Republic: artistic practice and manual labor, experimentation and function, tactile and optical perception. Chapter 1 examines the workshop's early years (1919–23), when its tapestries and carpets were understood as "pictures made of wool" and weaving lacked a theoretical armature. Expressionist artists like Kandinsky and Itten saw painting as a conduit to the artist's soul, while weaving was too domestic and laborious to hold significant depth. Setting these objects and texts against contemporaneous Marxist debates about labor, this chapter considers the vexed status of abstraction in the Weimar Republic. The second chapter examines the initial theories of weaving, written by Anni Albers, Helene Schmidt-Nonné, and Gunta Stölzl between 1924 and 1926. As the school abandoned its purely experimental beginnings and catapulted itself toward a technological future, a modernist theory of weaving was born. Harnessing the functionalist (*Sachlichkeit*) discourse of the Neues Bauen movement (Adolf Behne and Walter Gropius), they specified the use of textiles in architectural space. Chapter 3 examines how weaving student Otti Berger drew on László Moholy-Nagy's arguments regarding the "optical" nature of photography to develop a complementary theory of tactility as it pertained to cloth. While close-up photographs of Bauhaus textiles in magazines and brochures worked to sell the workshop's products, Berger reflected on the simultaneous visuality and "hold-ability" (*Haltbarkeit*) of the woven medium.

The fourth chapter shifts direction somewhat. In 1932, Otti Berger began to seek intellectual property protection for her textile fabrication techniques. Identifying herself as a patent "author"—an "inventor" in a design world mostly marked by anonymity—she would also define her craft anew. What she developed through patent applications (in dialogue with her patent attorney) was a theory of textiles for the modern age, a language that harnessed legal rhetoric (not quite a medium, but an apparatus, nevertheless) with that of functionality and "properties."

The book's conclusion examines how the writing of Anni Albers quickly expanded after she immigrated to America with her husband, Josef, in 1933. Through texts published in magazines or catalogs and ultimately in two books—*On Designing* (1959) and *On Weaving* (1965)—she considered terms like *medium* and *design* as they integrated and, in postwar America, increasingly eclipsed the work of *craft*. In this chapter, Albers is set into dialogue with several significant and incongruent voices on media from this moment.

As the chapters demonstrate, the weavers' texts at once posit the specificity of their craft—how it was, for instance, specifically gendered—but also the way in which any such definition was inseparable from other fields. Their texts point to the social and artistic worlds that shaped weaving as a distinct entity with specific parameters, and the particular practice through which it was reenacted or transformed.[72] The chapters thus show how the entwinement of one disciplinary space with the next is, on the one hand, specific to textiles but, on the other, is a general case of media. And it is of this condition that the weavers' writings remind.

Thus, for the purposes of this book, weaving is as much a craft and medium as it is an apparatus (*dispositif*), in the Foucauldian sense. It is as much a specific practice (set of materials, tools, and way of putting things together) as it is a "heterogeneous ensemble consisting of discourses, institutions, architectural forms . . . propositions—in short, the said as much as the unsaid."[73] Weaving is at once *this* particular technique as opposed to *that* one (say, painting or architecture), and also the network that in various concrete, practical, and theoretical modes links together the competing discourses of modernism.

WEAVING LABOR IN THE WORKSHOP

> The [mass] ornament, detached from its bearers, must be understood rationally. It consists of lines and circles like those found in textbooks on Euclidean geometry. . . . Both the proliferations of organic forms and the emanations of spiritual life remain excluded. The Tiller Girls can no longer be reassembled into human beings after the fact.
>
> —SIEGFRIED KRACAUER, "THE MASS ORNAMENT"

Before the Bauhaus weavers wrote, before weaving had a theoretical armature to secure its status as a medium-specific craft, weaving was what Gunta Stölzl would later call "a picture made of wool."

A tapestry from 1921–22 by weaving workshop student Hedwig Jungnik is a good example of such an artifact (see Plate 1). Unlike a bolt of cloth whose fabric might cover, in various dimensions, a bed, pillow, sofa, or window, this small "picture" has a clear beginning and end. Framed by its four sides, it serves little other function than to hang on and decorate a wall. Within these parameters, the tapestry has a distinct composition, one in which waves and circles ebb and flow in and around angular forms. Curved shapes appear to sit below a plane of strongly contoured circles, while sharp, diagonal lines simultaneously cut across the composition and lie beneath the surface of repeated waves. Monochromatic diamond shapes hover behind and in front of the flowing activity, while an arc, toward the lower left, creates an illusion of three dimensions within this otherwise flat, abstract design.

Jungnik's tapestry is a good example to begin the discussion, for it resembles a specific kind (indeed, a style) of pictorial abstraction found in the prewar practices of the

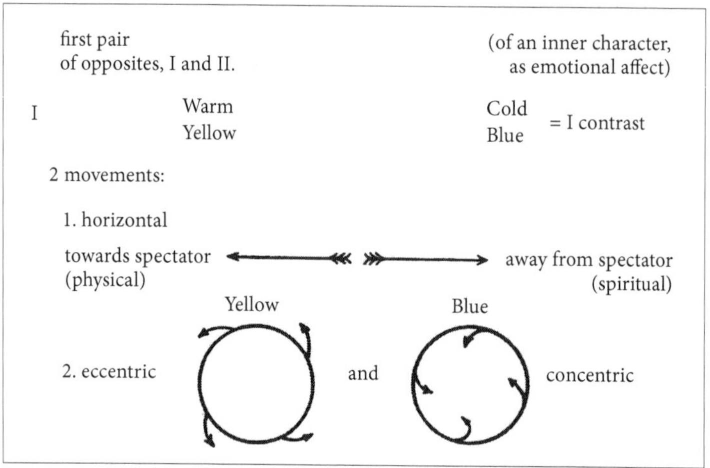

Wassily Kandinsky, Table 1 (excerpt) from *On the Spiritual in Art,* 2d edition (1912), in Lindsay and Vergo, *Kandinsky: Complete Writings,* 178. Re-created by the author.

Munich-based expressionists, especially the Blaue Reiter group, which grew out of international movements in impressionism, cubism, symbolism, Jugendstil design, and the teachings of the Dachau colorist Adolf Hölzel.[1] It is this particular brand of early-twentieth-century expressionism that through a number of side steps found its way into the design work of the Bauhaus workshops, as the school's earliest form masters Johannes Itten, Lyonel Feininger, Georg Muche, Wassily Kandinsky, and Paul Klee offered courses or at the very least broadcast a set of ideas about form and color.[2] In the lectures of Itten, Klee, and Kandinsky especially, students were introduced to so-called basic principles in form, methods for arranging shapes in an abstract composition, principles they then translated into various household items: cradles, toys, ceramic teapots, carpets.

But there are many differences between the form masters' pictorial principles (based on painting and drawing) and Jungnik's tapestry. In the latter, three white lines made from markedly thick strands of yarn jut out into the viewer's (physical) space, beyond the picture plane, drawing attention to the body of this entity. And determined by the woven process—the alternating elevation of warp and weft—the compositional activity of the tapestry is marked by its surface's pits and falls. The interlocking grid produces an optically resonant field, but it also draws attention to the material fact of the weave.[3] The boundaries of geometric forms are not "set free from [the] space" around them, as Wilhelm Worringer had observed among the modern artists obliquely referenced in his 1907 doctoral thesis—ideas later promoted by the likes of Kandinsky and Franz Marc.[4] Rather, these shapes issue from the physical network of threads—compromised, one might say, by their settling of differences between material and form. (The compromise also suggests a reduction in value of the latter.) Thus on the left side of Jungnik's tapestry, a circle enveloped in the crest of a wave flows from the tangible construction of interlocking weft and warp beginning at the textile's edge. The shape is not imposed onto the material, as when patterns are printed on blocks of plain cloth, or when paint delineates forms on the surface of primed canvas. Rather, if this wall hanging yields a composition of shapes and color, it is clearly formed *from within* the weave.

"A picture made of wool," Stölzl's short, descriptive phrase of this sort of object from the Bauhaus weaving workshop, thus foregrounds a fundamental problem, one that has gone unexamined in the literature concerning the Weimar Bauhaus weaving workshop and the feminine status of the medium—even as Anja Baumhoff, for example, points to the unjust standards by which her textiles were measured:

In retrospect, the former Bauhaus student and weaver Anni Albers . . . realized that her works on paper were categorized as art, but that a similar motif in textile design was suddenly regarded as craft. Along with that went differences in status, prestige, and price that, from the viewpoint of the women producing the work, were unjustified.[5]

Baumhoff astutely identifies a problematic method of evaluating "similar motifs" among "works on paper" and weaving "as craft."[6] But the terms of the comparison, as understood by Albers, also leave us with a predicament in terminology, or of categorical boundaries—a predicament from which several overlapping questions about these media ensue.

For a definition of a *picture* in this context, we could begin with the simplest characterization of it, spelled out in Kandinsky's *Point and Line to Plane,* published in 1926 as number nine of the Bauhaus Books series. This text, which Kandinsky began writing in 1914 and then resumed in 1923 based on notes gathered for his courses, set out to identify a picture's "basic elements": form, color, plane.[7] So Kandinsky begins with a statement that seems to derive from the empirical fact of the object: "By plane we understand that material plane which is called upon to accommodate the content of the work of art."[8] A picture is that composition or field of forms and colors that occupies another field, a substrate, a "material plane" of canvas or paper.

Following the reasoning of Kandinsky's definition, already we are faced with a problem, if not a contradiction, at the core of Stölzl's statement, "ein Bild aus Wolle." For to say that a picture could be "made (out) of wool" undoes the implicit separation in Kandinsky's schema between the picture and the plane that it occupies. In Kandinsky's painting *On White II* (1923), for example, the artist arranges the shapes and colors in the center and on top of a white rectangular field. The painted white surface—beneath the compositional figure of abstract forms—itself overlays a canvas, which only works to create a layer of distance between the structural support and the artist's idea. Through the flat white gesso, the material difference between the canvas and the paint forming the "picture" is maintained, or rather reinforced, by a layer of paint-glue. In Jungnik's tapestry, by contrast, the design and the surface are one and the same—they are made from the same material and process. The woven design is *built* in tandem with its physical matrix, so the tapestry's picture is not imposed onto a material ground but, rather, embedded in and transformed by the different kinds of threads and structures used in the process. So while another weave—the canvas—provides the forgotten, or neglected, structural ground for painting's content, the visual design of the tapestry cannot pretend to detach itself from, or supersede, the material through which it is *made* on a particular apparatus—the loom.

Still, there is no neat way to define the significance of the pictorial at the Bauhaus in Weimar. The word *pictorial* is problematic on several counts: while the resident painters argued for the making of pictures as an autonomous category and activity, Gropius's

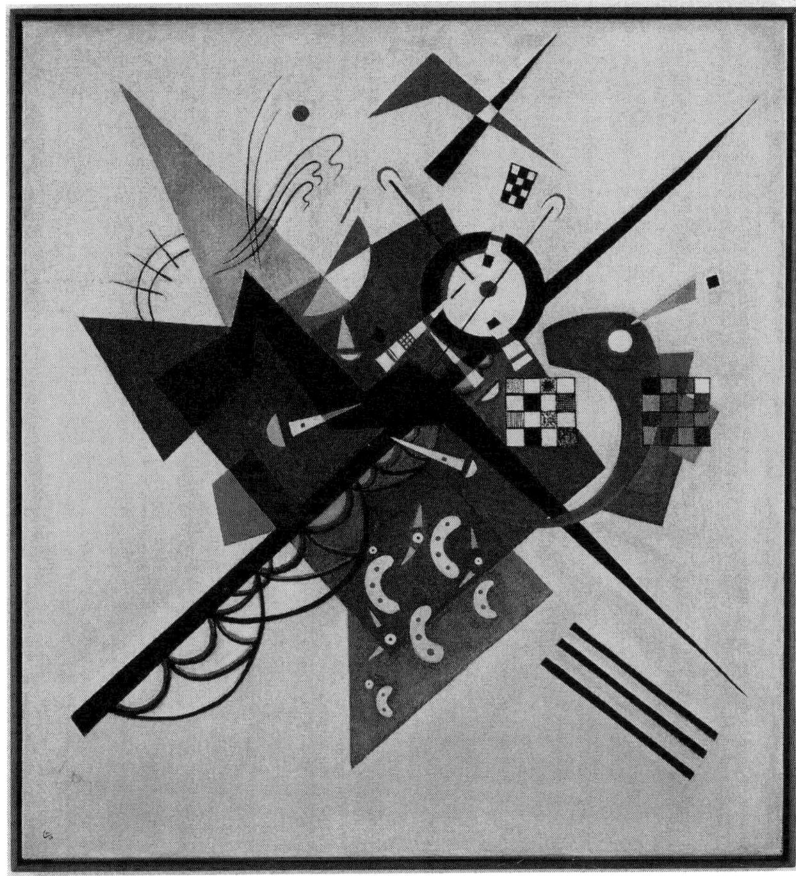

Wassily Kandinsky, *On White II (Auf Weiss II)*, 1923. Painted during the Bauhaus years in Weimar. Oil on canvas, 105 x 98 cm. Musée National d'Art Moderne, Centre Georges Pompidou, Paris, France. Photograph copyright CNAC/MNAM/Dist. RMN-Grand Palais / Art Resource, NY. Copyright 2013 Artists Rights Society (ARS), New York / ADAGP, Paris.

educational outline for the school regarded pictorial theories as a mere stepping-stone for the design of practical objects. And just as often as the Bauhaus literature suggests a unity in the pedagogical approach to design theory—based on the "ABCs of [triangle square circle]"—the pedagogy of distinct painters (Kandinsky, Itten, Klee, and so on) and later graphic designers (Moholy-Nagy, Herbert Bayer, and Joost Schmidt) gives us divergent views on that planar, graphic field.[9] But insofar as ideas about painting at the Bauhaus (particularly in the years between 1919 and 1923) came from the discursive ground of expressionism, the defining characteristics of a picture are laden with a language of the *spiritual* and the *emotional*. As the expressionist proponent G. F. Hartlaub wrote, "Colors are symbols for feelings," and "forms . . . become ecstatic gestures of the soul."[10]

Back to Jungnik's picture: even as we recognize a pictorial composition with its basic formal elements of circles and squares, we also see a network of threads, some rough, others smooth. As warp and weft intersect, the ground is physically animated through the optical and material resonance of the plane. What in painting is a passive ground, a receptive container, is activated within weaving. The material and structural matrix of the woolen picture functions to break down several binaries: figure and ground, form and material, passive and active. Indeed, what seems to be a mere description, "picture made of wool," ultimately begs several questions. What does it mean to use the criteria of one medium (namely, painting, as defined by the rhetoric of expressionism) to define the parameters of another (weaving)? Further, how does this comparison, bound up in the material transfer of one medium to another, help determine weaving's value as an "applied art" in this context, where painting's ideas are "applied"—or, rather, we might say, embedded in a different medium? Perhaps the salient question to be asked in light of Stölzl's statement: what was a "picture" at the early Bauhaus (1919–23) and at this moment in Germany, and what did it mean to make that Bauhaus picture in wool? And finally, why, or how, does this craft accrue a gendered value? Rather than compare the work on paper or canvas and the same motif in weaving—and bemoan the arbitrary hierarchy that divides them—it may be more productive to draw out their differences, to show how those morphological similarities and medial ruptures produced more confusion than clarity.

When we are forced to confront a picture made of wool's terminology, those differences also point to limits, and as such the periphery, or excess, of a field.[11] A stylistic resemblance between pictorial weavings and abstract paintings forces an acknowledgment not simply of the "intermingling" of object categories, but also the value that sets one version above another. Neither medium (weaving nor painting) was so internally unified, even if painting claimed for itself to be the original idea to weaving's mirror—or, rather, its matter. Just as quickly as the form masters conveyed their abstract theories of form, these ideas were applied by the craft workshops. Thus, the borders of nonobjective painting touched on that zone characterized as the "ornamental," "decorative," and "manufactured." And the haziness of this line was best actualized in the weaving workshop, where the weavers created pictures while laboring over a loom.[12] The comparison, as we will see, helped to produce weaving's feminine status, but it also doubled back, contaminating any definition of an expressionist picture.[13]

Unstable Foundations

Like Feininger's expressionist cathedral printed on the cover of Walter Gropius's manifesto, which appears to rise up out of the rubble while simultaneously collapsing inward, the early years of the Bauhaus were anything but stable (see image in the Introduction). From the beginning, the school was caught up in two, somewhat related problems: first of all, the political, cultural, and economic instability of the Weimar Republic after the war in the wake of the Versailles Treaty; second, the internal debates among the Bauhaus faculty about the status of art versus craft. "There is no essential difference between the artist and the craftsman. . . . Let us create a *new guild of craftsmen,* without the class distinctions which raise an arrogant barrier between craftsman and artist," Gropius declared, setting the tone for this postwar manifest. In light of runaway inflation and newly minted poverty out of the ashes of Germany's former bourgeoisie, a smoothing over of class differences seemed pertinent to this otherwise well-to-do cultural figure. Craftsmen, or rather the "hands of a million workers," would be harnessed to lead a future unity of disciplines—"the crystal symbol of a new faith." Indeed, Gropius's proclamation and manifesto seemingly harnessed a Marxist rhetoric and rejected the distinctions between craft and art because it befitted a landscape in which things and buildings had to be remade, and in which communities (or classes) were being redefined in the immediate aftermath of social upheaval—a war, the loss of a regime, a new political system. But the broken barrier was not received kindly by Gropius's new staff of painter-masters, and so, it turns out, the declaration of class unity accompanying Feininger's woodcut only yielded dissension amid the ranks.

If the early Bauhaus seethed with conflicting ideologies and goals in 1919, two particular personalities were the main churners of the soup. On the one hand there was Gropius: a German architect from a family of architects and a member of the Deutscher Werkbund, a design guild whose foundational goal had been to merge handicraft with industry in the interest of the German state's competitiveness in mass production.[14] On the other, there was Swiss-born Johannes Itten, a painter as well trained and practiced in elementary school pedagogy (the Kindergarten philosophy of Friedrich Fröbel) as he was in early-twentieth-century Viennese abstraction (the textbook approach of Hölzl). Itten arrived at the school in its founding year and would quickly establish the fundamentals of the *Vorkurs* (basic course) based on his belief that the individuality of each student could be activated through proper pedagogical techniques. While Gropius handled the finances and politics in the early years, he left many of the curricular decisions to this expressionist painter.

The curriculum's initial manifestation was in certain respects an outcome of Itten's influence, but it also reflected a widespread distrust of industrial technologies and their role in the devastation of World War I—a distrust that Gropius understood and hoped to harness in his appeal to student applicants. His initial "Recommendations for the Founding of an Educational Institution," presented to the Saxon State Ministry in Weimar in January 1916 before he left for the front, had complemented and extended the Werkbund ideology.[15] The school, this document explained, would help "bridge" the gap between artistic education and industry, acting as a "counseling service" for German companies, trades, and crafts. After his return from war in 1918, however, Gropius saw the value in promoting a Romantic vision of art and craft education—inspired by the nineteenth-century Arts and Crafts movement and Ruskinian ideals. His 1919 "Manifesto and Program"—a pamphlet sent to potential students—thus projected the image of a medieval *Bauhütte* (guild) in which a "working community" of artists and craftsmen could produce together in harmony. Although largely the same program, the emphasis shifted over these two years through a linguistic sleight of hand. While the crafts were meant to bridge the gap between education and industry in 1916, by 1919 craft was projected in an alliance of artisanship with the fine arts, an approach more in keeping with German expressionism's spiritual-utopian ideals. *Craft*, in other words, was redefined as a product of workers to the service of idealized communities rather than, say, industrialists.

Again, the newly phrased goals of the Bauhaus were concisely illustrated in the Manifesto's cover print, a black-and-white wood-cut created by his friend the Berliner Secessionist Lyonel Feininger. A sharply expressionist, pseudo-Gothic cathedral rises toward the sky, lit from behind by a great spiritual sun that casts forth beams of energy. Capturing perfectly the sentiment of German postwar culture in the wake of war, Gropius's new educational program and Feininger's print reflected the expansion of expressionism in German culture (which had by then saturated the fields of painting, sculpture, architecture, literature, music, and film). Even if Gropius was, as historian Marcel Franciscono argues, still concerned with the practical and economic potential of cultivating a relationship to industry, he managed to frame—indeed, market—the program to students using the language of the medieval *Bauhütte*, a *Gestamt-kunstwerk* of craft workshops and art.[16] What Gropius established in early 1919 perfectly suited the postwar obsession with self-reliance and finding harmony in nature, sentiments expressed in the back-to-nature *Wandervogel* movement that had captured the imagination of so many of Germany's disillusioned youth at the time.

But this shift from "industry" to "the cooperative effort of all craftsmen" was not just a clever marketing tactic aimed at appealing to and harnessing the power of "wandering" young students; it was economically pragmatic as well.[17] The Thuringian government had initially solicited Gropius in 1916 to take over Weimar's School of Arts and Crafts—from his Werkbund colleague Henry van de Velde, who had to resign on account of his Belgian nationality. After the war, however, the new government also asked Gropius to head the Academy of Fine Arts. With this in mind, the young architect proposed to merge the schools into one entity: the Staatliches Bauhaus in Weimar. The "ultimate aim of all visual arts," he would proclaim, "is the complete building"—a complete building, in other words, that could share resources, especially since the workshops' equipment, with the exception of the weaving workshop, had been almost entirely dismantled. The rejection of the barrier separating art and craft, often highlighted as a radical break with traditional categories, was in some ways an economic necessity that came with a lack of resources or equipment.

Indeed, although Gropius's ideological objectives were instrumental in the school's foundation, the curricular framework he established and the choices he made, according to historian Elaine S. Hochman, were largely made under pressure from various cultural, political, and economic forces within the early Weimar Republic.[18] Hochman argues, for example, that the director's need to appeal to different funding sources from the Thuringian state—itself caught between the progressive forces of the Social Democratic Party and the still-present conservative Wilhelmine bureaucratic apparatus, and alternately swinging between Right and Left administrations—was largely responsible for the school's accommodation of divergent cultural tactics.[19] Similarly, Gropius's involvement in the Arbeitsrat für Kunst (AfK [Work Council for Art]), formed by the expressionist architect and former Werkbund colleague Bruno Taut, helped shape his conception of the *Bauhütte*.

The AfK was associated with the Novembergruppe, which drew its name from the communist-inspired November Revolution of 1918 that overturned the government and led to the establishment of the Weimar Republic in August 1919, and the RGA (Politischer Rat geistiger Arbeiter [Council of *Geistig* Workers]). Like the RGA, the AfK was in solidarity with Berlin's Workers' and Soldiers' Councils, but it also, according to Hoffman, grew out of the artistic community Bund zum Ziel, founded in 1917 by the writer Kurt Hiller.[20] As Hiller's apolitical and utopian goals were aligned with proletarian movements, his promotion of a "*geistig* community" held inconsistencies, found in the very coupling of "community" with "geistig," as Hochman notes: "Usually translated as 'spiritual' or 'intellectual,' *geistig* really means something more. Its truest meaning derives from the Cartesian division between body and soul. . . . [and] relates to the soul and transcends the 'lower' values of the body."[21] When this notion of a *Geist* sought political allegiances in proletarian labor movements, whose concerns were about labor, the resultant entities (first the RGA, then the AfK) were rife with contradictions and conflicted programs. This was especially apparent in the experimental, speculative projects of the AfK's leading member, Taut, whose *Alpine Architektur* (1919) was designed to merge urbanism and agriculture in an organic unity.[22] The group known as the Gläserne Kette (the Crystal Chain), brought together by Taut in 1919, fancied themselves to be "imaginary architects," whose aim was not to build but, rather, create what they vaguely referred to as "the game," or the practice of dreaming in fantastical forms.[23] Taut's "Crystal" architectural work, in other words, attempted to lead a spiritual enlightenment of the people through architecture that, paradoxically, could not be built.

As Gropius took over leadership of the AfK from Taut in February 1919, its troubled agenda (regarding art, architecture, politics, and spiritual ideals), Hochman argues, would prove to be similarly challenging for the Bauhaus's curriculum. In his first speech to the Council on March 22, only a day before the Bauhaus school opened, Gropius resurrected an idealized model of a medieval craft guild. As a messianic artistic community, it "would enlighten and lead society to renew itself by 'sweep[ing] aside the divisions between their various artistic disciplines.'"[24]

A proposal by Gropius's student Walter Determann for a Bauhaus Development in 1920, like the weaving by Jungnik discussed earlier, encapsulates the challenges of this initial Bauhaus moment as it emerged out of the AfK (in the intersection of expressionism and architecture). If seen without the surrounding text, this *Siedlung* design might be mistaken for an abstract drawing by Itten—one in which an oblong pentagon is divided internally into geometric shapes (diamonds, zigzags, and squares) using a modernist palette of mostly primary colors. With the text, one understands that the Determann sketch is proposing a plan for an idealized "community," though the plan also, on second examination, divides that very community into perfectly executed, rigid geometries. Like this *Siedlung* proposal, the Bauhaus community in its early years was at once prescribed and inchoate, pragmatic and abstract, spiritually and materially inclined, espousing unity and dividing from within.

Indeed, as expressionist values butted up against the practical ambitions of the curriculum and Gropius's ideal of the built-house-as-total-work-of-art, the actuality of the school, split into factions, was anything but harmonious. The form masters—some

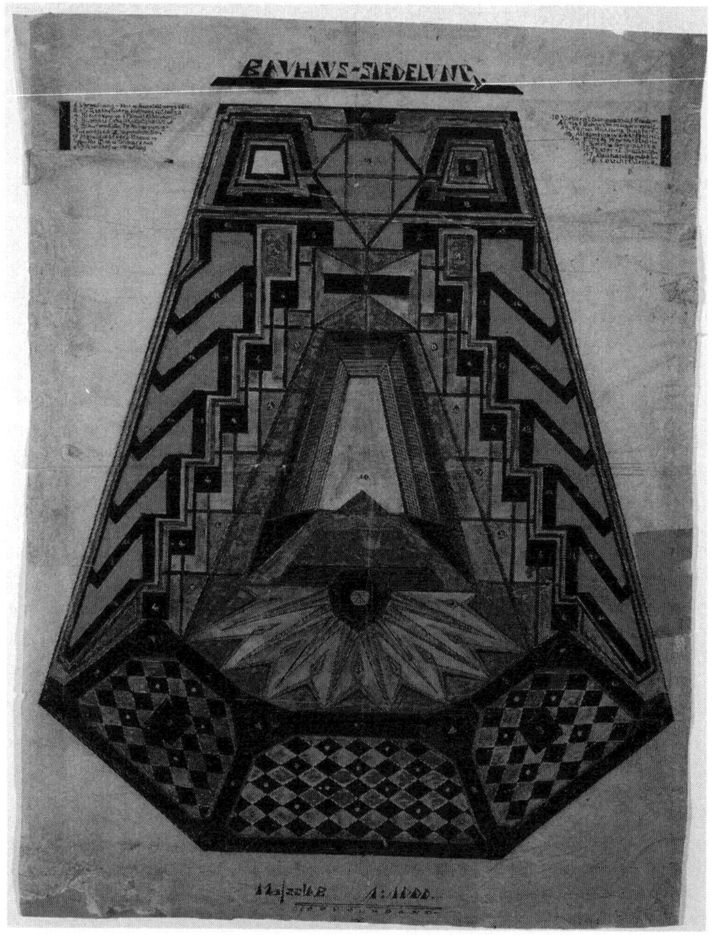

Walter Determann, site plan for "Bauhaus-Siedelung" (Bauhaus housing settlement), Weimar, 1920. Watercolor and ink on paper. Klassik Stiftung Weimar, Graphische Sammlungen. Gift of L. Determann. Source: Klassik Stiftung Weimar.

of which were from the former Weimar academy and resolute on maintaining the strong division between art and craft, in addition to those painters hired by Gropius—felt especially threatened by the centrality of craft in the curriculum. In spite of or perhaps because of the convergence of expressionist architectural designs and expressionist painting, the painters insisted in the school's Masters Council meetings that the Bauhaus could not fully abandon the practice of painting as an "end in itself."[25] Meanwhile, a student-run campaign against Gropius, organized by former students of the Academy, coincided with accusations from the Weimar government's most conservative politicians that the school was promoting the dissolution of German high culture.

Master Itten's *Vorkurs* exercises presented the single greatest alternative to Gropius's workshop curriculum. Although meant as a complementary course that provided students in their first year with so-called basic approaches to formal practice and work with materials, or the specific crafts of the workshops, the course ultimately took on a life of its own, a sense of its own purpose divorced from application and functionality. While the academic practice of painting had certainly dissolved in the cacophony of Itten's classroom chants and meditation exercises, the painter nevertheless created an atmosphere of relative autonomy. Some division between art and craft was part and parcel of the curricular design, and Itten's classroom pedagogy further enforced it.

Even Gropius, who initially proclaimed the breakdown of barriers, and whose manifesto insisted on a leveling of craftsmen and artists, found such categorical divisions to be useful. Not only did he keep the Workshop Masters from positions on the Masters Council of the Bauhaus (the seats were occupied by Masters of Form only), but he also created a hierarchy within the domain of craft that reflected in large part his own interests as an architect. As Baumhoff explains, any definition of *craft* was split internally:

In fact the democratic tradition which is associated today with the Bauhaus was undermined by an ambiguous conception of craftsmanship and by a conception of art based on male genius, which differentiated between three categories of art: fine art *(Kunst)*, such as painting and sculpture; arts-and-crafts *(Kunstgewerbe)*, like pottery and weaving; and handicraft or craftsmanship *(Handwerk)*, such as carpentry.[26]

Gropius ultimately elevated craftsmanship (*Handwerk*) above the merely applied arts (*Kunstgewerbe*), assuming that the latter required less skill and the former, associated with the tectonic art of carpentry, yielded a more direct pathway to building. His ultimate goal: the elevation of architecture to art—a status that had troubled architecture throughout the nineteenth century.[27] In some sense, the differentiation between handicraft and merely applied arts and crafts carried the weight of Gropius's architectural anxiety. Moreover, Baumhoff continues, this division spoke to Gropius's larger concern about the flood of women entering the school:

These categories were themselves gendered: high art and handicraft were male domains, but arts-and-crafts was a female occupation, with comparatively low status. While the first Bauhaus statutes, such as its admissions policies, explicitly prohibited sexual discrimination against women, the *de facto* Bauhaus policy did just that. This was due to the fact that craftsmanship was traditionally a male sphere in Germany. Women were excluded from most of the old handicrafts, and also from most of the art academies until the early 1920s. When Gropius wanted women to become craftsmen he knew that they could hardly *be* professional handicraftsmen but that they could only *do* arts and crafts.[28]

Identity and *being* versus (merely) *doing*: categories helped differentiate the objective hierarchy or status of the diverse crafts taught at the school, as Baumhoff suggests, but they also helped decide which crafts best fit (or not) into Gropius's curricular goals. (Pottery was dropped when the school moved to Dessau—perhaps neither masculine nor feminine enough, or perhaps too encumbered by then out-of-fashion Romantic ideals—and textiles would soon take up their role within the architectural frame.) The problem of *mere doing* that Baumhoff brilliantly points out indeed subtended the gender of the weaving medium in the early years. Doing without thinking (without ends) seems to be the operational difference. The initial absence of "professional" affiliation combined with a lack of a theoretical armature made weaving a (feminine) distraction from "real" craft in this already unstable institution—a workshop practice merely done.

Expressionist Pedagogy

Although the *Vorkurs* only became compulsory in 1921, Itten established the course's principles and the primary methods by which he approached teaching immediately upon his arrival. Itten was hired by Gropius at the encouragement of the latter's first wife, Alma Mahler, who had befriended the artist in Vienna. Through his methodical approach to the study of "counterpoint in painting," as well as his interest in Eastern philosophies (specifically Persian Mazdaism), Itten's lectures widely influenced the students' work and daily activities at the school.[29] Itten took a leave of absence from the Bauhaus in 1920 to study the Mazdaznan religion in Switzerland, where certain cults had popularized the practice, and when he returned, dressed in a robe with his head shaven, he acted as a spiritual leader to the students.[30] But even as early as the fall of 1919, his spiritual bent toward Theosophy conditioned the way in which he managed the classroom, where the ultimate goal was to "translate this spiritual program into aesthetic practice."[31] The initial Bauhaus curriculum thus adopted a decidedly spiritualist rhetoric, even if its approaches and aims remained incoherent. Next to Gropius's goal of building an architectural *Gesamtkunstwerk* and medieval guild, there was Itten's pedagogy involving the choreography of chanting, meditation, and vegetarian diet.

During his tenure as the leader of the *Vorkurs*, Itten focused on "freeing the creative powers" of the students, so each class began with breathing and physical exercises, intended to create "mental and physical readiness for intensive work." Itten felt that the "training of the body as an instrument of the mind is of the greatest importance for creative man."[32] As Franciscono notes,

Perhaps the most original aspect of Itten's pedagogy—the foundation upon which the *Vorkurs* was built, and as far as the Bauhaus was concerned its most problematic aspect—did not come primarily from orthodox sources of professional art education but rather from the liberal Rousseau-Pestalozzi-Froebel-Montessori reform tradition of child education, which had as a basic tenet that education is essentially the bringing out and developing of inherent gifts through a guided process of free and even playful activity and self-learning. This tenet is behind . . . the practice of . . . retrain[ing the student] from the beginning by means which initially include by-passing the intellect in order to reach what is conceived to be his natural, unlearned, creative center.[33]

Itten's class thus merged Rousseau-inspired educational reform with the language of Steiner's Theosophy, Eastern meditation, and an expressionist-romantic interest in the artist's inherent "creative center." Itten also schooled the students in Hölzel's theory of "counterpoint in painting," with a strict analysis of the Old Masters to emphasize the basic, objective rules of contrast in design. Mysticism met pseudo-scientific objectivism. With the study of a basic vocabulary of forms and textures, the students developed abstract compositions that were meant to explore the full possibilities of elemental contrasts. But these forms were also charged with a certain symbolism and metaphysical significance. In 1916, before arriving at the Bauhaus, he declared: "Square: calm, death, black, dark, red; Triangle: intensity, life, white, bright, yellow; Circle: infinite symmetry, peaceful, always blue."[34] And in *Design and Form*, an account of his teaching methods at the Bauhaus, Itten would stress that forms are characterized, first of all, by different spatial directions.[35] The direction of forms is conveyed to the student first in the experience of the body, and then understood abstractly in the mind, or "felt without moving the body." Thus, the formal square would correspond to a strict horizontal and vertical axis and manifest in tense or recurring angular movements; the triangle would be designated by a diagonal axis and expressed through a diversity of angles in bodily motions; finally, the circle would suggest fluid motions, as in the rotation of an arm in space.[36]

Itten's notion of contrasts ultimately yields what he would define as a rhythmic effect. Rhythm, in Itten's theory, is the vital characteristic of the work, combining all contrasts of form, color, and texture. On the topic, Itten writes: there is "great power in everything rhythmical. The rhythm of ebb and high tide changes the shorelines of continents; the rhythmic dances of African tribes, lasting for days and nights, drive people to ecstasies."[37] By definition, a "rhythm can repeat itself in a characteristic regular beat, in up and down, strong and weak, long and short," as in the repetition of "points, lines, planes, spots, volumes, proportions, textures, and color." But rhythm, he notes further, "can also be irregular, continuous, in free flowing movement." In Itten's account, rhythm stands as the great force of the composition, as repetition or as experiential movement.

A notebook by Gunta Stölzl from Itten's *Vorkurs* in 1919 recorded Itten's teaching: "In form is movement, ceaseless movement. [Movement] is the rising of the world. . . . we do not yet comprehend it, we feel it."[38] Through lectures and demonstrations, then transcribed in Stölzl's journal, Itten's expressionist pedagogy

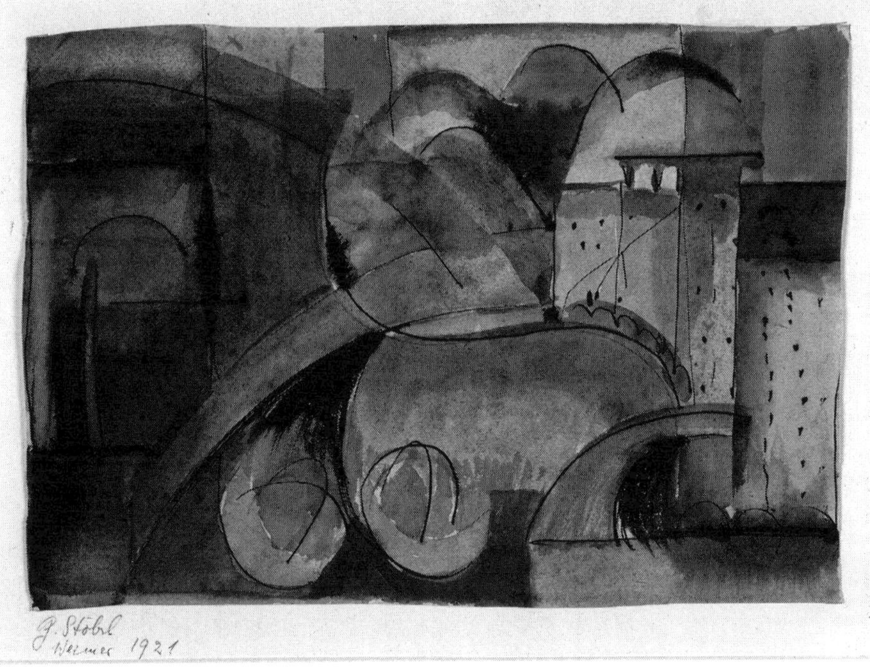

Gunta Stölzl, *Untitled,* 1921. Watercolor on paper. Photograph by John Stoel.
Copyright 2013 Artists Rights Society (ARS), New York / VG Bild-Kunst, Bonn.

entered the weaver's pictorial practice. As "felt" but not "comprehended," the idea of movement within form can be seen in Stölzl's many watercolors, such as a work from 1921. Yet some of her
watercolors, also sketches for potential weavings rather than ends
in themselves, make it apparent that the weaver was considering
the technical limitations of weaving (see Plates 2 and 3). A pictorial weaving, she no doubt understood at this point, is not simply
the transfer of a picture into wool; rather, it has its own "ideas."
In a watercolor sketch for a wall hanging, Stölzl begins to think
through a specific apparatus: the loom, its heddles raising and low-
ering the warp in alternating sequences. The alternating rhythm
of the geometric and linear pattern internalizes the parameters
of the weaving grid, the grid of interlocked threads that limit the
formation of curves. So when Itten's notion of rhythm meets the
work of the weaver, the painter's combined esotericism and scientific language of formal reduction become increasingly difficult

to pull apart. Stölzl's drawing projects a contiguous relationship between rhythm, as such, and the physical technique required by the loom: the feet that press treadles, then the hands that help to shuttle weft through the opening of the shed—the tent of warp that momentarily opens up, allowing for a rhythmic vertical-horizontal connection to be made.

Expressionist Theory

If the Bauhaus's foundations had some irregularities owing to Gropius's and Itten's complex background and goals, these also stemmed from the inconsistencies that marked the expressionist movement's different voices—the various artists, critics, activists, and art historians, such as Wilhelm Worringer, author of *Abstraction and Empathy* (1907), and Paul Fechter, author of *Der Expressionismus* (1914), who advocated on behalf of the movement.[39] In the sixteen years between 1905 and 1921 in which expressionism held a strong, albeit socially marginalized, artistic position in Germany, the movement generated texts by G. F. Hartlaub proclaiming its alignment with spiritual mysticism and Rudolf Steiner's Anthroposophy, as well as a collection of poetry edited by anarchist poet and social critic Ludwig Rubiner who connected expressionism to proletarian politics.[40]

While a call for an engagement with politics was often crucial to certain expressionists, like the members of Der Sturm and the Novembergruppe, it was most often in the language of spiritual transcendence that its proponents addressed the relationship between art and society. Thus, the critic Herbert Kühn would write: "Expressionism is—as is socialism—the same outcry against matter, against the unspiritual, against machines, against centralization, for the spirit, for God, for the humanity in man."[41] In their alignment with the workers' movements, the expressionists espoused a return to an "anti-materialist" preindustrial age and identified artists as the spiritual leaders of the modern world.

Groups such as Der Blaue Reiter, led by Kandinsky and Franz Marc in Munich, and Die Brücke, begun by Dresden painter Ernst Ludwig Kirchner, shaped the artistic standards of the movement. Kirchner's Brücke, begun around 1905, meanwhile identified what he saw as a specifically German form of modern painting, readily denying his painterly debt to international (specifically French) modernist movements, such as cubism, and emphasizing instead the importance of German Gothic and "primitive" art for his approach to painterly practice. The artists of Der Blaue Reiter, on the other hand, located metaphysical significance in the "universal" pictorial elements of form and color, and claimed for painting the capacity to siphon Spirit into art as though through its pigment-stained surfaces. Where Kirchner maintained an emphasis on representational figuration in order to express the subject's inner state, Kandinsky sought to express inner thoughts and feelings through the abstraction of color and form from nature. In spite of their differences, however, both groups spoke of the importance of subjective experience for shaping the forms found in the work of art. Thus a picture, in this context, necessarily accomplishes the truthful manifestation of the artist's soul. Referring to the work of these painters, Paul Fechter wrote: "Landscapes of souls are created without any landscape features, musical states are transposed into colors and lines; the distance between emotions and expression is shortened here to its minimum."[42] At the foundation of expressionism was an assumption that the work of art can be a direct expression of the artist's interior "landscape." Likewise, the painter's brush, as a tool at the service of the artist's will, enabled him to battle the materialist forces of the industrial world.

The version of expressionism that entered the Bauhaus was especially influenced by the writings of Kandinsky. When Gropius finally arranged for Kandinsky to come teach at the Bauhaus in 1921, the students had already, in part through Itten's teaching, absorbed the Russian-born painter's ideas about composition or color as the expression of Spirit. Gropius mentioned in a letter to Kandinsky how much the students looked forward to his mentorship even before he began teaching there.[43] His *Über das Geistige in der Kunst* (*On the Spiritual in Art*), which first appeared in 1911 and described the limits of painting, was undoubtedly considered essential reading among the young *Bauhäusler*.

Taking on the Theosophically inspired rhetoric of his moment, Kandinsky begins his eponymous text by citing the failure of his present society to address spiritual development.[44] "Our souls, which are only now beginning to awaken after the long reign of materialism, harbor seeds of desperation, unbelief, lack of purpose."[45] Accordingly,

Art, which at such times leads a degraded life, is used exclusively for materialistic ends. It seeks in *hard material* the stuff of which it is made, for it knows no finer. Thus, objects whose portrayal [or reproduction (*wiederzugeben*)] it regards as its only purpose, remain the same, unchanged. The question "What?" in art disappears *eo ipso*. Only the question "How?"—How will the artists succeed in recapturing that same material object?—remains. This question becomes the artist's "credo." Art is without a soul.[46]

Kandinsky's belief is typical of much expressionist rhetoric, in suggesting that a turn to the expression of the soul could potentially lead a way out of the mechanical nature of the modern world—in which there is, as he says, too much emphasis on the mere "stuff of which [stuff] is made." He aims to reinvigorate the interior life of the artist, and by association culture in general. Thus the theoretical opposition between economically or technically tainted work (labor) and nonmaterial or spiritual experience is invoked throughout Kandinsky's text. Kandinsky insists that too much attention to the material (the physical substance but, even more, the method or reproduction) is problematic for the advancement of art—that is, when the "How?" takes precedence over the "What?" and the methods of artistic practice become a rationale. Kandinsky thus seeks in art that which, while necessarily activated through the material properties of color and connected to the senses of the spectator's or artist's body ("the soul," he writes, "is closely connected to the body"), supersedes all technical means.

Internal necessity (innere Notwendigkeit), Kandinsky's category for the principle of art, is the term around which Kandinsky's thesis develops and, it could be argued, becomes undone. Here we find the roots of his text's tautological mess: the work's content may follow the principle of internal necessity (spirit), but the harmony that "sets the soul vibrating" rests on the manipulation of color and the particular formal properties of the work, where form is "the expression of inner content."[47]

Referring to the hermetically sealed space of painting, the term *internal necessity* thus proposes that a painting, for instance, should express its limits or definite rules and conditions so that the "abstract element [can] come to the fore."[48] In an examination of "the inner value of one's materials . . . , i.e., . . . of color," or the "inner sound of a given form," the work's internal necessity is "laid bare."[49] But related to the category of art more generally, internal necessity reaches beyond the limits of the concrete form, and its manifestation through a medium, to contact a spirit—an interior of a different sort. And so the *internal* refers not just to the particular, material conditions of painting, but also to the artist's emotional and psychic life, as his "eyes [are] directed toward his own inner life and his ears turned to the voice of inner necessity."[50] The internal properties of painting establish *direct* contact with the interiority of the artist, such that "as a servant of art," his work "express[es] what is peculiar to art in general (element of the pure and eternally artistic . . .)," as well as the "limits of a particular art."[51] What is established through internal necessity, in other words, is a "mystical necessity"—found not "in the external, but in the root of roots—in the mystical content of art."[52]

Indeed, in this term *internal necessity* two distinct elements (the space of the work and internal space of the soul) correspond to one another as in an analogy, but also with one another, as if across a direct passage from the artist's soul to the work to the receptive viewer. (Here the diagram by Kandinsky with which I started the chapter comes into relief.) While the work is hermetically sealed, its passage to the Spiritual World is guaranteed through the interiority of the artist, who gives to that work its mystical guarantee, as if it flowed unhampered from his soul to his hand through the brush to the surface and on to the viewer.[53] In order for the internal necessity of the work to connect metonymically to the inner necessity found in the soul, Kandinsky's idea relies on a kind of transparency between these two surfaces. In other words, an art, such as painting or music, if it is to cohere to its internal limits, can never get caught in the web of its means. Painting eventually overcomes the process by which color is applied to canvas to become the (now seemingly unmediated) direct expression of meaning in external form. Hence, the painter eventually seeks in colors and forms their abstract and universal significance: red as square, blue as circle, yellow as triangle.

In Jean-Joseph Goux's comparison of Kandinsky's writing to Hegel's *Aesthetics,* he argues that the artist's movement toward "pure composition" requires that painting lose its reference to "external nature."[54] Like Hegel, according to Goux, Kandinsky seeks in art that which is the least tethered to the ground; so where Hegel identified the remnants of material sensuousness in painting as that which made it inferior to music or poetry in the progression of the arts toward Spirit, Kandinsky proposes an alternative to painting's conundrum: pictorial abstraction. "If painting wishes to be exalted to the free sky of spirit, it must cut the bonds that imprison it to 'matter,' it must embrace the abstract means by which poetry, according to Hegel, presents an idea," writes Goux.[55] Painting has to "*become sound,* as it were, in order to rise to the ranks of idealism: sound that, as Hegel says, is of an abstract nature, expresses the 'ideality of matter.'" Thus, Kandinsky paradoxically effaces the material conditions of production in order to ensure "the spiritual transparency of meaning."[56] Leah Dickerman, by contrast, has argued that such a reading of Kandinsky as "concerned with a primarily transcendental immateriality and purity" is too "simplistic."[57] The sensual, indeed bodily, aspects of perception (found especially in his discussion of synesthesia) are key to the artist's practice and theory. Insofar as the harmony of colors are "based on the principle of *touching* the human soul," Dickerman argues, bodily perception is integral to the soul. Nevertheless, these two visions of Kandinsky are more in sync than it would seem. While Dickerman emphasizes the significance placed on the spectator's physical, sensual, and psychic experience of color in painting, and Goux emphasizes the drive toward a transcendental experience, both authors agree that Kandinsky seeks in color an "unobstructed conduit to the interior."[58] Perception is about overcoming the fetters of production; so the medium of painting is at its height of specificity when it becomes a transparent vehicle of communication—or becomes medium-less.

Crucial here is the way in which Kandinsky's understanding of painting is less about its materiality than its function as a conduit between different internal realms. Here it helps to cite a short text he wrote for *Der Sturm* in 1913, which summed up his division between the inner and outer dimensions of art:

As long as the soul is joined to the body, it can as a rule only receive vibrations via the medium of feelings. Feelings are therefore a bridge from the nonmaterial to the material (in the case of the artist) and from the material to the nonmaterial (in the case of the observer).

Emotion—feelings—the work of art—feelings—emotion.[59]

One might say that painting's development in the properties of abstract form and color is that which opens the work beyond its "external expression" to feelings, to an emotion or the soul of the artist (another internal realm). Thus, it is across this phrase *internal necessity* that two, seemingly incompatible terms—*material constraints* and *spiritual interiority*—are forced into a collision. Although Kandinsky sought to construct a cohesive picture of spiritual significance, a careful reading of his text reveals several knots: his language for determining art in general and the medium of painting in particular was, from the start, rather vexed by an insistence that abstraction could provide a direct, practically unmediated correspondence between the inner and the outer, the soul and external form, albeit through the "medium of feelings" (not of canvas and paint).

Weaving's art would eventually find the snag in Kandinsky's theory: as a picture is interwoven with its material, a different kind of external enters into the apparently sealed limits of the pictorial medium. Perhaps we could even say that weaving undoes the seal on the hermetic realms of the work and, as such, the realm of the soul. In its use of a technique known as Smyrna cross-stitch, one picture made of wool produced in 1922–23 by the workshop weaver Lore Leudesdorff speaks to Kandinsky's conundrum of mediation. Leudesdorff's small carpet, enframed by a border of fringe on two sides, uses an array of colors—cadmium red, pink, blue, brown, white, and black—to create a field of intersecting dynamic forms and lines. Even more than, say, Kandinsky's *White Line No. 232* from 1920, Leudesdorff's composition lacks a centering principle as the malformed patches of color are strewn across it according to no identifiable schema. Color appears to rise from the woolen surface as if spontaneously—more like a fungal growth pattern than a notional presentation of Platonic geometries. But then, on closer inspection, the overall grid of the knotted surface—the ground through which the pile of colored yarn figures a composition—curtails this spontaneity. We can barely discern shapes or lines, for the organic-ish forms are so disrupted by the digital field from which they emerge. The composition ultimately conforms to the rectangularity of the structural ground, the "stuff of which it is made," so the would-be sinuous curves of arcs are noticeably made jagged, squared off. Indeed, these forms are not the product of the smooth, gestural stroke of a painter's brush—a hand moving unrestrictedly across a surface. They are clearly developed through a different procedure. As the woolen surface overtly mediates the picture's content, Leudesdorff's picture thus draws up new kinds of metaphors. Sensuous colors, realized through the heavy wool they saturate as dye, point toward the production and distribution of commercial, chemically dyed threads, or the difficult economic and political conditions through which wool entered the Bauhaus in the first place. The work induces one to ask not after the "spiritual significance" of its colors but after the means of its manufacture, whereby its pattern arises from the Smyrna technique of stitching threads into another, cloth substrate or backing.

Leudesdorff's small, stitched carpet indeed compels us to pose some questions. If an abstract composition can be carried into wool—into and through a new medium (the means of a certain craft)—what happens to the spiritual content conveyed by painterly forms and colors? Is the picture or the Soul (the what) still there, despite a transformation of the substance and the method (the how), or despite the fact that these properties are now stitched into the plane, calling forth an economic reality? Moreover, can the work still carry significance if it provides no mimetic picture of the external world, or if it has no oracle (Kandinsky) to speak of its invisible, supernatural forces? Or is it just a decorative object without meaning or subjective depth?

Or to reverse this line of questioning, is painting really so internally unified if its constituent elements of color and form can so easily be "applied" (in a "domestic" practice of stitching) to another medium? Even as Kandinsky's internally necessary picture reaches toward another, spiritual space, it too must confront the sensuous Other of its own means.

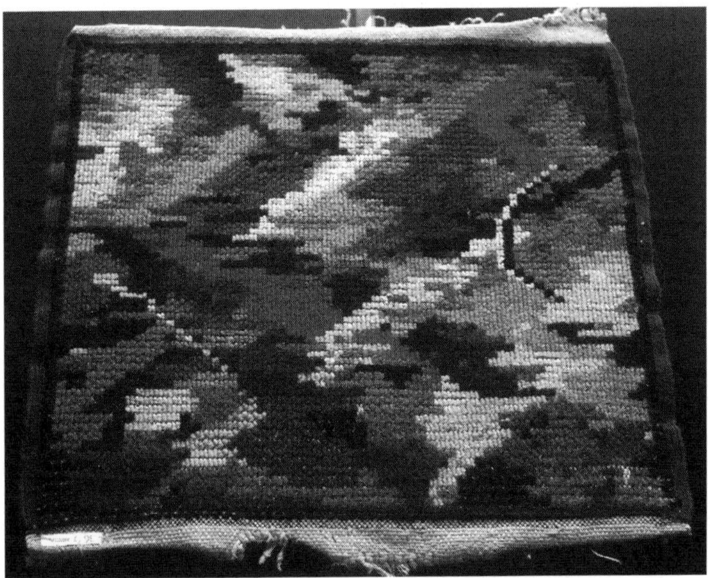

Lore Leudesdorff, Smyrna carpet, 1922–23 (detail: back). Photograph by T'ai Smith. Bauhaus-Archiv Berlin.

Or perhaps more to the point, is painting so autonomous, so spiritual, if any dialogue between painting's internal and external "limits" require reconciliation through textual rhetoric, *another* medium. "Painting in particular" has only accessed the "spiritual in art" through, one might say, a linguistic sleight of hand, and language that figures forth the "soul" in color. What differentiates Kandinsky's painting (as art) from Leudesdorff's carpet (as craft)? The answer: another frame, a book like *On the Spiritual in Art*.

Of course, this latter question and its implicit problems were acknowledged by Kandinsky himself. A prolific and at times beautiful writer who composed as many essays on art as he did letters and poetry, Kandinsky often and somewhat anxiously interpolated his texts with comments on the incommensurability of writing and painting.[60] Interested in the analogy of abstract painting to music, he understood the problems of translation on several levels. And so just as Kandinsky argued for painting's formal specificity, he found himself simultaneously excusing and complicating his own act of writing on the "language" of color in painting: "It is clear," he notes, "that all the descriptions employed for these quite simple colors are extremely provisional and clumsy. . . . The different tones of the colors, like those of music, are of a much subtler nature and awaken far subtler variations in the soul than can be described in words."[61] Mere words can never truly capture the essential vibration of a tone within the artist or a spectator's being. Diagrams and "tables" (another kind of picture) can help "explain" the "emotional effects" of color interactions on a "spectator," but toward the end of his chapter on the "Language of Forms and Colors" he insists that the "forces hidden in the various arts [painting, music, poetry] are themselves fundamentally different."[62] Words and tables only ever provide an approximation.

Thus, precisely that through which Kandinsky seeks to explain his theory of art to a wider public is also that which complicates painting's (form and color's) claim to specificity, or its capacity to express the soul any more, say, than an abstract pattern found in a piece of fabric. The well-crafted armature of Kandinsky's "language of forms and colors" defined abstract painting's internal necessity as a direct expression of the soul, but it also bound his pictorial practice, from the get-go, to the vehicle of words.

The Picture of Labor: Practice without Theory

Departing from (but also misconstruing aspects of) Kandinsky's argument, Itten would later focus on a discussion of the painterly process (the how). Arguing that painting was able to maintain its soul—in spite of the material conditions of industrialism or war—due to the nuances of the brush, Itten focused on the particular process that connects the artist to the surface of the picture:[63]

The beginner becomes aware of the elastic point of the brush only when he . . . feels the form and is ready to follow this feeling. Brushes are superior to charcoal as expressive media because they achieve richer nuances. Charcoal always produces the same dark stroke whether it is applied with a right or a left slant. But the brush allows rich variation.[64]

Itten thus contends that painting is the most successful means for the "creative release" of the subject's interiority, because its tool has the capacity to register gradations in the artist's movement.

Nevertheless, given that artistic practice is a process—one that derives from the physical movements of a body—Itten ends up being rather distressed by any potential proximity to labor. Warding off the space in which one practice meets the conditions of the other, he defines artistic process according to a movement from *Arbeit* (labor) to *Spiel* (play). In a letter to a friend, written in December 1919, he stresses the ultimate ascendance of the latter:

Our play [*Spiel*]—our celebration [*Fest*]—our work [*Arbeit*]

. . . Build the Bauhaus—construct it—ordain it—diverse forces—bring diverse forces into unity—build up diverse forces into an independent organism—the game of strengths into harmony, add to the celebration.

Play becomes celebration—celebration becomes labor—labor becomes play.

It appears to me the highest completion of our human activities is that our play becomes labor and labor becomes celebration and our celebration becomes play.[65]

Where at first Itten appears to suggest a circular relationship between each element (*Arbeit, Fest, Spiel*), by the end of the text everything becomes play. The "highest completion of our human activities" is when play overcomes labor. Although the question of labor and physical processes in general are related for Itten, he ultimately imbues labor with free play, thereby casting the material conditions of production aside.

Pictorial weaving developed out of painting's language of form and color, but it produced the picture differently, making a matter of wool and its apparatus. Take Stölzl's abstract design for a wall hanging (1923) mentioned earlier, where the layers build rhythmically, alternating colors and horizontal bands, and clearly cite Itten's counterpoint theory of rhythm, of contrasting form and color. But as the piece is rendered in the wall hanging, one begins to see the tension between the matrix of weaving and Itten's pictorial theory. Contrasting material features, such as silky versus rough, or shiny versus matte, as well as contrasting textures, show that the formal design is not merely stamped onto the material but is significantly transformed by the process. Itten's and Kandinsky's formal theories inspired Stölzl's design—the abstract forms that appear within its matrix—but the textile medium also alters the two-dimensionality of the initial sketch. Any counterpoint theory is realized but also textured anew. Now seen in the wall hanging, moreover, the design recursively figures the vertical building of the weft, where, like the stacking of bricks, the addition of layers is predicated on the completion of previous layers.[66] Weaving's practice and material, or rather its labor and ground, now provide the condition for the design. The abstract pattern or rhythm is no longer the impetus—the idea (or sketch) that initiates and dictates the system of manufacture—but is that which is generated by the system (the mode of production).

We have only to think of Marx, whose early writing on "sensuousness" set a different tone for the way that "material" would be construed. Initially working from Feuerbach's materialist critique of Hegel's "abstract thinking," Marx further suggests that raw material was never that—simply "raw"—an unmediated substance to be formed by the willing mind. It is bound to human activity (in "social intercourse") and, as such, the productive forces of history.[67] Sensuousness thus denotes the materially perceptible state of objects or the state of man's senses vis-à-vis objects (or nature), as it did for Feuerbach, but now it also pertains to the nexus governing objects and subjects as they develop in social intercourse. The "sensuous external world . . . is the material on which [the worker's] labor is realized, in which it is active, from which, and by means of which it produces."[68] Even that which comes from nature as "raw" has a history, another kind of materiality—one that emerges in a social and economic field; it is always already subject to sensuous activity, always already mediated. Threads are not simply the physical *Stoff* (of wool, cotton, or artificial silk [*Kunstseide*])[69] but are also products of the material history through which they enter the Bauhaus and link it (metonymically, one might say) to the industrial and domestic production of thread and textiles in Germany in the nineteenth and early-twentieth centuries—for example, the loss of access to wool and cotton after the First World War, sparking the weavers' experimentation with Germany's newly developed, man-made materials derived from trees, like *Cellophan*.[70]

Moreover, if Marx's discussion of sensual materials and objects is important to weaving, it is especially so insofar as it is used to exemplify the relationship between the worker and his labor in a capitalist economy, whereby labor has become "abstract labour, absolutely indifferent to its particular specificity"; it is "a merely formal activity, or, what is the same, a merely material [*stofflich*] activity, activity pure and simple." (Ironically, it seems, the specificity of textile production as it came under capital is that it was the first to erase its specificity, and yet also, at the same time, was never able to escape its "merely material activity.")[71] In his *1844 Manuscripts* Marx cites statistics and the writings of political economists and social critics, continuously identifying the textile industry as a concrete example of "estranged labor" under capital.[72] The worker's process at the loom, no matter how physically active, is ultimately passive: the machine owns his or her body, not vice versa. And this discourse carried on into the twentieth century. Indeed, the practice of weaving emerged in the popular imagination of Weimar Germany through literature and newspaper reports as an industry that exemplified the worst conditions of industry,[73] as in Gerhart Hauptmann's 1892 play *The Weavers,* which was widely read and performed across Germany during the 1920s.[74] The play's first scenes portray impoverished country weavers who work at their looms from home and sell their products to a local, unsympathetic businessman. Hauptmann describes the loud, whirring, repetitious murmur of the looms, which permeate the space of the workers. The characters' bodies are bent over and crooked to fit the apparatus that causes their poor posture and health; they are seen to submit physically, and by implication spiritually, to the mode of production that subsumes their identities, yielding entirely to the demands and logic of the apparatus. Thus Bauhaus weaving was not just associated with domestic labor but emerged in the metaphorical space created by such texts. Even while the Weimar institution aspired to create an unalienated version of workshop labor through a romanticized model of the premodern craft guild, the textile medium had absorbed this entrenched association.

The entwined categories of labor and weaving in the nineteenth-century discourse of political economy (and its critiques) remained central to broader theoretical debates in the Weimar moment. In Max Weber's *General Economic History,* published in 1923 from lectures written during the winter of 1919, for example, he focuses on labor within the historical development of capitalism, yielding important questions about the status of modern textile production as a particular kind of work.[75] Weaving is an exemplary case in economic history, Weber notes, and particularly crucial for a social theory of modernity: "The decisive factor in the triumph of the mechanization and rationalization of work was the fate of cotton manufacture," whereby factory machines first took over production from the manual loom.[76] But even prior to its mechanization by modern technology, Weber argues, weaving was already systematized on account of its loom and spinning wheel apparatuses, which were often owned by an entrepreneur. Textile production was the first historical instance in which the social organization of the shop instituted a schematic division of labor and subsumed, or abstracted, the labor process. To describe an early textile shop, Weber summarizes a sixteenth-century English text:

Two hundred looms are collected in the workroom; they belong to the enterpriser owning the establishment, who also furnishes the raw material and to whom the product belongs. The weavers work for wages, children being also employed as workers and helpers. For feeding the workers, the entrepreneur maintained a complete staff of provision workers, butchers, bakers, etc. People marveled at the industry as a world wonder . . . the looms were brought together in the house of the owner. This fact represented a considerable advantage to the entrepreneur; for the first time disciplined work appeared, making possible control over the uniformity of the product and the quantity of the output. For the worker there was the disadvantage—which still constitutes the *odious* feature of factory work—that he worked under the compulsion of external conditions. . . .[77]

So whereas Marx would argue that the "capitalist character of manufacture" beginning sometime in the eighteenth century would divide workers from one another and also within, Weber observes that "the worker was [already] entirely separated from the means of production" in preindustrial textile workshops.[78] Weber finds in this historical phenomenon a precedent for every model of work thereafter. Textile mills establish the ground for the capitalist mode of production.

The way in which Weber frames the category of labor can be defined technically, but its implications are sociological, involving, most significantly, fundamental gender divisions: "In general the oldest form of specialization is a strict division of labor between the sexes."[79] In agrarian society, between working the land and taking care of the household (where producing vessels for cooking, braiding mats, spinning, and weaving were of concern), "woman was a continuous worker, the man an occasional one." Though Weber shies away from designating value to the category of labor, a careful reading of his text yields considerably value-laden connotations. The terms *mechanization* and *rationalization,* used to describe the "odious feature of factory work," are, after all, highly charged (with a certain amount of loathing and anxiety). Thus, in Weber's case, the division of labor that he describes has philosophical consequences, deriving from a tradition that puts form in opposition to matter, and purpose, reason, or telos against the material flux of history. So when Weber notes the religious significance of "labor" in *The Protestant Ethic and the Spirit of Capitalism,* one can hear the tones of valuation. Where labor (the means) is spiritualized in Protestant discourse, it is routed through a notion of an "end," whereby work is a reflection of God's will and at the service of God. And from another vantage, regarding the "masculine" work of medicine men and blacksmiths, Weber notes their claim to spirituality or "magic."[80] "Men's work," such as curing illness or appropriating territory through war, is seen to have "ends," leading on to some greater goal.[81] "Women's work," such as tilling the soil or producing textiles for the household, by contrast, is considered a mode of maintenance, a form of "pure labor."[82] In the Western tradition, women's labor historically lacks a spiritual, magical, or otherwise theoretical dimension. The labor of women is described as an odious precursor to the estranged factory labor of the nineteenth century.

The practice of Bauhaus pictorial weaving, one might say, similarly lacked theoretical purpose, a spiritually nuanced goal. Thus the painter Georg Muche actively distanced himself from the weaving workshop, for which he acted officially as form master.[83] Like Johannes Itten, the weaving workshop form master before him, Muche continued to regard weaving pictorially, not as an independent form. And without a theoretical dimension or goal, weaving remained in his eyes a manual craft, an example of pure labor, a means without ends. In a piece of writing from 1923, Muche expressed his sole interest with the weavers: to set a plan for organizing the workshop and the weavers' labor more "economically."[84] The piece is titled "Suggestion for the Economical Organization of the Weaving Workshop" and is scrawled across four handwritten pages in which he constructs diagrams and lists of the workshop's technical costs. Less concerned with setting a teaching agenda or with the workshop's formal products than the organization of its workers, Muche never developed a theory for thinking about weaving's practice and the relationship among wool, form, and color—the pedagogical categories for which he was apparently responsible as form master. Instead, he writes of the weavers' labor, their pay for sold pieces, and the ways in which the workshop can function more productively. Rather than view weaving as a distinct craft with a specific form or technique, Muche regarded the workshop as a potentially lucrative resource for the school. In December 1922, the weaving workshop had grossed an impressive amount of money for the Bauhaus, selling more products and at higher prices than any other workshop during an exhibition of Bauhaus products in Zurich.[85] But despite (or because of) their economic success, the weavers continued to occupy a low status within the school's hierarchy of media. As the social and economic history of textiles haunted the Bauhaus weaving workshop, the textile medium, it seems, was dismissed as mere labor, as ornamental form without "intuition," whose "inner sound" could only ever "simulate internal necessity."[86]

Ornament: From *Kunstwollen* to Labor

The significance of ornament had at the end of the nineteenth century been a topic of much debate in art history, having everything to do with an opposition between technique, or manual labor, and the idea of an "inner impulse." In *Stilfragen* (Problems of Style) from 1893, the Viennese Aloïs Riegl presented a history of style that sought to redeem ornament for art history, to elevate its status. But in order to do so he explicitly resisted the reductive "technical-materialist" idea of ornament initiated by the writing of Gottfried

Semper in the 1850s and 1860s, which saw transformations in ornamental style as the result of developments in technique.[87] As a harsh critic of the kind of positivism he saw in Semper's writing, Riegl attempted to recast ornament in the language of "psychological motivation," arguing that the "artistic impulse" of an era, not its technology, was the foundation of different ornamental styles. "The invention of line," he wrote,

took place during the natural course of an essentially artistic process. . . . All [the cave dwellers] needed to do was arrange them according to principles of rhythm and symmetry. . . . The Geometric Style of the cave dwellers of Aquitaine, therefore, was not the material product of handicraft but the pure fruit of an elementary artistic desire for decoration. . . . All of art history presents itself as a continuous struggle with material: it is not the tool—which is determined by technique—but the artistically creative idea that strives to expand its creative realm and increase its formal potential.[88]

Ornamentation, like the invention of line, was thus founded on a "human desire" to decorate, or to increase an idea's "formal potential."

The question through which Riegl frames much of his argument about ornament, in particular with regard to geometric style, involves a response to the claim by Semper that tectonic forms, geometric motifs, and linear patterns originated from the integration of the technique of interlocking threads. Semper claimed that "textiles should undoubtedly take precedence because they can be seen, as it were, as the primeval art from which all other arts—*not excepting ceramics*—borrowed their types and symbols."[89] Riegl vociferously attacks this idea throughout his introduction and first chapter, returning to the claims about weaving technique again and again, only to "reduce the importance of textile decoration to the level it deserves."[90] What is interesting here is how Riegl's textual anxiety—perhaps related to his own status as a curator of textiles at the Kunstgewerbemuseum in Vienna—emerges in the moment of his portrayal of the weaving medium. Textiles, he concludes, are merely a "subset, equivalent to any other category of surface decoration." While arguing that sculptural forms in clay or metal objects were in fact the original historical site from which patterns emerged, according to a creative impulse or will of a people

(*Kunstwollen*), or human agent, to decorate and thereby communicate, Riegl has to rid textiles of their *theoretical* (or formal) import for other media. And so his text must assume (perhaps even more than Semper's) that methods of thread interlacing are merely technical developments used for the purpose of clothing the body, that weaving is nothing more than a tool. Although in Riegl's *Stilfragen* the term *ornament* seems at first to transcend technique and become connected to creative impulses, it now signals two layers, two oppositional forces. Textiles become a merely material, technical ground, while a more artistic "will to form" or "inner impulse" transcends them.

By the early twentieth century, a discussion of ornament signaled, on the one hand, the proliferation of new technologies—as machines stamped out patterns in perfect uniformity—and on the other, the most odious conditions of capitalist manufacture, whereby physical labor was not just exploited but also "wasted." This is the argument that gave rise to modernist architecture, in the writings of Adolf Loos, who declared that ornament was a "crime," a measure of a society's degeneracy, but also a "devaluation of labour": "The producer of ornament must work for twenty hours to obtain the same income of a modern labourer who works for eight hours. . . . Ornament is wasted manpower and therefore wasted health."[91]

Subsequently, in Siegfried Kracauer's "The Mass Ornament," we see how the picture of labor is likewise intimately entwined with the notion of ornament. Drawing on the debate that entered early-twentieth-century discourse after Riegl, he ultimately unpacks the term through a Marxist analysis of labor. Although Kracauer's text was written in 1927, a few years after the expressionist period of the Bauhaus, his thought is apt here as a means to understand further the values through which weaving was feminized, or assessed as a mechanical medium at this moment in Germany. As "The Mass Ornament" addresses the problematic relation of industrial modernity to both labor and ornamental style, Kracauer relies on Riegl's assertion that ornament, in its earliest forms, organically surged up from human drives. In effect, Kracauer's text brings Riegl's art historical and psychological vocabulary into the domain of social critique—using it to naturalize the notion of an original, preindustrial "humanity." Drawing on Riegl's language, Kracauer appreciates how premodern communal groups apparently endowed "ornaments with a magic force . . . burdening them with meaning to such an extent that they [could not] be reduced to a pure assemblage of lines." He then contrasts the premodern ornament with the more abstract manifestation of ornament in Weimar society, with its "body culture" based in mechanical processes. The specific cultural form of the performing Tiller Girls, which he calls the "mass ornament," aligns, according to Kracauer, with the social forces of Taylorist production. The very question of labor is inscribed within the gymnastic activity of female bodies in the public spectacle, as the larger configuration of the spectacle assigns each part, the position of each girl, to the ornament's geometric form. For Kracauer, this modern spectacle's organization of bodies signifies a dehumanized world, one lacking freedom or subjectivity:

The patterns seen in the stadiums and cabarets . . . are composed of elements that are mere building blocks and nothing more. The construction of the edifice depends on the size of the stones and their number. It is the mass that is employed here. Only as parts of a mass, not as individuals who believe themselves to be formed from within, do people become fractions of a figure.[92]

For Kracauer, the organic life force of communal relations should ideally yield another, more organic or "Realist" shape.[93] Thus for all of his admirably progressive politics when it comes to the issue of women's work, Kracauer uses the abstracted figure of the female body to launch his critique of capitalism.[94] Ultimately, the social theorist's description and analysis of the Tiller Girls resonate with the expressionist's "feminization" of pictorial weaving as purely ornamental and, one might say, *too* abstract. Both apparently lacked inner meaning or subjective depth:[95]

The [mass] ornament, detached from its bearers, must be understood rationally. It consists of lines and circles like those found in textbooks on Euclidean geometry. . . . Both the proliferations of organic forms and the emanations of spiritual life remain excluded. The Tiller Girls can no longer be reassembled into human beings after the fact.

Kracauer's assembly line of Tiller Girls links by analogy to the workshop of loom apparatuses that determine the weavers' bodies. For if the apparatus organizes the configuration of the body, then the ornament is not "formed from within." In Kracauer's rhetorical framework, where the aspiration is toward meaning, truth, and enlightenment, the Tiller Girls submit to the apparatus of the mass ornament and thereby lose their subjectivity, their identity as "human beings." Likewise, the overtly mechanical relationship between the weaver's body and the tool inscribes itself into the geometric, ornamental figures that through the technical process are woven into the fabric. Both pictorial weaving and the Tiller Girls are more abstract than the ornament that bears "a surge of organic life," a "direct link" to a "communal group," or artistic interiority. Like the rationalized means of mechanical labor, they appear without "ends," lacking subjective interiority or theoretical value—abstract and yet also tethered to the body.

Locating the Subject

The gendered status of weaving at the Bauhaus is the topic to which, in the end, the question of labor points. This feminization happened through actual policies that created a hierarchy between art and craft and moreover aligned a certain workshop with a certain gender. But this gendering was not simply achieved through an association with a sexed, social category named "woman," or even with a status as "mere craft"; weaving's femininity, it seems, hinged on an inability to determine the medium's subject—its "I." Indeed, the gendering of weaving at this moment concerns perhaps most of all an anxiety over the *source* of agency. Human freedom, bound up with a notion of an autonomous interiority, proscribes a linear relationship between the body, the intellect, and the tool. What makes weaving feminine is the fact that the agency of its practitioner is put into question. For if weaving is nothing more than a technical medium, governed by the mechanics of an apparatus, then it induces passivity in its practitioners, thereby subjecting (or subjugating) the weaver and her work. So it was less an association with women that feminized the medium at the Bauhaus than a general assessment of the relationship between subject and object that the medium (apparently) entailed. The pictorial tapestry or carpet's ornamental composition, having been reworked according to the arbitrary workings of the (capitalist) apparatus, apparently lacked the depth of the true picture, painting. The weaving medium was infected to its very core by (abstract) labor.

Yet if weaving was feminized on account of its complex industrial history and accrued meanings, the expressionist notions of "freedom" or "expression" were, in parallel, neither spontaneous nor natural associations. (It took an application of Riegl's argument that ornament could arrive out of an artist's inner impulse rather than material means, after all, to free abstract painting from other, more odious instances of ornament.) In fact, the rhetoric surrounding painting struggled to ensure the autonomous agency of its maker at every turn. The language that accompanies Kandinsky's or Itten's pictures, linking them to a spiritual, metaphysical, or symbolic world beyond the material space of the canvas and paint, was produced through a discourse, another kind of apparatus. Abstract forms and colors, otherwise lacking in content, thus appeared in the work of these painters laden with meaning. But the expressionist painting's so-called depth paradoxically lies in the flat space of the picture, in the terms of abstraction. And many critics used the label of the decorative to denounce the works of Kandinsky and Klee; in kind, these artists worked just as stridently to avoid any such connection. For Kandinsky, it was in abstraction that a medium like painting could find its true identity, its "own language." But for Max Beckmann, another expressionist painter who criticized the Blaue Reiter group, it was precisely abstraction that led painting toward "the dangers of the flatness of the applied arts."[96] Abstraction brought painting into proximity with mechanical reproduction, even as abstraction was deployed by Kandinsky to ward off society's materialist forces. The two conditions were in battle within the very same field. Some practitioners of expressionism thus found themselves working nervously against an association with "tapestries and wallpaper," for the picture potentially slipped into mass-produced ornament, form without meaning. This is precisely where the difficulty of drawing boundaries and limits emerges, and where the language of the mechanical touches the language of abstraction, such that the integrity of the picture breaks down.

Pictorial weaving, like the mass ornament, thereby showed the limits of painterly abstraction. It is even apt to say that weaving was the Other that painting aspired to overcome at this moment in order to shore up its identity. Especially since it lacked a textual theory of its own, Bauhaus weaving before 1923 was feminized, made to compare to painting as an inferior version. But the comparison also threatened the coherence of painting's picture—one that expressionist rhetoric would have sought to maintain. At once bound up with the mechanical space of labor and a formalist pedagogy of "lines and circles," weaving exploited the picture's frame: the decorative in painting became the picture in the decorative object of weaving, thereby unraveling painting's already tenuous relationship to the spiritual. Though this process was also happening in the historical life of the Bauhaus, as it moved to embrace technology and left the rhetoric of spirituality behind, weaving as pictorial might have been especially threatening. The apparent labor underpinning weaving technique established weaving's inadequacies in relation to painting, but as it reworked the barriers between art and labor, technique and interiority, pictures and the matter of wool, it also made painting at the Bauhaus all the more uneasy—grasping at an identity in order to ward off the threat of its dispersal.

Here we return to Stölzl's brief statement from 1926, "a picture made of wool," used at once to describe and reject the expressionist practices of the early weaving workshop. If, as Foucault suggests, a "statement is always an event that neither the language (*langue*) nor the meaning can quite exhaust," Stölzl's phrase is then "linked not only to the situations that provoke it, and to the consequences that it gives rise to, but at the same time . . . to the statements that precede and follow it"[97]—those of Kandinsky, Itten, Weber, or Kracauer. It points to the full range of paradoxes, conflicts, and fictions that would saturate the Bauhaus institution and Weimar culture.

But in addition to complicating the narrative around the Bauhaus's expressionist moment, Stölzl's statement also reveals something very particular to the Bauhaus weaving workshop's craft. Its specificity, it seems, lies not just in the material conditions of its own medium but also in its contingent relationship with, and struggle against, other media. As weaving registers the Bauhaus's internal contradictions, these debates inform its feminized status, but they also enable weaving to produce something else—something that is neither a picture nor pure technique. Stölzl's wall hanging from 1923 was produced at the moment of the Bauhaus's "consolidation" or "new unity"—as the members of the workshops began thinking about what it would mean to conceive prototypes for industrial manufacture. Hence, Albers would later note, while looking back at this moment from the perspective of 1938, that the "repeated pattern adopted for machine production" in later textiles had "derived from" a section of Stölzl's pattern.[98] And the weavers soon began to define their practices in opposition to the picture made of wool, increasingly emphasizing, through writing, the material structure and function. Though they continued to draw on the terminology developed by painting's form and color theories, those elements would become part of their textiles' functional life. As the weavers began to write on their medium—shaping it through a theoretical language—they took on (and complicated) the language of another discipline. After painting came architecture.

2

THE USE OF TEXTILES IN ARCHITECTURAL SPACE

Without a theoretical armature—a group of texts specifying weaving's dimensions and goals—the workshop's production of tapestries and carpets remained, for the first few years of the Bauhaus, a medium without ends. This state of practice without theory changed dramatically when several weavers, between 1924 and 1926, stopped focusing on pictorial objectives, began thinking through the requirements of the loom and malleable threads, and spelled out their aims using choice words. Through woven experiments and essays that considered the particular dimensions of their practice, the workshop embraced the rhetorical strategies of architectural criticism.

The vocabulary of *function, purpose,* and *utility,* promoted through pamphlets and speeches by Neues Bauen architects and critics, began seeping into the Bauhaus after 1923. This was when Johannes Itten left, having lost support for his esoteric curricular ideas, and when Gropius reassessed the school's curriculum with his opening lecture for the 1923 exhibition. "Art and Technology" together, he declared, must create a "New Unity."[1] Recognizing that economic development in the manner of production was necessary for the institution's survival, the director called on the workshops to begin integrating artistic with business requirements—"to industrialize" their practice in the creation of *Normenstücke* (standard products).[2] Gropius recruited László Moholy-Nagy, who would shift the curricular focus toward modern media like typography and photography; and he hired Emil Lange as the Bauhaus *Syndikus* (manager) to help broker deals between the workshops and buyers, and to ensure the timely production of goods for sale. Turning away from a model that joined art and craft in dwellings like the Sommerfeld House (1920–22), which showcased finely carved interior walls by student Joost Schmidt and stained-glass windows

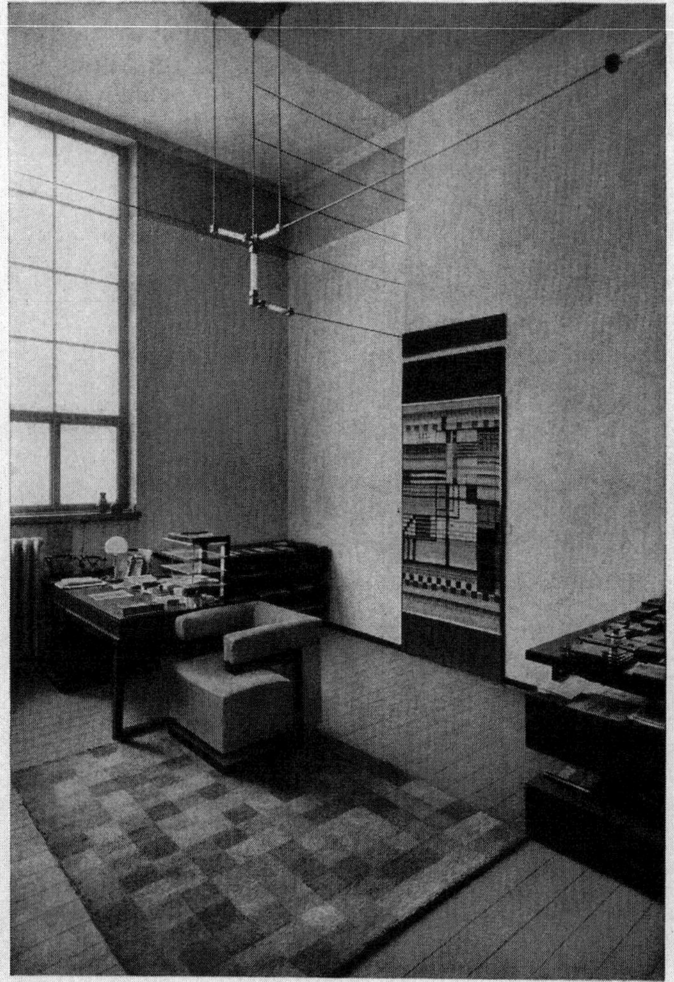

Page from Walter Gropius, *Neue Arbeiten der Bauhauswerkstätten, Bauhausbücher, Nr. 7* (Albert Langen Verlag, 1925), 13. Director's room in the Weimar Bauhaus, 1923. Floor carpet by Gertrud Arndt; wall hanging by Else Mögelin; ceiling lighting by Walter Gropius. Photograph by Lucia Moholy.

by Josef Albers, in 1923 Gropius backed the ascetic white box called the Haus am Horn. The first house sponsored by the building contractor Adolf Sommerfeld had been conceived as "an experimental worksite" (*Versuchsplatz*) for creating a "patented system of precut interlocking timbers" made from salvaged ships.[3] But Gropius soon determined that Georg Muche's sparsely white *am Horn* design—a look he had already deployed, for example, as architect of Jena's Municipal Theater (1921–22)—was far more consistent with the look of technological progress and the functional housing economy. The ideal was now to conceive well-designed *Baukasten* (modular prefabricated building systems) and prototypes for industrially fabricated household items like upholstery and curtain fabric or metal teapots and lamps.[4]

Yet if measured in monetary terms, this initial phase of Bauhaus functionalism between 1923 and 1926 was hardly successful. The school continued to struggle financially for several more years. Gropius's 1923 lecture envisioned the Bauhaus's future somewhat accurately, but as a theoretically inspired plan his new program took several years to take root. The workshops still employed a handicraft approach better suited to creating unique (and expensive) applied-art objects for wealthy patrons rather than industrially manufactured items for the masses.[5] Despite Moholy-Nagy's espousal of technology and promotion of new materials like nickel and chromium for the metal workshop, the objects produced there were still crafted with traditional hand tools used by copper- or silversmiths.

The functionalist rhetoric did, nevertheless, change the workshops' ambitions. The new ethos found its way into the 1923 exhibition *Internationale Architektur,* organized by Gropius with the help of architectural critic Adolf Behne, the leading advocate of the *moderne Zweckbau* (modern functional building).[6] And following commissions from individuals and distributors after the 1923 exhibition, the weaving workshop was "particularly quick off the mark in finding representatives to handle its retailing," as historian Anna Rowland has observed.[7] As the weavers embarked on the next phase of their practice—creating *Meterwaren* (fabric sold by the meter) for 1924 Leipzig trades fairs held in the spring and fall, and for the Werkbund exhibition that September—they began writing on the basic elements of their craft, appropriating the language of utility. But in order to make industrial textile "types," they first had to comprehend their field's constituent parts: its materials, techniques, and functional applications.[8]

By replacing compositional questions with functional ones, the earliest writings on weaving grasped the importance of having a theoretical plan, a discursive frame. The new language of the modern functional building borrowed from Behne and Gropius served them well. But in applying *Sachlichkeit* theories to their "adaptable" textile objects, they also invoked another discourse, seemingly outside the purview of architecture: the Weimar *Frauenbewegung* (women's movement). As manifestos and marketing material found in the hippest journals of the day, the texts on Bauhaus weaving by Anni Albers, Gunta Stölzl, and Helene Schmidt-Nonné aimed to give their workshop a voice by arguing for what was called the "woman's field at the Bauhaus."[9] Indeed, these texts functioned doubly: drawing on the language of architectural functionalism, the weavers attempted to define weaving as an internally defined medium so that it could be *specific*—so they could specify their practice and their textiles' functions—but this language was also harnessed to justify their craft and methods of production to the school's business manager and to an audience of potential users.[10] In order to be specific, it turns out, the woven object (whether a prototype for curtain fabric or a one-of-a-kind blanket) had to be imagined as useful for something or, rather, someone else—i.e., a largely female clientele or dweller who uses and cleans that piece of fabric. At once modernist, or insistent on the distinctness of this thing and its space of practice, and acknowledging a specifically modern civic identity (perhaps the German *Neue Frau* who had only recently received the right to vote but was still, nevertheless, a *Hausfrau*), early weaving theory joined together the rhetoric of functionalism, modern marketing, and the new women's movement.

Nascent Theory

In the convoluted territory between the school's expressionist past and its architecturally oriented, functionalist future, a modernist theory of weaving was born. Soon after returning from the Leipzig trades fair that fall, the young student Annelise Fleischmann (later called Anni Albers, upon marrying Josef) published her first essay,

"Bauhausweberei" (Bauhaus Weaving), in *Junge Menschen*, a Weimar magazine that billed itself as speaking to "the spirit of the young generation."[11] Through her carefully crafted text—the first of its kind on weaving—Albers proposed a future of mass textile production even as she advocated for experimentation and a renewed approach to design through handloom weaving. She was quick off the mark to apprehend Gropius's suggestion at the September Werkbund exhibition: swaths of bolt fabric should be displayed next to one another "in rows," not set off in a "pretty arts and crafts arrangement, i.e., a higgledypiggledy scattering of the individual products according to a purely visual point of view."[12] Nevertheless, Albers declared that the way toward mass production must come through an understanding of the craft.[13] Progress can only be made through the convergence of handicraft and mechanical production.

Important to understanding Albers's first essay is that she came to the Bauhaus at the beginning of the curricular shift. She began her education there in 1923, occupying a generation of students younger than Stölzl or Benita Koch-Otte, who arrived in 1919 and obtained their basic training under the influence of expressionism and the postwar *Wandervogel* movement that permeated the school under Itten.[14] Although the two older students would later concede that the pictorial approach was limiting, they remained committed to explorations with color and dyeing.[15] Albers, more inclined to use threads in neutral tones, ultimately favored an investigation of materials, experimentation in woven structure, complex methods for double-weaving on an eight-harness loom, and using industrial technology, like the Jacquard.

Still, the young weaver was not necessarily gung-ho about industry. The younger student came to the Bauhaus the year that Gropius and Lange decided it would be necessary to pursue the creation of a limited liability company separate from the school (Bauhaus GmbH) to help sell and market the school's designs to industry. Anxious about dilettantism and confronted with complaints about the workshop's slow production schedule and inability to meet orders, Lange and Gropius tried to establish a system for preventing waste and meeting deadlines for production.[16] So while weavers like Albers must have seen the benefits of such a system (she was able to earn her keep while a student), it surely frustrated

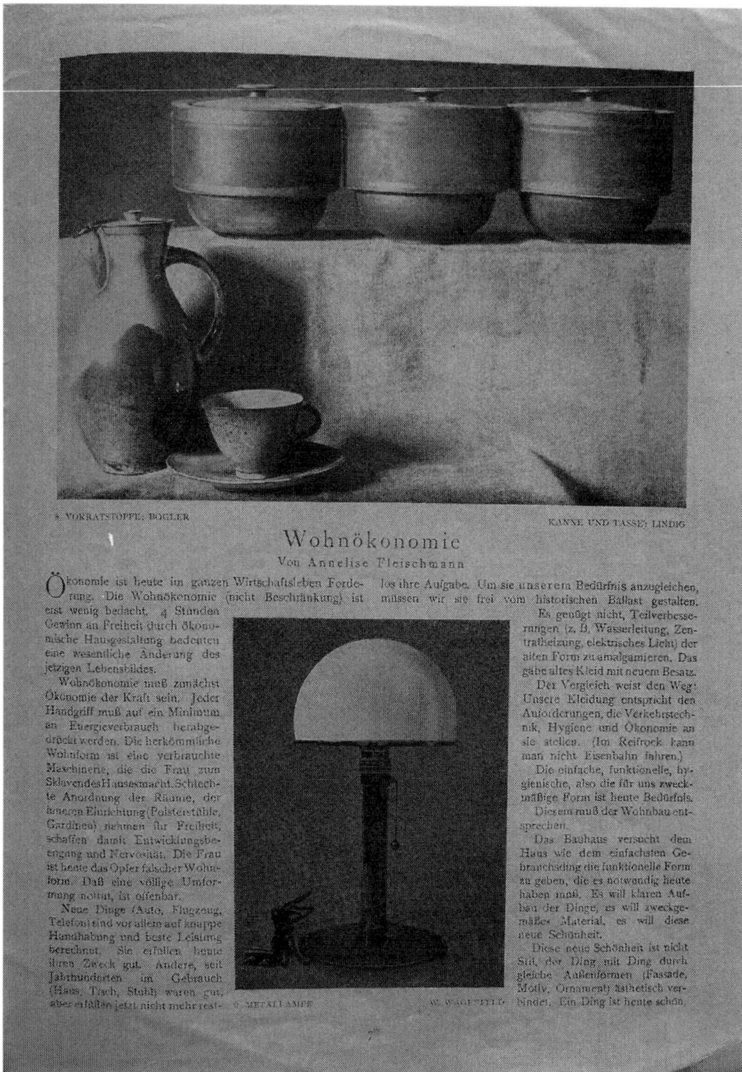

Wohnökonomie

Von Annelise Fleischmann

Ökonomie ist heute im ganzen Wirtschaftsleben Forderung. Die Wohnökonomie (nicht Beschränkung) ist erst wenig bedacht. 4 Stunden Gewinn an Freiheit durch ökonomische Hausgestaltung bedeuten eine wesentliche Änderung des jetzigen Lebensbildes.

Wohnökonomie muß zunächst Ökonomie der Kraft sein. Jeder Handgriff muß auf ein Minimum an Energieverbrauch herabgedrückt werden. Die herkömmliche Wohnform ist eine verbrauchte Maschinerie, die die Frau zum Sklaven des Hauses macht. Schlechte Anordnung der Räume, der inneren Einrichtung (Polsterstühle, Gardinen) nehmen ihr Freiheit, schaffen damit Entwicklungshemmung und Nervosität. Die Frau ist heute das Opfer falscher Wohnform. Daß eine völlige Umformung nottut, ist offenbar.

Neue Dinge (Auto, Flugzeug, Telefon) sind vor allem auf knappe Handhabung und beste Leistung berechnet. Sie erfüllen heute ihren Zweck gut. Andere, seit Jahrhunderten im Gebrauch (Haus, Tisch, Stuhl) waren gut, aber erfüllen jetzt nicht mehr restlos ihre Aufgabe. Um sie unserem Bedürfnis anzugleichen, müssen wir sie frei vom historischen Ballast gestalten.

Es genügt nicht, Teilverbesserungen (z. B. Wasserleitung, Zentralheizung, elektrisches Licht) der alten Form zu amalgamieren. Das gäbe altes Kleid mit neuem Besatz.

Der Vergleich weist den Weg: Unsere Kleidung entspricht den Anforderungen, die Verkehrstechnik, Hygiene und Ökonomie an sie stellen. (Im Reifrock kann man nicht Eisenbahn fahren.)

Die einfache, funktionelle, hygienische, also die für uns zweckmäßige Form ist heute Bedürfnis.

Diesem muß der Wohnbau entsprechen.

Das Bauhaus versucht dem Haus wie dem einfachsten Gebrauchsding die funktionelle Form zu geben, die es notwendig heute haben muß. Es will klaren Aufbau der Dinge, es will zweckmäßiges Material, es will diese neue Schönheit.

Diese neue Schönheit ist nicht Stil, der Ding mit Ding durch gleiche Außenformen (Fassade, Motiv, Ornament) ästhetisch verbindet. Ein Ding ist heute schön,

Page from Annelise Fleischmann (Anni Albers), "Wohnökonomie," *Beilage der Neuen Frauenkleidung und Frauenkultur,* no. 21 (1925): 7–8. Bauhaus-Archiv Berlin. Copyright 2013 Artists Rights Society (ARS), New York / VG Bild-Kunst, Bonn.

her early interest in experimentation with techniques. Following a summer in which Gropius canceled "all experimental work in the workshops" and insisted that everyone "work productively, replicating Bauhaus models" in advance of the fall fair, Albers's November 1924 essay sought to remind herself, fellow workshop members, and perhaps Gropius himself of the benefits of experimental craftwork in the creation of good design.[17]

Indeed, expressed in Albers's nascent theory of weaving were the contradictions generated by the "state of flux," circa 1924, between the Bauhaus's early adoption of a medieval handicraft approach and its fantasy of a future mode of assembly line–ready design, ready for business.[18] Considering the reality of her workshop—the fact that its best-selling products were pretty shawls and unique blankets for bourgeois female patrons—the young student crafted a flexible text that addressed, all at once, weaving's past, present, and future.[19] On the one hand, traditional handwork is projected as the best means to gain contact with the material and process of weaving. On the other, machine work and mass production are understood as tools belonging to the textile's inevitable future. The goal is to exploit the limits of the craft in this experimental phase in order to yield better products for industry. Making a case for experimentation in an environment that otherwise insisted on furthering an industrial image for the school (Gropius) or simply selling well-crafted items to a wealthy, largely female, clientele (Lange), Albers attempted to bridge two modes—to change the minds of traditional buyers of applied-art items and industrialists alike.[20]

Albers begins her essay by noting that weaving is an "ancient craft" whose basic structure (the intersection of vertical and horizontal threads) changed little with modern tools of mechanization. What these new modes brought about, however, was an essential estrangement from the material and the means. Addressing the fundamental question of process and practice, the different relationships between weavers and apparatuses—bodily operated floor looms and industrially sized machines—and the implications for the practitioner's sense of the material or the fabric with all of its tactile specificity, Albers's text seems at first to idealize older working methods. There is an appreciation for a now-lost method, once performed by the broad, nonbourgeois population (*Volksschicht*) of weavers, who had a "more direct connection to their material" through their ethnic identity (*Rasse*). But a romantic vision of the *Volk* and their weaving practices seen at the start of her essay gives way to a different story—one that expresses the fantasy of a new, improved method of design for industrial manufacture. The vision of a future functionalist method of fabric production is, according to the essay's conclusion, rooted in a history of experimental handicraft.[21]

This is not to say that the utopian relationship between craft and industry projected by Albers's essay was entirely uncritical. At the middle of her narrative comes the discussion of the sociological and physical conditions that hang over the proliferation of poorly designed products. Albers comments on the division of labor between design and craft in the textile industry—the fact that the draughtsman (*Zeichner*), who stands as "the isolated intellectual," has taken over the design process from weavers. And of the weavers she expresses concern that they have lost a connection to their technique as well as a "feel" for the material. The first modern theory of weaving thus engages critically with the apparatus—the loom and a mode of production—that distinguishes weaving from drawing as a means to design. In this way, the essay significantly confronts the division of labor, the modern means of industrial production. Her critique of a society that values efficiency and speed over slow but more variable handwork reminds one of earlier critiques by John Ruskin and William Morris, except that in Albers's text the focus turns toward the problem of intellectual design (pattern making) usurping the design process from the craftsman or laborer. The goal of the Bauhaus weaving workshop, in Albers's mind, was an "attempt . . . once again to produce [textiles] through a holistic contact with the material," to "try anew to teach this feeling," in order to arrive at "[all] hand and technical possibilities."[22] But also, echoing Marx, Albers advocates for a reorganization of weaving labor, to make room for fabric things that might better connect makers and users with their environment and others. What her text outlines is a future for modern Bauhaus hand weaving in a technical world—one whereby the weaver's handwork and experimentation at the loom would generate formal, technical, and material developments in design, but also by implication new and improved relations between human subjects and woven things.

The text was not uncritical, yet her essay functioned to convince and educate its audience—of (female) buyers who asked for slight variations in color on the patterns offered, and (male) industrialists who sought replicable prototypes—in the benefits of modern design emerging out of good craft. Albers's first theory of weaving was thus generated as something of a marketing campaign—a practice, as we shall see, that she learned from the school's director and that would become common to the workshop's theoretical writings on weaving.

Speculative Weaves

Following Albers's essay and a budding interest from textile manufacturers in their designs, a kind of excitement in thinking through the basic elements of the craft yielded experimental samples and books of notes on them. The weavers attempted to arrive at a model of utility fabrics, as a young design student might, through hit-or-miss research on the loom. These laboratory experiments often lacked a direct application to architectural space and were definitely not useful for industry, but they did serve another function: they gave rise to further developments in weaving theory.

A box of textiles containing ten or more samples made circa 1925–26, located at the Bauhaus Archive in Berlin, can be read against the terms of Albers's nascent theory. In these small squares of cloth, the students combined different thread materials, colors, formal treatments, and a variety of different weaves, often within a single item; thus one might accurately call these experimental samples "speculative weaves." Just as Albers imagined a future practice for Bauhaus weaving, a fantasy in which craft and industry could come together, these objects picture a future state of textile prototypes, still unachieved. Taking seriously Albers's critique of the design intellectual, who creates patterns on paper but has no contact with the material, students instead drafted the samples on a common floor loom, through a manual exploration of the conditions of that apparatus and various materials in thread.

Many items in this and a related archival carton are attributed to the weaving student Gertrud Arndt (born Hantschk), who entered the weaving workshop reluctantly in 1924 after coming to the Bauhaus in 1923 (the same year as Anni Albers) with the hope of pursuing architectural training under Gropius. But given that the Bauhaus only advanced a small clique of men through the construction course, that there was no architectural workshop until 1927, and that she was a woman all thwarted her initial ambitions.[23] Thus her interest in structure found expression in investigations of a different medium, which she studied until 1927.

Somewhere between the pictorial work that characterized the school's early years and the more functional, though achromatic textile prototypes of the late twenties and early thirties, the small, experimental weaves found here approximate well the still-experimental direction of the late-Weimar and early-Dessau moment.[24] Compare, for instance, a Gobelin cover from 1924 by Martha Erps-Breuer with Arndt's fabric samples (see Plates 4 and 5). Each is woven using the simplest materials: cotton and wool in the Erps-Breuer cover, cotton in the sample, and each takes advantage of the layering of weft and the juxtaposition of thickness among the threads to achieve a complex pattern of contrasting tones and texture. While the cover's scale and compositional variety is a bit more impressive, and the samples do include the larger weave's subtle detail of embedded patterning, the little prototypes nevertheless yield a distinctly balanced arrangement in stripes.

In one of these experimental objects from the workshop's first year in Dessau, the interlacing of viscose and mercerized cotton threads (which absorb brilliantly colored dyes) with the raw colors of natural fibers yields a sumptuous composition of color and texture. Still largely determined by a formal interest in compositional arrangement, the resulting experiment remains a contained spatial-color field, a thing framed by its four sides. And just as pictorial weaving continued to influence the weavers' experiments at the loom, the Bauhaus's form and color theory instruction, taught primarily by Klee and Kandinsky, greatly influenced this student's formal play. So a luminous array of blue stripes in this sample's upper half is juxtaposed with a field of yellow on the lower, as though repeating the diagrammatic and dynamic layouts of Klee's pedagogical sketches. Even before he was assigned to provide a course dedicated to the weavers in 1927, Klee's teaching and theories influenced his enthusiastic protégés, who took fastidious notes in his courses, and whose notebooks reveal page after page

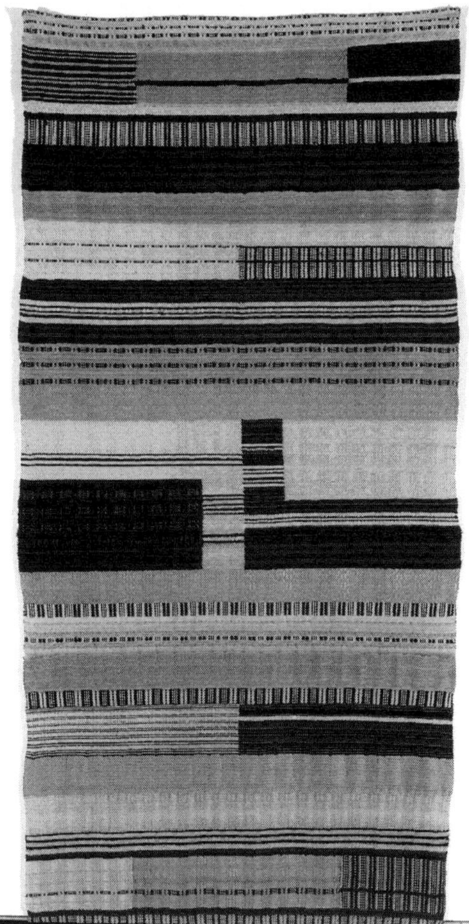

Martha Erps-Breuer, cover, 1924. Wool and cotton. 230 x 113 cm. Bauhaus-Archiv Berlin.

of diagrams informing their workshop experiments with fiber.[25] "Artistically," Arndt relayed to interviewers years later, "we were with Klee and Kandinsky. They were our heroes."[26] So in these speculative weaves, the study of compositional properties and materials, Klee's ideas about *Bewegung und Gegenbewegung* (movement and countermovement) continue to outweigh any interest in the final product.[27] It is not surprising that Arndt recalled her education in weaving with a bit of disdain: "I never wanted to

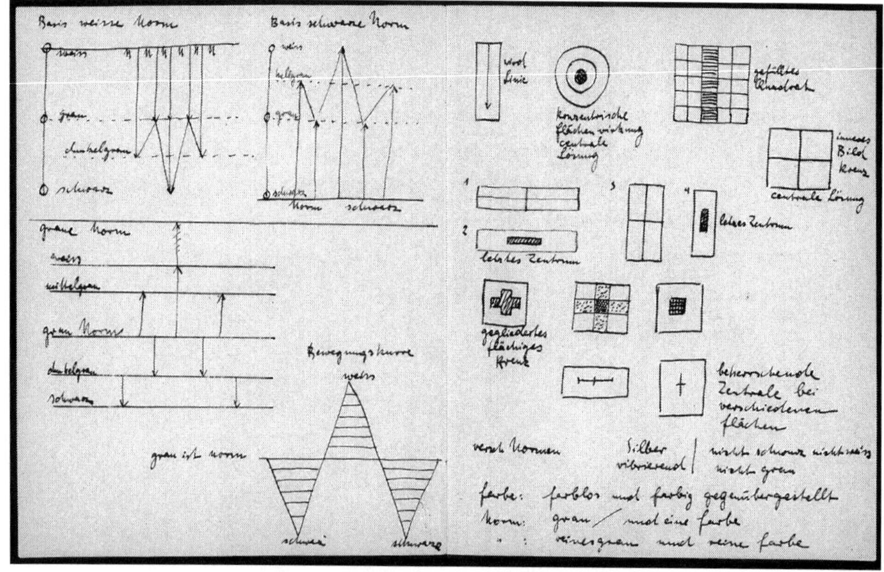

Gunta Stölzl, page from notebook for Paul Klee's course, n.d. Bauhaus-Archiv Berlin.
Copyright 2013 Artists Rights Society (ARS), New York / VG Bild-Kunst, Bonn.

weave. . . . No, not at all. All those threads, I didn't want that. No, that was not my thing." Among these samples we find threads handled carelessly, with evidence of hastily introduced weft and selvages that are uneven.

Nevertheless, the weaver's "free" (if also hasty) experimentations on the loom supported, and were supported by, a new theoretical program, which designated the workshop's woven work—quite unlike their watercolors, drawings, or notes from the theory classes—as experiments working toward a function. With descriptors like *Vorhangstoff* (curtain fabric) and *Möbelstoff* (furniture fabric) added later, the workshop's objects would meet their application; the end use or purpose (*Zweck*) would come into the object equation. Thus the designation of *experimental* used here to describe these prototypes implies the scientific objective of their work, as typically defined: "An operation carried out under controlled conditions in order to discover an unknown effect or law, to test or establish a hypothesis." In the case of these woven things, any free exploration of the "pure" means of color or form is to some degree driven by the fabric's hypothetical utility, its future status as an entity that incorporates and adjusts to the architectural environment.

But again, these samples are not quite functional, at least insofar as they imply a future—a possibility of use after the kinks have been worked out and finished samples have been formed—but little use in the present. As swatches no larger than a few inches square, they provide less information about their potential use than they do evidence of the weavers' processes and mistakes. Many reveal in their surface the trace of a rethought plan, somewhere toward the middle of the progression of the weave, as in a sample given the Bauhaus Archive inventory number 353a, where the experiment seems to yield a hiccup in the weft. These speculative weaves are neither truly pictorial nor properly functional; their makers were more concerned with working through ideas at the loom—an application of Klee's pedagogical philosophy of movement und countermovement, to the back-forth of weft through warp, or to the juxtaposition of disparate materials and textures (shiny viscose and rough wool). Rather than realizing a utilitarian goal, these proto-prototypes can only signal the fantasy of a future mode, a function not yet achieved. They are, as woven stuff, what might simply be referred to as "things": the results of experimentation that are sufficient neither as objects for human use nor as works of art: "Temporalized as the before and after of the object, [their] thingness amounts to a latency (the not yet formed or the not yet formable) and to an excess (what remains physically or metaphysically irreducible to objects)."[28] These fabric leftovers, in a box, in an archive, are excessive, pointing more toward the weaver's budding theories than practical use.

Related to the samples is another category of things, perhaps even more useful. Lying somewhere between thingness and theory (in its most applicable sense) are the weaving instruction books (referred to as *Unterrichtsmaterial* or *Bindungslehre*), several of which were written and compiled by different members of the workshop, including Stölzl, Koch-Otte, and Otti Berger.[29] These reference manuals were not simply of pedagogical value in the classroom but provided a record of their makers' working thoughts on the practice. (Indeed, the larger history of the *Bindungslehre* is connected to a lineage of mill books used by master weavers and textile mill owners since the eighteenth century to note formulae for threading looms, diagrams of looms and other machines, drafting patterns, textile samples, and notes.[30] Such books could be described as theoretical tracts written by and for weavers, a specialist audience.)

For now, it seems pertinent to focus on Stölzl's *Unterrichtsmaterial zur Materaillehre*, which was likely compiled sometime after 1925 for the use of her students.[31] Here, one can find cut swatches of industrially produced commodity fabrics, undoubtedly acquired as scraps from a textile mill or shop and pasted on pages next to descriptions (see Plate 6). These typewritten texts describe and analyze the swatch systematically: the fabric type (i.e., taffeta, Chinese crepe, cotton jersey, muslin, etc.); its function (clothing fabric, curtain fabric, tablecloth); the materials used for the warp and weft (wool, cotton, rayon, etc.); the colors of the threads as well as the thickness of the fabric; the technique used to make the pattern on its surface (weaving, knitting, brocade, printing, Jacquard); and last, the cost of the particular fabric per meter. Stölzl's instruction manual can be seen as a kind of secondary-source text, used to analyze the successes and failures of earlier fabric documents. Harnessing an analytic method, she breaks down the fabrics into a set of data. Indeed, the diagnostic language seen on the page to the side of the swatches will reappear (only slightly transformed) in the two lists in her theoretical essays: one list of material properties particular to textiles (color, thread, structure), the other list providing examples of textile types (carpets, curtains, upholstery). Both kinds of texts analyze properties, aiming to show where these industrial fabrics might go if the technique were better handled or if the Jacquard or mechanical loom were traded for experimentation on a handloom. Stölzl, in other words, had to destroy these fabrics quite literally (by cutting them up and pasting them in a book) and metaphorically (through an analytical dissection of their properties) in order to use them for her pedagogy and the development of a new approach to thinking about weaving. The book's usefulness to the weaver's theory was predicated on an analytical destruction.

In the experimental textiles and instructional manuals coming out of the workshop, the weavers were just beginning to grapple with the relationship between their practice and an orientation toward the use of fabrics within dwelling space. Between 1924 and 1926 their work attempted to integrate and then surpass pictorial objectives. (Stölzl wrote in her diary at the time: "The weavers [were] . . . happy to have found another means of expression, besides watercolors and oils. . . . Naturally, one learned very quickly *that weaving could not be a picture.*")[32] While their speculative weaves were not quite ready for use, the weavers began to define their *Gestaltungsgebiet* through experimentation in order to locate its parameters. Very few designs for architectural textiles were actually generated in this moment; it took until late 1926 to establish a rhythm in the new Dessau workshop. What did result from these investigations were two important texts by workshop members Stölzl and Schmidt-Nonné.

Before turning to a discussion of this development in weaving theory, however, it seems important first to examine the contradictions that abound in the texts by Behne and Gropius, who initiated the *Sachlichkeit* language in the workshops. For here, it turns out, functionalism was not a simple attention to "use," but a means to advocate for modern form.

Functional Words about Form: Behne and Gropius

Sometime in 1926, as the workshops were moving into the new building in Dessau, the medium of architecture took over as the conceptual touchstone of the school, a position that painting had occupied in the Bauhaus's early years. Even painter Oskar Schlemmer, as head of the stage workshop, would now advocate for following an architectural model in the development of sets and costumes. Defining the stage as "after all architectonic," Schlemmer considered his workshop to be the perfect setting to explore the "integration of artistic ideals with craftsmanship and technology." So like other workshops at the Bauhaus, he "direct[ed] all activities together toward architecture."[33]

The words of architectural critic Adolf Behne, a prolific writer and advocate for the Neues Bauen movement, along with Gropius's 1923 exhibition *Internationale Architektur* (which Behne helped to prepare), were mostly responsible for this shift.[34] Indeed, the Bauhaus students would have been familiar with the writing of Behne, who harnessed words like *Zweck, Funktion,* and *Sachlichkeit* in his book *Der moderne Zweckbau* (The Modern Functional Building) and in essays on that topic.[35] With the pervasiveness of such terms, most of the *Bauhäusler* were inspired to get on the same architectural train.[36] Gropius, meanwhile, was emboldened to reharness his Werkbund roots and to frame not just architecture but also the products of the workshops with these functional terms in hand. In some sense copied from Behne's analysis of the functional house and pasted onto his new program for the workshops' future prototypes, functional ideas buttressed new thinking about design's "use" in the modern home, now "appropriate to [modern man] and his time." Soon after the *Internationale Architektur* exhibition, Gropius set out to publish a promotional book on the workshop's activities.

Important to keep in mind in this discussion is the slippery history of certain words. Historians have noted how the use of *Zweck* (function, purpose) and *Sachlichkeit* (objectivity, functionalism) were inconsistently applied throughout German architectural modernism.[37] After a primarily "organic" moment that came out of architectural expressionism, a hard-edged moment and definition of functionalism ensued, ultimately spearheaded by the economic collapse of 1929. At this point, as Hilde Heynen comments, "functionality" in the public housing movement was increasingly "thought of in terms of cost-effectiveness."[38] The already economical ethos of Ernst May's Frankfurt developments, Grete Lihotzky's Frankfurt Kitchen, and the Neues Bauen concept of the *Existenzminimum* became, after 1928, "subordinate to the purpose of being of service to as many people as possible with the (inevitably limited) means that were available."[39] Thus, the year 1926, at the middle point of this functionalist history, reveals quite a bit about this passage.[40] For at this juncture what emerged was a profound anxiety about the movement's supposedly organic origins and the viability of its economic future. Indeed, the beginnings of architectural functionalism, as explained by historian Rosemarie Haag Bletter, have been underestimated by the American audience of European modernism, who tend to gloss over some of the productive contradictions at stake in this term, especially when it is understood to be synonymous with utilitarianism. While Henry Russell Hitchcock and Philip Johnson in *The International Style* hold Hannes Meyer (the Bauhaus's third director) responsible for an overexaggerated "anti-aesthetic functionalism"—thereby distancing themselves from Meyer's failures—their text also contributes to the simple equation of "Bauhaus functionalism" with Sullivan's dictum "form follows function," after which the concept seems to exist as a positivist "law or mathematical theorem."[41]

The understanding of functionalism was especially vexed between 1923 and 1926, and Behne's *Moderne Zweckbau* is an important touchstone for thinking through the contradictions at this time. For Behne, the relationship between form and function did not fit a neat theorem, let alone opposition. The fact that form, or facades, had taken over from organic functions (thinking of the house as a tool) in the past several centuries in Europe was not simply a matter to be inversed; rather, according to Behne, a new "compromise" between them was required.[42] In fact the problem of form was more important to Behne's theory than it would otherwise seem, though it was redefined according to objects (*Sachen*) rather than facades.[43]

To understand the contradictions at stake in Behne's first major discussion on the topic of architectural *Sachlichkeit*, it helps to unpack the book's layers. The chapter titles follow a dialectical progression that suggests that the history of modern architecture since the late nineteenth century is an interconnected progression of forms:

I. No Longer a Façade / but a House
II. No Longer a House / but Shaped Space
III. No Longer Shaped Space / but Designed Reality

In the first chapter, Behne introduces the trajectory of modern architecture, found first in the buildings of Otto Wagner, Alfred Messel, and Frank Lloyd Wright, who represent a shift from an attention to "style" in architecture, marked by its facade, toward a concern for the building as a whole.[44] The second chapter shifts to the description of industrial architecture and its relationship to the worker, mainly Peter Behrens's Turbine Hall factory built in 1909 for the electric company AEG.[45] Here *Sachlichkeit* is defined as it concerns the movement of workers in space, their need for light, or the requirements of organizing the factory space like a city with a railway at its center for the moving of heavy materials within it. The factory environment as a unit (the building, its workers, and the industrial tasks performed there) is the quintessential medium for the development of the functionalist plan.[46] But this notion of *Sachlichkeit* then moves into the space of another kind of building—namely, the dwellings designed by Henry van de Velde. Behne notes that van de Velde is able to shape space "from the inside," to arrive at expressive forms that "speak" the will of purposes and materials; as applied to van de Velde, functionalism is an organic and anthropocentric affair.[47] While Wright's sense of movement is made up of "immobile, technically determined, standardized, ready-made pieces," that are "absolutely 'expressionless,'" van de Velde injects empathy into function, through "curves and flourishes" that acknowledge and respond to lived, organic bodies, who "know no right angles and straight lines."[48] But van de Velde's functionalist ethos—"colored with a romantic, pantheistic tinge"—potentially goes too far, particularly when its consequence emerges in another architect, Hermann Finsterlin. (One might take *pantheistic* to mean antiquated, but also undisciplined, too tolerant of hybridity.) In Finsterlin what emerges is, in the movement of this dialectic, "the most radical dissolution of the house."[49] Behne thereby identifies several strains of functional attitudes.

This suggests that for Behne a concern with function is not the endpoint of the entire modern architectural development. Behne comments that while functionalism is important for grasping the movement of a body, "reality" could never fully take to the functionalist dream: "Functionalist deliberations are correct so long as they concern a specific matter, and they go wrong as soon as things have to fit together." While "a curve is a better biological transcription of real usable space," when it comes to the "matter of arranging several rooms together . . . a group of rectangular rooms" or buildings in a development is preferred.[50] In other words, a "romantic" functionalism comes at a price when it interfaces with society, insofar as the individual inhabitant's tendency toward curves and organic movement might eclipse social requirements. Moreover, good function is never enough, because without *form*, functionalism always runs the risk of effacing itself, dissolving into a romantic experiment or the invisible ground of its use. Hence, the resolution of the dialectic (found in the third chapter on designed reality) returns to the question of form in order to save functionalism from yielding its own dissolution. Here Behne writes: "Form is nothing more than the consequence of establishing a relationship between human beings. . . . Form is an eminently social matter. Anyone who recognizes the right of society recognizes the right of form."[51]

The definition of *designed reality* is a formal-social matter, so the relationship between function and form traverses a shift that doubles back and redefines each term. Where function originally supported the inhabitant's movement, and the Baroque facade denied it, now functional solutions are problematic insofar as they overemphasize the individual or the specific case. The "functionalist prefers to exaggerate the purpose to the point of making it unique and momentary," the problem related to a specific building, kind of worker, or resident— "a house for each function!" At this point, then, Behne cites Le Corbusier, the "rationalist architect," whose attention to form considers the "purpose broadly and generally as readiness for many cases," that is, for a social whole.[52] Although pure rationalism can be a problem when it becomes "rigid formalism," it is form that the architect needs to counteract the (individualist) dissolution of social accord.[53] Form is indeed central to *Sachlichkeit,* defined according to the "object" of architecture as an "instrument of human use," an "eminently social matter."

Yet for all of Behne's discussion of form as social, the critic's examples are telling. Speaking of Peter Behrens's Turbine Hall as the most *sachlich* of built factories, Behne would emphasize its form as its absolute virtue: the "body built here to house the working process was an *indivisible, unbroken whole. . . . The building was itself form, it needed no forms.*"[54] And concluding the book with the example of Dutch Theo van Doesburg, he adopts the designer's words on the "double function of the building: 'Function from the perspective of practice; proportionality from the perspective of art.' Function and play."[55] Form returns at the end of Behne's book in a more traditional guise—as a question of "rhythm" and the "relationship of masses" to create a harmonious entity.

Indeed, what becomes apparent in Behne's analysis of buildings as object-like is that they are defined, despite (or perhaps because of) their interface with society, as discrete units, forms, or vessels— rather like a teapot filled with water or a lamp emitting light. And this might even account for the contradictions found in the dizzying progression of Behne's argument. He begins by rejecting form as a matter of covering surfaces (facades), later to reject functionality that denotes adaptability to human bodies ("a house for each function!"), and ultimately to promote those buildings that uphold "proportionality" in formal play. Noticeably missing from nearly all of the book's one hundred illustrations of buildings and interiors are those objects of design that cover floors and furniture with cloth (only one page of photographs showing van de Velde's spaces includes carpeting). Of course his focus is the modern functional building, but it is not hard to imagine that Behne would have trouble recognizing fabric's particular version of *Sachlichkeit*. Flexible textiles in architecture would, perhaps, be too functional—far too lacking in a distinct form of their own. The language of functionality within the discourse of the Neues Bauen, no matter how diverse, could never quite accommodate the textile's profound adaptability.

When the vocabulary of functionalism was repurposed and applied by Gropius to his analysis of workshop products, Behne's conception of functional form was deployed not just as a vehicle for users but also as a way of challenging the existing framework of craft at the school. In three related texts published in 1925 and 1926, Gropius sought to market the Bauhaus's new products and redirect the workshop's goals. The first was an introduction to *Neue Arbeiten der Bauhauswerkstätten* (New Work of the Bauhaus Workshops), number seven of the *Bauhausbücher* series, written in 1924 and published in 1925.[56] The most cited of the three, "Bauhaus Dessau—Principles of Bauhaus Production," printed as a leaflet in 1926, was a shortened version of the book's introduction.[57] The third, "Where Artists and Technicians Meet," was published in the Werkbund magazine, *Die Form*, alongside photographs of airplanes and mechanical parts, suggesting that Bauhaus ideas on household objects had wide applications, equivalent to the most sophisticated machinery of the day.

In the 1926 leaflet, Gropius declares: "The development of present-day housing, from the simplest household appliances to the finished dwelling," must be a "rational" endeavor, akin to the requirements of modern life.[58] Thus he proclaims the "new attitude towards design" to be as much about a "resolute affirmation of the living environment of machines and vehicles" as "the organic design of things based on their own present-day laws." Gropius defines the direction of the new orientation of Bauhaus practice, a project that considers the objective "laws" of things and recognizes "simplicity in multiplicity, economical utilisation of space, material, time, and money."[59] While Behne's *Moderne Zweckbau* discussed the house as a tool for the dweller but hardly mentioned the tools of the architect, the designer's craft (his means) is integral to Gropius's consideration of the Bauhaus workshops—hence the focus on *Arbeit* (work) in the title of the book.[60] Still, craft emerges in "Principles" as a conflicted element within his argument. In the final three, rather ambivalent paragraphs, Gropius attempts to define something called *future crafts* as the means through which laboratory experimentation will ensure better quality prototypes. Yet at the same time he writes that the "Bauhaus fights against the cheap substitute, inferior workmanship, and the dilettantism of the handicrafts, for a new standard of quality work."[61] Future craft is separated from handicraft, which would signal the hand's tendency toward inaccuracy and frivolousness.

A discussion of craft is less overt in his article for *Die Form*— where Gropius attempts to outline the modern designer's practice as a meeting of the artist and the technician—but appears between the lines, nevertheless. Here, he discusses the process whereby "technical transformations" in the school's workshops are synthesized with "new modes of creativity"—"artistic" or "elementary insights" into material nature and form. Although not mentioned explicitly, the concept of craft underscores his discussion of the artist, whose "interest centres on the way technical articles are put together and on the organic unfolding of the manufacturing process." But it also applies to the engineer, whose "principles . . . are basically the same." Both recognize that a "thing (*Sache*) is determined by its nature and if it is to be fashioned so as to work properly, its essence must be investigated and fully grasped."[62] Gropius thereby details a synthesis of the artist and the engineer, a figure—perhaps a designer or a future craftsperson—whose "'work of art' must be made to 'function' in the spiritual as well as the material sense, exactly like the engineer's design, such as an aeroplane whose inescapable power is to fly."[63] Design practice, unlike applied arts, is a "rational" and "spiritual" affair, yielding objects, unmarred by the "dilettantish" mistakes, with surfaces that gleam like an airplane. A thing's formalized function is of the essence.

It is perhaps telling, therefore, that for his 1925 book on the workshops, the Bauhaus director paradoxically chose to display, not advanced textile prototypes for industry, but twenty-nine full-page images of wall hangings and one-of-a-kind blankets—all falling under the category of *Kunstgewerbe*. Gropius was somehow compelled to illustrate the weaving workshop using nice images of discrete items that resembled the proportional glass facades of his own buildings (like the new Bauhaus building), rather than ones that would actually function for architectural space. The one exception is a folding fabric room divider (a screen) by Dörte Helm from 1923, but even that object with its bold composition of rectangles and strong outline looks architectural. So just as he asked the metal and weaving workshops to display their hand-wrought teapots and fabrics in rows at trades fairs in 1924—hoping somehow to convince an audience of manufacturers that these items could be manufactured serially—his choices of textiles for *Neue Arbeiten* suggest that the book was more of a marketing tool than a site for purely

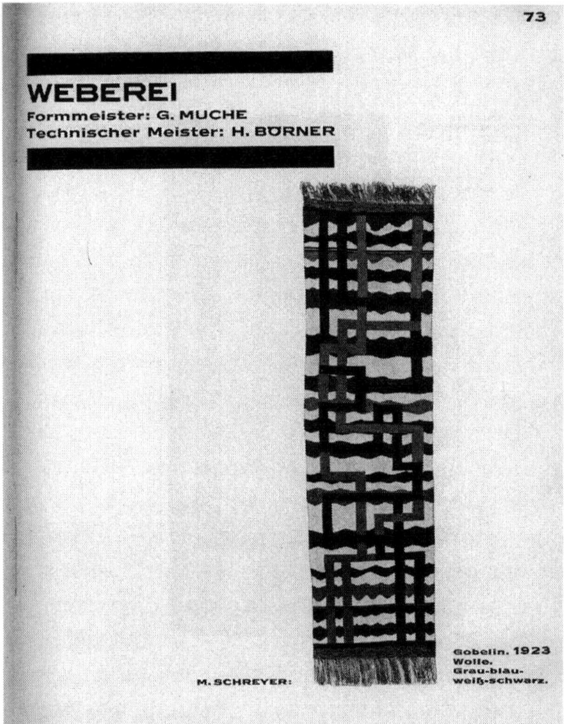

Page from Walter Gropius, *Neue Arbeiten der Bauhauswerkstätten, Bauhausbücher, Nr. 7* (Albert Langen Verlag, 1925), 73. M. Schreyer, Gobelin, 1923. Wool, gray–blue–white–black.

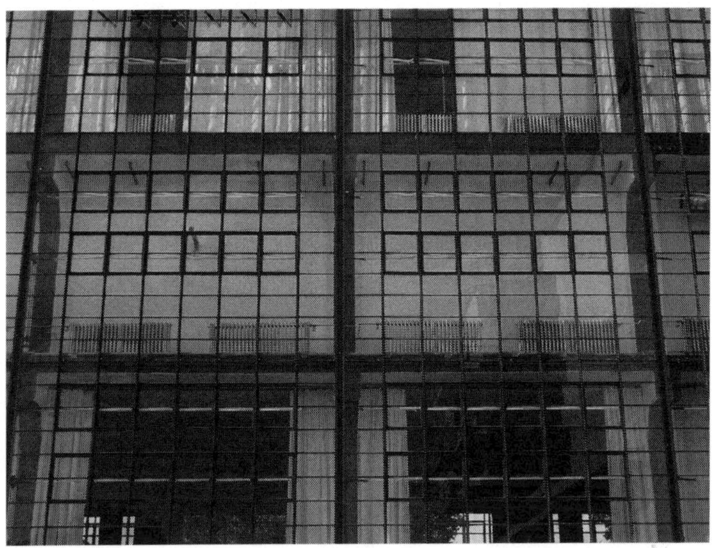

The Bauhaus building in Dessau, 1925–26 (detail: windows). Architect: Walter Gropius.

theoretical reflection. He knew who the weaving workshop's new clients were and thought they could be convinced by "architectural" imagery, not poorly lit, black-and-white images of plain-looking *Meterwaren*. His introductory theoretical text thus provided the armature through which otherwise arts and crafts objects could be seen differently—akin to machinery and curtain wall facades. It seems he understood the point made by Behne on the need for balance between function and form: good function is never enough.

The near lack of images of architectural fabrics for curtains or upholstery in 1925 illustrates the conundrum the weavers faced as they harnessed the new language of functionalism. As their objects evolved from well-framed "arts and crafts" items into adaptable, unframed things that spread across the surfaces of floors and walls or furniture, they had to generate essays to define their practice and its parameters. Functionalist ideals borrowed from the Neues Bauen discourse helped the weavers assert an identity for their textile medium in words, even as those ideals simultaneously undercut its visibility. Functionalism without form, the weavers no doubt grasped from Behne's and Gropius's texts, always runs the risk of effacing itself, dissolving into the invisible ground of its practice or use.

Adaptable Words about Fabric: Weaving Theory after 1926

The second and third essays on weaving came out in 1926, following the move to Dessau and in response to Gropius's developed program. Written by workshop members Gunta Stölzl and Helene Schmidt-Nonné, these two essays embraced the rhetoric of functionalism in their definition of the weaving workshop's practical area. With increased focus on the use of fabrics in architectural space, their definitions of the discipline began to address not just the practical dimensions of the craft but also the arena of dwelling, a particular site. By harnessing the Neues Bauen language of function, their essays sought to complicate the *Kunstgewerbe* picture of their work, and so they declared, avant-garde style, their revised intentions for textiles' utility in the modern world.

Repeating the major point made by Anni Albers's text from two years earlier, Stölzl's essay on "Weaving at the Bauhaus" in 1926 argued that practice on a handloom was vital to all investigations of textiles:

Since mechanical weaving today is not far enough advanced to provide all the possibilities offered by hand weaving, and because these possibilities are necessary for people to develop their creativity, we deal in particular with hand weaving. It is only by working on a handloom that one has enough room to play, to develop an idea from one experiment to the next, until there is enough clarity and specification about the model for it to be handed over to industry for mechanical reproduction.[64]

This was an argument, it should be said, that Stölzl (the workshop's technical master) had professed to the younger Anni Albers in the classroom—which leaves the question of its authorship rather unclear, or perhaps inconsequential. In any case, Stölzl's essay was reiterating the fact that the weavers sought to engage with their craft, not just with a definition of their object. The weavers realized through experience that the possibilities provided by a nonmechanical loom—with its multiple harnesses (4, 8, or 12) and treadles—were best understood through slow experimentation. To fully grasp all the options in woven structures afforded by an 8-harness loom, one had to thread the loom by hand. And to define or clarify these textile ideas for industry, a sustained exploration of threads and weaving technology was required.

One might say the argument for hand-weaving technique and experiment in Stölzl's 1926 essay served the simple function of defending the continuation of craft in the Bauhaus workshop. As the Bauhaus increasingly turned toward industry, they had to defend their seemingly retrograde methods. And the argument served another purpose as well: it helped to support Stölzl's battle against the workshop's form master, Georg Muche. He had purchased and wasted money, so she thought, on several expensive Jacquard heads and mechanical looms for the workshop upon moving to Dessau in 1925.[65] Stölzl and the weaving students found Muche's act to exemplify his general disregard, and even contempt, for the workshop's practice.[66] His interests remained firmly planted in his own painting and budding architectural career, and so Muche made his role as the form master into more of a business manager, to meet the demands of an increasing financial interest in the workshop's products, specifically its commodity fabrics, which had become increasingly well regarded as potentially profitable.[67] The Bauhaus weavers turned away from the language of painting, but they also rather defiantly rejected a simple transfer toward mechanics. In their rebellion against both, the students declared that Muche "was not needed in the workshop," and they ultimately engaged in a revolt against the school.[68] The entire student body (weavers and nonweavers alike) insisted on Muche's removal as the weaving workshop's form master and voted to replace him with Stölzl.

The turn against Muche was an interesting step in the weavers' move toward independence and recognition. In a feminist-like revolutionary act, they asserted that their medium was a specific material entity and practice, an area for "women's work." Gropius opposed this revolution, and he apparently asked Muche to "get a handle on the workshop," since he was uncomfortable with the uprising of the workshop against the institution and against one of the masters of form.[69] Nevertheless, the weavers' arguments were heeded and Stölzl took over as the workshop's leader. Writing in *Meister* by hand on her Bauhaus identification card where it once said that she "studied" there, the junior master asserted her new role and authority.[70] A revolutionary act thus inspired a modernist, theoretical enterprise: Stölzl was appointed head of the weaving workshop in 1926, and that year she set herself the task of determining the parameters and conditions of her weaving medium, or formal field (*Gestaltungsgebiet*).[71] Taking on her new didactic role, she declared emphatically and authoritatively in her first article on the weaving workshop:

In all fields of design today, there is a striving for universal laws and order. Thus, we in the weaving workshop have also set ourselves the task of exploring the basic laws of our field of specialization. Whereas, for instance, in the early days of our work at the Bauhaus, principles of pictorial images formed our foundation—a woven piece was a [picture] made of wool, so to speak—today it is clear to us that a woven piece is always a serviceable object, which is equally determined by its function and its [conditions of manufacture].[72]

Although a woven fabric is "an aesthetic whole: a composition of form, color, and substance into a unity," its applications are manifestations so diverse that woven pieces can only be explored through experimentation. To determine the specificity of her field, Stölzl both describes the entity's formal properties—the fact that it is a "surface" but also material, made up of threads in various structures, or the fact that its color could be "intensified or weakened through brilliance or dullness" of the surface—and addresses its multiple applications. "Since textiles can be put to such different uses, and have to meet so many different requirements," she writes, it's important to acknowledge the various demands required of blankets, curtains, carpets, or upholstery fabric. The entity's identity as a formal object emerges from certain conditions of manufacture but also from its (organic, lived) use in dwelling space. Thus, in its flexible identity, it is essentially multiple, even marked by several opposing terms: "It is a characteristic of [a] woven textile that it can be rough or smooth, hard or soft, light or heavy, matte or shiny,"

Stölzl's 1926 essay thus describes an object that hovers between painting—a composition or "thing in its own right" (*Ding an sich*)— and one whose function is a curtain, carpet, or upholstery fabric.[73] Where curtains and blankets are objects that "can be easily moved and changed," and carpets can be "incorporated into the layout of a room," having "a determining spatial function," the latter can also be an "independent 'thing in its own right,' whose form and color vocabulary" can express any theme.[74] Color and form as an abstract, autonomous terrain of inquiry remain integral to the object, even as it shifts toward use. Utility and formal concerns occupy the same matrix.

Several years later, in an article titled "Utility Textiles of the Bauhaus Weaving Workshop," for the July 1931 issue of the *bauhaus zeitschrift für gestaltung*, this theme of integration grows more intense. While she declares that there is a rhetorical "cleavage between . . . the *development of textiles* for use in interiors (prototypes for industry) and speculative *experimentation* with materials, form, and color," she also insists that any "cleavage" between utility and experimentation is *also bound* within the very structure of the woven prototypes.[75] Stölzl notes that through the "bond" (*Bindung*) of the fabric—that is, what she referred to as the "structure of the intertwining of the colors"—color, material, and functionality touch one another.[76] As several properties cross one another in the fabric's weave, there is a crossing of the fabric's functions—its "elasticity" or "flexibility"—with its aesthetic qualities of color, pattern, luster, or softness. This is evidenced in a series of four prototypes by Stölzl using cellophane from 1928.[77] Through its material juxtaposition with other threads in various colors (yellow, red, green, and white), the cellophane both produces a visual effect in the formal composition and functions—as a wall covering—to reflect light and illuminate architectural space. Moreover, developments in technology (such as new dyeing methods or mechanical treatments) equally determine the effect of woven fabrics in a room. Woven out of a binary system (the crossing of the warp and the weft), a fabric also interlocks the terms of this binary within its bond, thus holding the analytical distinction between horizontal and vertical, or weft and warp, in tension with their joining. Significantly, the model of fabric in Stölzl's 1926 and 1931 essays invokes both the binary system and the process that binds them. Once the fabric is woven, its properties such as color, material, form, and function are not so distinct from one another or from the functional end product. In any event, these properties suggest the dual nature of the textile object—its potential functionality and autonomy all at once.

Still, the question of form within functionalist discourse posed several problems for the weavers' theories. Their textiles adapted to modern architecture, as wall coverings, wall-to-wall carpeting, curtains, and upholstery—things that extend or "span" (as the German *Spanstoff* indicates) across floors, walls, windows, and furniture. But as Magdalena Droste has pointed out, the new functionality and adaptability of the weaving workshop's products in 1926 and 1927 helped erase their presence in photographs.[78] Whereas a teapot has discrete borders and relatively clear applications (a vessel to hold and brew tea), the same can't be said for a swath of fabric whose identity may shift depending on the context. Some wall-covering textiles may alternatively be used as curtains or upholstery.[79] Textiles have a uniquely integrated relationship to architectural space, helping to define it subtly or more obliquely, but their functional applications are so variable that their identity as an object is also conditional. As things with relatively "mobile" and "adaptable" functional parameters, as the weavers' theories would express, fabrics are difficult to pin down. Thus as the language of architecture came to frame the weaving medium, fabrics were incorporated into the building as surfaces, and their *sachlich* (objective) identity became less clear.

What is further interesting is that the practice and medium of the female weavers were explicitly and implicitly gendered in the weavers' texts. Women, Stölzl notes in her 1926 essay, were adaptable creatures, much like textiles. Hence she would write that fabric "design is concerned with a two-dimensional rendering that relates to all things surrounding it, *adapting and adjusting itself accordingly* . . . . the movability of the surface lends the textile its special character."[80] But also that weaving "is primarily a woman's field . . . the ability to feel and *adapt* strongly, more rhythmic than logical thinking are all predispositions with which the female character is generally equipped, which makes women particularly able to achieve great creativity in the field of textiles."[81] A structural resemblance between object and subject—however adaptable that (female) user is—only complicates the functional equation. The object's form is not merely the consequence of its functions; it also appears to reflect a predisposition specific to women. Textile subjects and objects bear a similar character.

Helene Schmidt-Nonné (wife of Joost Schmidt) also wrote on the weaving workshop's area, further claiming it as "the woman's field in the Bauhaus" (Das Gebiet der Frau im Bauhaus), as the title of her article suggests.[82] Her text, published in the August-September 1926 issue of *Vivos Voco. Zeitschrift für neues Deutschtum*, was an apparent capitulation to the form masters' disregard for weaving and to the idea that "this field of work is appropriate to a woman and her talents." Schmidt-Nonné seems to concede that weaving is a task more suited to woman's inherent talents or her attention to "details" than to man's "spatial imagination." And Schmidt-Nonné's text even appears to react against "the accomplishments of the Women's Movement," arguing that a woman's way of seeing is "so to speak, childlike, because like a child she sees the details instead of the over-all picture." What is established at the start of the essay is a clear binary distinguishing "intellectual" from "intuitive."

Yet through a subtle twist (or manipulation) of these essentialist assumptions, her argument also worked to dismiss Muche's role and position as the workshop's form master. Toward the middle of the essay, Schmidt-Nonné deploys essentialism to her advantage: "There are even indications," she writes, "that woman is counting on her limitations, considering them a great advantage." Women have the capacity to experiment with the details of the fabric surface and thus meet the dictates of "functional requirements." For even with wall hangings, Schmidt-Nonné notes, the "advantage of woven pictures over framed pictures is that they can be easily removed and folded into a very small space," a function more in keeping with a modern world determined by "airplane[s] and radio."[83] Schmidt-Nonné was in some ways repeating what Gropius had written in his introduction to the exhibition of 1923: "We want an architecture adapted to our world of machines, radios, and fast motor cars, an architecture whose function is clearly recognizable in the relation of its forms."[84] But the weaver turns this functionalist rhetoric of fast cars and airplanes toward an advocacy of weaving work, which, she claims, was an exemplary thing for the modern world, certainly more than painting but perhaps even more than architecture itself. Architecture is stationary and, despite itself, too focused on the relation of its forms. Schmidt-Nonné instead highlights the mobile capacity of the object itself. The soft object could contribute to the reconception of dwelling space, in the same way that a Murphy bed challenges, in the Ernst May apartments in Frankfurt, the specification of rooms for single functions. (With the installation of a Murphy bed, any room could also function as a bedroom.) Thus functionalism in the fabric was less about specificity (a specific object for a specific function) than it was about variability. The textile medium's soft flexibility made it suitable to change and to what might be referred to in today's context as "mass customization."[85] The fabric must meet the demands of mobile and economic living—able to be folded into a small space and put away in a drawer, used as a curtain or convertible wall divider. This would be important for the modern dwelling, whose requirements were determined by strict limitations on space.[86]

Functionalism served the weavers well: they used it to redefine their medium and to reject the logic that otherwise identified their practice as a "feminine handicraft"—as "domestic" (mindless) work with little purpose. The *Stoffgebiet* of weaving, they seemed to argue, is particular enough to deserve a theory: a rigorous description of its processes, or the "conditions of it manufacture," as well as its multiple functions. One might go even further to say that Schmidt-Nonné and Stölzl did a fine job of beating Gropius and Behne at their own rhetorical game. In their (gender-neutral) discussion of functional *Sachen* and architectural form, Gropius and Behne provided no discussion of *adaptability* and *flexibility,* terms that the weavers would use to identify the specificity of textiles. So with the weavers' description of a textile that out-functions cement-and-steel buildings, their theoretically defined "adaptable" object significantly challenges the formal parameters of functionalism.

Thus the weavers' theories of their medium also worked, perhaps in spite of their intentions, as a kind of feminist call-to-arms, a manifesto for recognition, in an institution that otherwise subsumed their work under the rhetorical and physical frame of architecture. An embrace of adaptability gained them a theoretical vocabulary and identity, even as it also in some sense returned them to a consideration of the domestic interior, the home.

The Function of *Frauenkultur*

Which brings us to the final, more obvious problem in the *Sachlichkeit* discourse. Insofar as it is a discourse of use, it must ultimately acknowledge the existence of the user. And these users are not (neutral) "humans" (as Behne or Gropius might suggest) but, rather, specific beings: some are artists or architects occupying a Bauhaus *Meisterhaus*, with a predilection for walls covered in neutral or bolder tones, while others are *Hausfrauen*, women who clean and fold fabrics and are well positioned to advocate for new designs in domestic housing. Of course this little fact was not lost on all writers about the Neues Bauen. In one book, architect Bruno Taut highlighted the "new dwelling" and the redesign of domestic space with an eye toward developments in another modern movement. The German women's movement or, rather, the women's "culture" it inspired (*Frauenkultur*), was put to service by this "new architect" in 1924, in a book that identified the new, female user as nothing less than a creator. *Die neue Wohnung: Die Frau als Schöpferin* (The New Dwelling: The Woman as Creator) sought to capitalize on the growing popularity of the women's movement among the female population. So Taut's book—something of a promotional campaign for his own dwelling designs—added a subheading that would equate the most advanced architecture of the moment with the language of feminist progress.

The utility of the *Frauenkultur* for architecture was clear enough in Taut's mind to put it front and center. As historian Mark Peach points out, Neues Bauen architects hoped that by "converting women to the cause of modern architecture" they would become the strongest advocates for new definitions space.[87] "Once the New Woman saw the light and began to demand the efficient, airy, sunny, and hygienic home foreseen by modern architects," Peach notes, "the movement could only succeed, given the influence over domestic issues supposedly wielded by women."[88] Modern architects figured that the changed psyche of the converted modern woman would help promote the cause of the New Dwelling. Taut wrote *Die neue Wohnung* the year he became head of the city planning board in Magdeburg, and the text signaled his shift in interest from the earlier expressionist architecture toward the "social and cultural implications" of designing new forms of dwelling for the masses.[89] At this point, Taut was determined to address the rising housing shortage in Germany's cities, and he hoped that a member of the Neues Bauen movement (or he himself) would be hired to meet the task. His argument depended on women's change of mind "in this [modern] direction." For, as Taut declared, "in order to even begin to build better homes the woman must emphatically demand them."[90]

By giving her a new, more economically designed living space, free of comfortable yet hard-to-clean drapery and other sentimental items (*Gefühlsdinge*), Taut even claimed to advocate for woman's best interest, reciprocating the camaraderie she might offer him in support.[91] He argued that his design would rid her of unnecessary emotional "nervousness" caused by the expectations of a traditional dwelling environment. But this attempt to align women's revolutionary goals and the "revolution of the household" had another, rather retrograde purpose, as found on the dedication page of his book:

Dedicated to women!

The century's pendulum has reached the bottom—ready for an upswing. What until that point was negation, now becomes affirmation with a new goal. Hitherto, woman was forced to turn her back on the home and now is turning toward it again. Mere critique [now] becomes a creative act. Critique is no longer reproach and reprimand, but a perspective on the new path.[92]

Instead of abandoning her maternal role for a career, with the new architect's help the woman could return to the dwelling (somehow) refreshed. In Taut's indictment of "critique" (or rather "reproach and reprimand"), he implores women to maintain their "Mütterlichkeit" (motherhood) in the face of modernity.[93] So while Taut uses the women's movement to aid in his book's popularity, his dedication also performs a preemptive tactic, by dismissing feminist criticism as obsolete. Were the woman to "turn her back on the home," Taut recognized, she would surely be in no position to advocate for the architect's New Dwelling.

The problems of the household would remain the sphere of the woman, even after she achieved the right to vote. Explicitly acknowledging rather than disregarding this fact, Anni Albers (still known by her maiden name Annelise Fleischmann) published her second magazine article titled "Wohnökonomie" (dwelling-economy) in 1925. It was not a theory of weaving per se, but it pinpointed the Bauhaus weavers' budding interest in the economic concerns and functional requirements of fabrics within modern interiors and initiated a dialogue on the function of cloth for the New Dwelling. Similar to the neologism coined by Le Corbusier, "dwelling-machine," which was translated into German as *Wohnmaschine*, the word *Wohnökonomie* (which Albers no doubt exploited to recall its precedent) was entirely in keeping with the economic agenda of Weimar society.[94] In her essay she was responding to the trend among German architects of praising "americanischen Hauswirtschaften," or American-style home economics, and its Taylorized system of efficiency applied to the household.[95] As Albers explains, "Economy is a requirement today in every area of economic life," yet "the *Wohnökonomie* . . . has been little considered. Four hours of freedom won through economic house design means an essential change in the current life picture."[96] Although the landscape of the Weimar economy had been up for continual review since 1919, perhaps even with respect to the newly minted working woman, the sometimes severe consequences for the housewife were only beginning to come under scrutiny. "The traditional form of the household," she writes,

is an exhausting machine that makes the woman a slave to the home. Poor arrangement of rooms and interior furnishing (seat cushions, curtains) steal her free time, thereby limiting her development and creating nervousness. The woman today is the victim of a false *Wohnform.* That we must perform a full remodeling of this form should be obvious.[97]

Published in the pages of *Neue Frauenkleidung und Frauenkultur*'s special issue on the Bauhaus (following an article by her soon-to-be husband, Josef Albers), the weaver's article harnessed the concerns of the Weimar housewife-cum-working woman. Albers could diagnose, in part from experience, that the New Woman required an economical rather than a "false *Wohnform*," that she wished not to be a slave to the home. So in focusing on upholstered chairs and curtains, Albers suggested that any path toward de-enslaving the woman and remodeling the household form had to begin with a reconception of household fabrics. The way she combines the discourse of architecture, technology, and the women's movement sets the stage for the method by which later texts from the weaving workshop would frame the medium. What her article does is to join economic, architectural, practical, textile, and so-called women's questions in a concise, modernist manifesto using the neat language of combined pragmatism and utopian aspiration: "Our clothing accords with the demands that transportation, hygiene, and economy pose to it. (In a hoop skirt one cannot ride the railway.)"[98] The design of chairs, lamps, houses, and clothing is required to meet the demands of current social life, and the solution is, she argues, not the creation of a new "style (facades, motifs, ornaments)" but, rather, the design of a single reproducible "type," like telephones that simply fill a function and nothing more. Her task was to explicate in the clearest terms possible the interior design ideas that pervaded the Bauhaus after 1923 by using the language of *Frauenkultur*. And in adapting this movement's language, Albers was able to frame textile products for a new audience of Neues Bauen–friendly women.

The questions of gender and women's culture were indeed central to the discussions. But as the new functionalist architecture came to depend on the language of the women's movement in order to advance its own goals, the reliance would yield several problems for its functionalist ethos. Functionalism was in some sense a theory of specificity—specific spaces for specific functions—and yet the specificity of the New Woman was perhaps too specific. The incorporation of *Frauenkultur* into functionalism, on the one hand, neutralized the women's movement into the clean "white cubes" of the new architecture and, on the other, gave it a "feminist" tint. This was especially the case as Taut's ideas on the New Dwelling were (re)harnessed, in turn, by the women's movement.

Both Albers's essay and Taut's book in fact preceded a series of texts found in magazines concerning a parallel interest in the refashioning of the household's economy (or mechanics of operation) and the fashioning of the New Woman and/or Housewife as an active agent of society and culture. Taut's book, as well as the New Dwelling's style and functional operation, suddenly became a popular topic of discussion in the press.[99] Women's organizations and periodicals debated the significance of the new architecture, particularly in response to Taut's conception of the *Idealwohnung*. Between 1925 and 1926, a number of texts in *Die Frau: Monatschrift für das gesamte Frauenleben unserer Zeit* addressed the problem of coordinating a career with the duties of the household.[100] Most texts merely reiterated the new architecture's theories.[101] Others, however, adapted the rhetoric to a field of debates about "Wohnungsbau und Haufrauen," shedding new light on the significance of functionalist thought.[102] Again, the influence from Taut and Le Corbusier to the magazine's female readership and writers was not a one-way street.

The women's movement had been grappling with the double bind of the housewife in modern society, in addition to addressing the most pertinent concerns of the bourgeois woman and/or the female intellectual, at least since 1894, when the Bundes deutscher Frauenvereine began to lead its charge. Figuring how to balance *Hausarbeit* and *Kopfarbeit* (mental, or intellectual work) was a central mission of *Die Frau*.[103] Throughout its history, from 1893 to 1944, the magazine was interdisciplinary in its scope and addressed a range of topics and fields from religion, philosophy, and the arts to economics, education, social injustices, and female labor.[104] For example, Grete Lihotzky's essay on the "Rationalization in the Household," published in the first year of *Das neue Frankfurt,* identified areas—like the kitchen's design, good lighting, and well-chosen wallpaper—that would be useful to the reformation of the dwelling for the New Woman.[105] But it also made the point that the Frankfurt Housewives' Association had recognized "for more than a decade . . . the importance of relieving the housewife of unnecessary burdens and have spoken out for central management."[106] Similarly, "Frauenanteil an der Lösung der Wohnungsfrage" (Women's Role in the Solution of the Dwelling Question) by Dr. Edith Jacoby-Oske, expressed concisely the sentiment of that moment—that women's concerns were central to the questions and solutions of the new architecture and were leading the charge.

Nevertheless, multiple viewpoints were knotted up in the women's movement, and not all of them were in agreement about whether to remodel the home. While male architects perceived the movement as a straightforward revolutionary force, in fact the feminine revolution between 1923 and 1926 was rupturing at its seams from the inside, with women antagonistic to the new requirements of outside employment in addition to work in the home. As Detlev

Peukert notes, the women's movement had to recognize that the image of the efficient housewife was far different from reality:

On the face of it, these new efficient methods of household management were time-saving, but the result was not necessarily to make women's work easier. Women were still stuck with the double burden of housework and a job, or they were expected to spend more time on housework and child care in order to meet the norms of modern family life that were being promoted. Conforming to new standards of hygiene or interior decoration similarly took more time, not less.[107]

A plain return to motherhood and home seemed to some women in the wake of economic and social upheaval a practical solution to the uncertain roles imposed by modernity. Members of the Bund für Mutterschutz (League for the Protection of Mothers) sought, following WWI, to reinvest a Wilhelmine ideal of motherliness (*Mütterlichkeit*).[108] Marianne Weber, for instance, saw the "special cultural mission of women" to be the restoration of morality and civilization based in the household.[109] There was also the fact that some women activists during the Weimar Republic often supported the idea of a separate female sphere in spite of their interests in equal rights. Historian Ute Frevert explains that suffrage movements wanted "conditions allowing the free development of the female character" at the same time that they sought emancipation.[110] Much of the feminist discourse at this moment hardly included a radical critique of gender roles.

Marketing Modernism

One might say that the specificity and complexity of the *Frauenbewegung*'s views on the New Dwelling underpinned the organizational logic of the Bauhaus weaving workshop. Stölzl, for example, found it rather useful that Gropius wanted to separate female students from the other *Bauhäusler* by establishing a women's class. Anja Baumhoff diagnoses this act as an internalization of sexism: "A precondition for her employment in the weaving workshop was her willingness to accept gender ideology."[111] Though surely the case, Stölzl may have had other motivations for creating a separate sphere for the development of the (adaptable) "female character"—one of which was to secure a space in which the specific conditions of her medium could be explored without the direct oversight of (male) masters and business managers. Moreover, she was undoubtedly savvy about her audience: a bourgeois female clientele newly reinvested in the home and perhaps interested in an affirmation of applied-art practices like weaving. The act of establishing the women's class was thus engaged in a larger debate in the Weimar Republic concerning woman's place in modern society and in the New Dwelling, but it was also, quite simply, good marketing. (Even before the culture industry actively capitalized on feminism in the 1970s, the weaving workshop—like Taut and the writers for *Die Frau*—had participated in this process.)[112] And so we note the complexity of the weavers' theories: the adaptation of modes of advertising was paralleled by a simultaneous capitulation to, and critique of, traditional gender dynamics. Perhaps Stölzl figured that the language of adaptability would leave clients feeling as though functionalism might also work for them—an apparently feminine brand of functionalism.

One key feature of Bauhaus textiles, in fact, was their ability to adapt to particular color choices—as evident in a table or aisle runner, designed by Stölzl and reproduced by Helene Börner for a female client who asked for "black with fresh blues and greens" in lieu of shades of purple.[113] This object—initially developed as a pictorial wall hanging—came in a design of layered, intersecting rectangles that adjusted easily to the length requirements of a given runner, while its abstract geometry was flexible enough to account for variations in color desired by the customer (see Plate 3). (Indeed, it might be said that these picky clients with "feminine" tastes helped inspire the workshop's prescient model of flexible manufacturing, as suggested in Schmidt-Nonnés article.) So when Stölzl's 1931 essay argued that an "understanding of and feeling for the artistic problems of architecture will show us the right way," she was still speaking to her object's female users, using a coded language of adaptability. If she had internalized the sexism of the masters, it was not just in the organization of the Bauhaus women's class but in her view of, and appeal to, the workshop's female buyers.

Thus as the writings of the weavers initially developed using the language of functionalism, their theories were not simply *about* an object; they were also often speaking *to* a certain subject—the New Woman, a specific consumer who was accommodating the ideas of the New Dwelling. Bauhaus weaving theory, as it was established between 1924 and 1926, was a modernist articulation of an object and practice, but it was also a means to explain and justify why the weavers did what they did, or why a client might pay for an expensive Bauhaus fabric. The particular recipient of the message (the gendered user), it seems, was an important part of this medium-specific, form-functional equation.

WEAVING AND PHOTOGRAPHY

There remains an aspect of weaving to which I have alluded in previous chapters but never properly addressed: fabric's tactility. The Bauhaus weaving workshop explored the possibilities of color and formal composition through the interlacing of threads, tacitly placing it in comparison to painterly composition and architectural function. Yet the specific palpability of threads and cloth surfaces required a new set of terms. Architecture's rhetorical strategies regarding functionality and space were only partly sufficient, so photography became the next medium whose language was harnessed. With this development, one weaving student named Otti Berger addressed the limits of the visual and the tactile within modernism and its media.[1]

From 1928, the year Hannes Meyer replaced Walter Gropius as director, until 1933, the year the Bauhaus finally closed, photographs for brochures, advertisements, and magazine articles actively marketed the weaving workshop's textile designs to a wider public of merchants and potential customers. Whereas images of the Bauhaus 1923 exhibition and one of Gropius's Weimar office from 1924, for example, displayed the workshop's carpets and wall hangings next to other furniture, as some of several elements in architectural space, the July 1931 issue of *bauhaus zeitschrift für gestaltung* revealed exquisite, carefully lit close-ups of fabrics.[2] Bauhaus textiles moved into the public image bank just as photography was beginning to flower at the school. A flurry of images quickly saturated the field of industrial design, and like all of the products generated by the workshops, weaving soon depended on the photographic medium to give it status and definition in the world. Perhaps more than any other workshop entity, weaving had the fortune of gaining a place in the spotlight, for the intimacy of a woven texture was particularly suited to the scrutiny of the lens. The slight

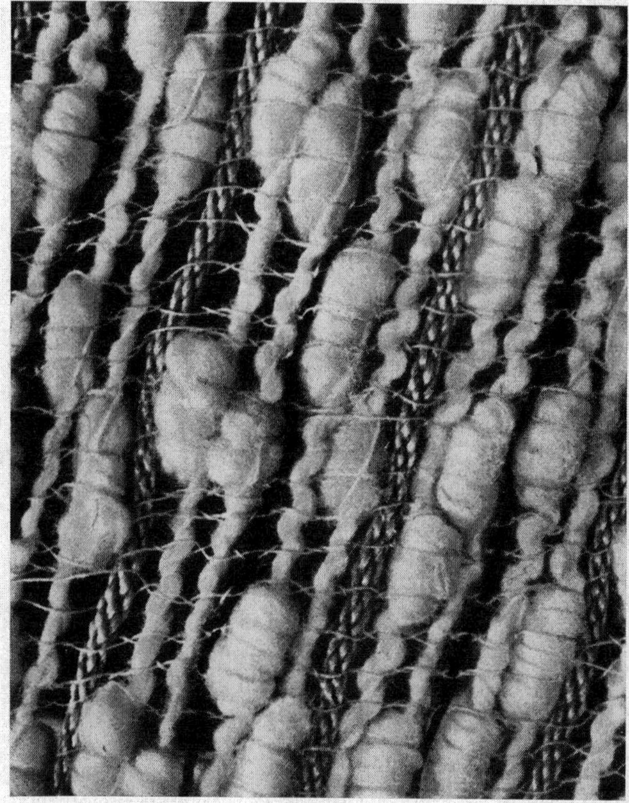

Cover of *bauhaus zeitschrift für gestaltung,* no. 2 (July 1931). Textile by Margaret Leischner, "drehergewebe Noppenstoff," 1930. Issue design by Josef Albers. Photograph by Walter Peterhans. Bauhaus-Archiv Berlin.

swellings, recesses, and shadows produced by the crossing of weft and warp, the way the fabric folded or creased, or the subtlety of the tactile sensations generated by wool against cellophane seemed infinitely refined when framed by the sharp focus of a precise optical apparatus.

The beautiful full-page spreads of textiles in the special weaving issue of *bauhaus zeitschrift* fell in line with the recent advertisement photography that had been developing for at least a few years. The cover's photograph of a textile design by Margaret Leischner taken by Walter Peterhans had already been published in 1930 in the Czech journal *ReD* for a special issue on the school. Alongside an image of Anni Albers's soundproofing and light-reflective fabric documented by Zeiss Ikon (the camera lens manufacturer), Peterhans's photograph helped to present textiles as structurally, materially, and industrially sophisticated products. With detailed, close-up photography, the textures came into focus, and with framing that implied the potentially infinite dimensions of swaths of fabric, the photographs highlighted the textiles' tactile conditions.

The increased frequency of photographic presentations of weaving at this time was in part responsible for prompting Berger to theorize an aspect of cloth that had largely gone uninvestigated, until her essay "Stoffe im Raum" (Fabrics in Space) of 1930. The Bauhaus weaving workshop had been exploring the formal, structural, and functional possibilities of textiles, explicitly placing their medium in comparison with architecture, and had developed theories that harnessed the language of the Neues Bauen. But to understand further the specificity of their craft, Berger sought a different, if related, route. Through a subtle and perhaps counterintuitive response to photography, she insisted on the tactility of different materials (the smoothness of silk or the roughness of jute, for instance) as well as the fabric's contact with the kinesthetic movements of the body within architectural space (with curtains or upholstery fabric). Indeed, although Berger may not have realized just how polemical her article was (it was seemingly ignored by the larger Bauhaus circle), its theory of weaving resonated with debates that were critical to this moment. Berger's essay participated in a discussion on the sensory status of objects, drawing on a paradigm within art circles in which the optical was distinguished

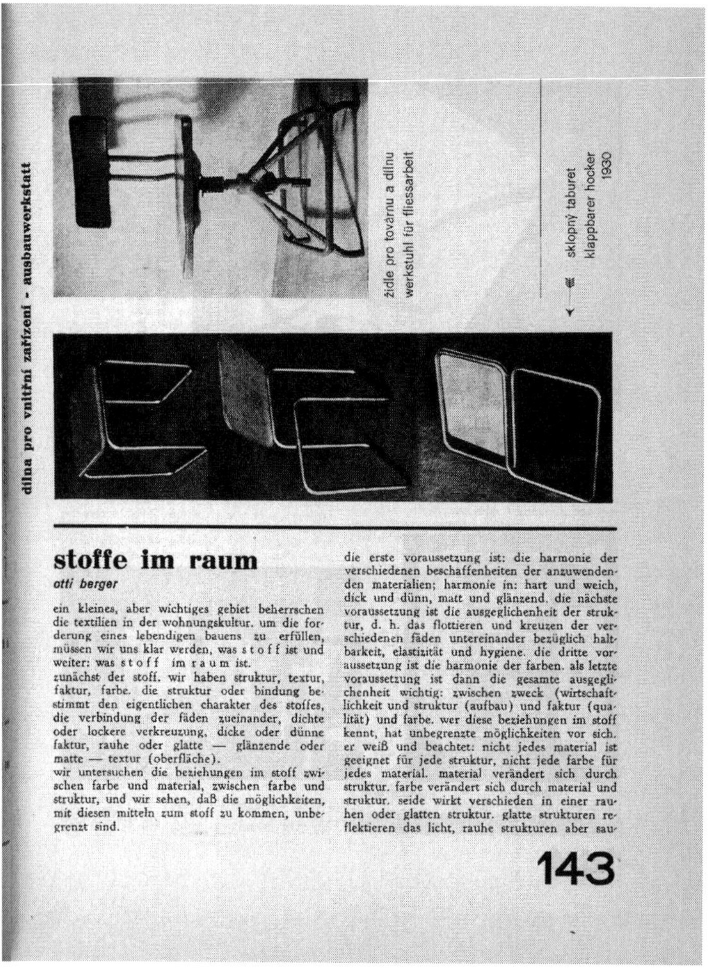

stoffe im raum

otti berger

ein kleines, aber wichtiges gebiet beherrschen die textilien in der wohnungskultur. um die forderung eines lebendigen bauens zu erfüllen, müssen wir uns klar werden, was s t o f f ist und weiter: was s t o f f im r a u m ist.

zunächst der stoff. wir haben struktur, textur, faktur, farbe. die struktur oder bindung bestimmt den eigentlichen charakter des stoffes, die verbindung der fäden zueinander, dichte oder lockere verkreuzung, dicke oder dünne faktur, rauhe oder glatte — glänzende oder matte — textur (oberfläche).

wir untersuchen die beziehungen im stoff zwischen farbe und material, zwischen farbe und struktur, und wir sehen, daß die möglichkeiten, mit diesen mitteln zum stoff zu kommen, unbegrenzt sind.

die erste voraussetzung ist: die harmonie der verschiedenen beschaffenheiten der anzuwendenden materialien; harmonie in: hart und weich, dick und dünn, matt und glänzend. die nächste voraussetzung ist die ausgeglichenheit der struktur, d. h. das flottieren und kreuzen der verschiedenen fäden untereinander bezüglich haltbarkeit, elastizität und hygiene. die dritte voraussetzung ist die harmonie der farben. als letzte voraussetzung ist dann die gesamte ausgeglichenheit wichtig: zwischen zweck (wirtschaftlichkeit und struktur (aufbau) und faktur (qualität) und farbe. wer diese beziehungen im stoff kennt, hat unbegrenzte möglichkeiten vor sich. er weiß und beachtet: nicht jedes material ist geeignet für jede struktur, nicht jede farbe für jedes material. material verändert sich durch struktur. farbe verändert sich durch material und struktur. seide wirkt verschieden in einer rauhen oder glatten struktur. glatte strukturen reflektieren das licht, rauhe strukturen aber sau-

143

Page from Otti Berger, "Stoffe im Raum," *ReD* (Prague), Bauhaus special issue, vol. 3, no. 5 (1930), 143. Slavic and Baltic Division, New York Public Library, Astor, Lenox and Tilden Foundations.

from—and opposed to—the tactile.[3] At the time her text appeared next to Peterhans's photograph in *ReD*, theorists and critics of photography had been embracing its status as a quintessentially modern form, what László Moholy-Nagy called the "purely optical" conditions of light through a lens.

So in order to grasp the significance of fabric's tactility, Berger turned to the medium that both brought her own object to view

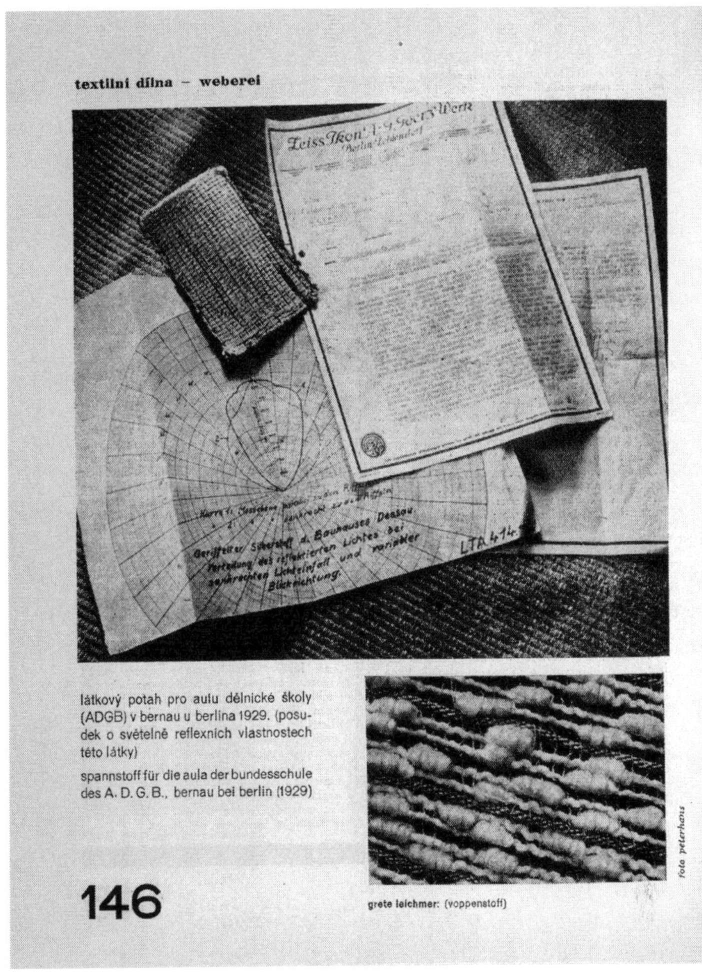

Page from Otti Berger, "Stoffe im Raum," *ReD* (Prague), Bauhaus special issue, vol. 3, no. 5 (1930), 146. Slavic and Baltic Division, New York Public Library, Astor, Lenox and Tilden Foundations.

and simultaneously presented a counterpoint to her objectives for a theory of weaving. Drawing on her teacher Moholy-Nagy's language and proclamation of photography as an inherently optical art, Berger countered, "A fabric is not only an optical object."[4] Rather, "Most important in cloth is its tactility. The tactile in cloth is primary."[5] She sought to differentiate textiles, to give them a specifically tactile theory and identity, and so she seized, through a twist, the language that was most apparently anathema to fabric's materiality and the process of handweaving.

Still, despite Berger's passionate interest in determining what could be felt but not seen in textiles, her texts do not so much posit a strict division between visual and tactile experience as specify the latter against, but also within, the former. As I will show through an analysis of "Stoffe im Raum" and two unpublished essays, Berger often points to a reciprocity between optical and tactile elements within woven objects and as they function within space. And through an implicit consideration of a debate in photography that had been evolving since 1927, she points to a particular problem that occupied the apparently pure, optical nature of the lens. Indeed, "facture"—most explicitly revealed in the photographs of cloth texture, but also in Moholy-Nagy's interest in high-contrast photographs of wrinkles or dried fruit—was a particularly laden subject for the light-based medium's apparent immateriality. It seems Berger was aware that the tactile sense had a particularly problematic history in the discipline of art. By showing how a study of cloth requires a reflection on tactility, she also queried the limits of the visual as modernism's prized term of formal inquiry. If modernist photography claimed its identity as the conveyor of optical truth—pure light and shade—afforded by its transparent lens, then weaving reminded that the notion of photographic "objectivity" depended on a tactile, opaque surface.

But before moving on to a thorough analysis of Berger's theory, it is necessary to take a detour, to lay out the optical-tactile dyad as it first emerged in the work of the late-nineteenth-century art historian Aloïs Riegl and later infiltrated the language of photography—specifically in the discussions concerning the visual representation of facture and texture. These are found in the writing of Moholy-Nagy, the Neue Sachlichkeit photographers, and another Bauhaus affiliate, the Hungarian critic Ernst (Ernö) Kállai.

Riegl's Paradigm

Riegl's seminal *Spätrömische Kunstindustrie* (Late Roman Art Industry) is often cited for the degree to which it helped shape debates within interwar German visual culture, and was crucial to the Bauhaus discourse.[6] Of particular interest to artists in the 1920s was Riegl's discussion of tactile and optical modes of perception—the way he framed the relationship as one of dialectical contact, or reciprocal interdependence. Indeed, both Berger and Moholy-Nagy are largely indebted to Riegl for the specific way that he brought the terms *haptisch* and *optisch* to the artistic table.[7] In Riegl's account of shifting modes of perception and production from ancient Egypt to the Greek Classical to the Late Roman period, the art historian outlines what at first appears to be a clear progression from the haptic (through nearsightedness, or *Nahsicht*) to the optical (through distance vision, or *Fernsicht*).[8] But the path toward an optical *Kunstwollen* is marked by a battle that leaves the winner with the (repressed) memory of its other. While optical perception takes the privileged position in his account, Riegl recognizes the degree to which these terms always collide. Thus the art historian lays out an opposition between two sensory modes only to show how they are interdependent aspects of perception. And just as tactility is the necessary precursor to an optical mode in the history of art, so, too, touch is a physiological precursor to vision within our perception of space. The touch of a surface paves the way for another mode of perception—particularly where extension in space can be identified through visual attributes such as light and shade.

The interdependence of these perceptual modes is elaborated most clearly in *Late Roman Art Industry* in the chapter titled "Architecture," in which Riegl performs an empirical analysis of sense perception to explain how space is grasped by a viewer. Employing a physiological methodology, the art historian recalls scientists in the field of optics, who in the early eighteenth century began to study the perception of depth and three-dimensional objects. In 1709, George Berkeley asserted that because vision can observe only two-dimensional patterns of light and color in order to perceive forms and distance, human beings require a memory of depth achieved through touch in order to see three dimensionally.[9] Although this idea of tactile memory in depth perception had been upended by the science of optics long before Riegl's 1901 text (nineteenth-century optic science emphasized the role of stereoscopic vision in depth perception), Riegl would continue to rely on this model: "Wherever the eye recognizes a coherent colored plane of one and the same stimulus," he writes, "there arises the notion based on experience of the tactile unpenetrable surface of a finished material entity."[10]

The memory of that experience generates, through a "complicated process of thought," a capacity in the viewer to mentally flesh out into three-dimensional form "the two-dimensional surface that our eyes actually perceive," and to see depth where the visual perception of color and light would otherwise yield flat planes.[11]

Although touch is at first crucial to grasping space, according to Riegl, it is quickly superseded by vision and "subjective thinking." He further writes about touch, regarding its possibilities and limitations:

Definite knowledge about the enclosed individual unity of single objects we obtain only with our sense of touch. It alone procures us knowledge about the inpenetrability of the borders, which enclose the material individual. These borders are the tactile surfaces of the objects. Yet what we touch immediately are not extended planes, but only individual points. Only through repetition of the perception of impenetrable points, one and the same material individual following quickly another and located in proximity, can we arrive at the notion of an extended plane with its two dimensions of height and width. Hence, this notion is no longer obtained with immediate perception by the sense of touch, but rather with a combination of several perceptions which pre-suppose necessarily the intervention by a process of subjective thinking.[12]

Hence, there is a crucial difference between an "objective surface" (*objektive Fläche*), as exemplified in low-relief carving that we perceive tactilely, and a "subjective surface" (*subjektive Fläche*). The latter, whose depth is formed illusionistically and which we perceive at a distance, such as a deep-relief Roman carving, we perceive optically but also through a combination of subjective thought. (This would become particularly evident in perspectival painting.) Touch is important as a precursor, but the eye, through the help of the mind, can overcome it.

Riegl thus relegates touch to the lesser of the two senses, maintaining that the eye is capable of a quicker and more reliable synthesis. So over the course of the history that he outlines, Riegl's argument traverses a series of shifts that often double back to reinvest the value of vision—such that sensory interdependence is clear in one moment only to be erased in the next. Through the help of the mind, vision can overcome its dependence on touch. Once "the

eye" becomes in the modern period "the most important record-
ing organ," projecting forms are mainly "disclosed through shadows."[13] A kind of visual texture, as found for instance in the light
and shade of photography, performs what, through distance from
a material object, cannot be haptically conveyed.

Still, Riegl's optical-tactile paradigm is ambivalent. After all,
the role of (tactile) memory is exceptionally important to his
favoring of the subjective process of mental synthesis. Despite his
apparent telos of optical perception and production, Riegl's argument consistently returns to touch through the (subjective) recol-
lection of objective impenetrability and extension in space that it
provides. So the two terms converge again and again, creating the
impression that even a purely optical mode of perception (such as
that deployed in the *Fernsicht* of Late Roman sculpture), can only
grasp the material texture through the eye's roving touch of that
form's shadows.

Neue Sachlichkeit, Neue Optik, and the Problem of Facture

The ambivalence of Riegl's paradigm surfaced most conspicuously
around the Bauhaus, albeit as a subtext, in debates on the nature
of photography; for, to use Riegl's logic, the distancing mechanism
of the lens may simultaneously provide us with an intimate view
of surface texture.

Through sharp-focused, black-and-white images of automobiles and street scenes but also fashion and faces, magazine pages
glistened with detailed images of metropolitan life. The new love
affair with the medium coincided with the publication of Albert
Renger-Patzsch's *Die Welt ist Schön* and with several exhibitions,
including *Film und Foto*, as well as the publication of *Foto-Auge*
(Photo-Eye) by Franz Roh and Jan Tschichold, and *Es kommt
der neue Fotograf!* (Here comes the new photographer!) by Wer-
ner Gräff, which were all part of a trend in the arts labeled Neue
Sachlichkeit. A cultural landscape of popular illustrated magazines further fostered a saturation of photographs in the pages
of the Werkbund's *Die Form* and the Bauhaus's own mouthpiece,
the *bauhaus zeitschrift für gestaltung*. The latter featured a special
issue on photography in 1928, heralding the "experimental" work
of Moholy-Nagy and citing photography's privileged role within

modern culture.[14] Then, in 1929, under the leadership of Walter Peterhans, a dedicated course in photography became part of the Bauhaus curriculum. Taking center stage within discussions, *Fototechnik* made even the question of architecture seem peripheral to the school's aims.

In his theoretical exploration of photography, film, and photograms, Moholy-Nagy emphasized visuality by defining the essence of the photographic medium as the *Gestaltung des Lichtes* (design of light). Frequently employing the adjective *optisch* in his texts, Moholy-Nagy regarded it as pertinent to the "optical apparatus of the eyes" but also to the technique whose very existence depends on the capturing of light and shadow. Throughout his Bauhaus books *Malerei Fotografie Film* (no. 8) and *Von Material zu Architektur* (no. 14) and in several essays from the late 1920s and early 1930s published in *bauhaus zeitschrift, Die Form, De Stijl, i10*, and *Photographische Korrespondenz*, Moholy-Nagy claimed that photography was the quintessential, indeed prototypical, medium for the modern world—one in which human perception had been radically altered by the proliferation of images in magazines and on cinematic screens.[15] According to one essay on "Photography in Advertising" from 1927, the fact that "today everything is concentrated, more powerfully than ever before, on the visual" made photography a particularly privileged site within contemporary culture.[16] But photography was also a modernist medium that could be defined in the "purest" (least commodified) of terms. Moholy-Nagy makes his argument along these lines clearest in 1928, in "Fotografie ist Lichtgestaltung," where he argues that "representational meaning" is not important for photography, least of all for the photogram, which allows an "unmediated optical experience."[17] The photogram, for example, "reveals a sublimated, radiating, almost immaterial effect."[18]

The name Neue Sachlichkeit (typically translated as "New Objectivity") in this context came to signal a style of photography and evoked the world of "common experience"—as the term had been promulgated by the critic G. F. Hartlaub. Hartlaub originally applied the term to expressionist painting that was less utopian, and more *sachlich*, or more closely in touch with the social and modern world of people and things. But according to Rosemarie Bletter, Hartlaub, "who had coined the label [Neue Sachlichkeit] in

1923, believed the term to have become meaningless by 1929 . . . [and] his complaint about its misuse tells us a lot about its volatility over a brief six-year period."[19] So by 1929, when the label came to reference photography, the difficulty and inconsistencies of the term had consequences for debates among the myriad of photographers associated with it.

Thus the conversation about and definition of Neue Sachlichkeit photography were conflicted, and several debates arose about the role of experimentation versus pictorial realism (as advocated by Renger-Patzsch). Moholy-Nagy was seen by many to be the adversary, engaged as he was with the more abstract possibilities of the medium and the development of a related movement around the terms *Neue Optik* or *Neues Sehen* (New Vision). Even at the center of many discussions, Moholy-Nagy stood in for a kind of experimentation that was seen to be "overly photographical"—meaning "emotionless and dead" because it was concerned with the workings of light.[20] Renger-Patzsch's photographs, according to the critic Hugo Sieker, sought to define photography as "the medium of absolute realism," where "even the smallest pore of a leaf becomes a sucking funnel, and the tiniest hair a revelation of some essential vital function."[21] Sieker insisted that the "sharp objectivity" of photography "always calls for *detail*."[22] So the very purpose of the photographic lens was up for question. The photographic realists highlighted the "pureness" of the camera's access to "fact," evident in the play on the word *Objektiv* for "lens"—as though the lens did not mediate but rather provided an objective view on objects and details.[23] In contrast, Moholy-Nagy, in promoting photography as a form of "production" over "reproduction," concerned himself mainly with the optical effects shaped by the camera lens' mediation of light. Paradoxically, in either case the question of objectivity seemed to hinge on the problem of light and its relationship to the material's tactile surface.

The debates about photography came to a head for the first time in 1927 over the problem of texture. Some critics, in particular Moholy-Nagy, recognized that tactility was necessary to the evolution of this quintessentially modernist visual medium. Indeed, the tension in photographic theory became evident in a number of debates spearheaded by the remarks of Kállai, a former advocate for constructivism. Kállai, who was increasingly pessimistic about the merging of art with technology (ironically just before he was appointed editor of *bauhaus zeitschrift*), sparked a debate in the pages of *i10*, beginning with the comment that "photography is incapable of [painting's] impressive degree of materiality and palpability. To be sure, it produces marvelously clear and distinct reproductions of reality. . . . [But] the plastic invigoration of the image, its orchestration, so to speak, through facture, is lost to photography."[24] Unlike painting, in which the palpable dimensions of paint and the canvas support are "in tension" with the image,

the gelatin of the light-sensitive layer and the paper texture offer no resistance against . . . the image's grain. The plane . . . is a pure, transparent mirror surface where all forms and tones can come into view without resistance . . . [and their] combination, effected through the action of the photographic material, is one of *complete optical neutrality.*[25]

By the end of 1929, following a second *bauhaus* issue dedicated to photographic work and theory,[26] Kállai made his critique of the "new vision" in photography (and more specifically the *Film und Foto* exhibition) even more direct, in an editorial collaboration with Renger-Patzsch, "Postcript to Photo-Inflation / Boom Times." The authors begin:

That endless series of exhibitions and publications has moved abroad for a while. Let us quickly take advantage of the reprieve and come to our senses before it is too late. It's time to say some things which no one wanted to hear at the peak of the commotion. You will perhaps argue that *bauhaus* too has brought out a photo issue. Correct. To be honest, by now we're almost regretting it.[27]

This reactionary "regret" was significant, because while he admitted to participating in the photo boom, he simultaneously expressed his discomfort with the medium's tendency toward "recipes" of "new, interesting visual effects" over "aesthetic standards and craft," which to some degree Kállai still associated with the technique and texture of painting.

This regret was previously woven into the Bauhaus magazine's 1929 issue on photography and film. Either commissioned or written by Kállai, a short, anonymous text of incomplete sentences titled "Augendemokratie u. Dergleichen" (Eye-democracy and That Sort of Thing),[28] aligns the photographic apparatus with democratic social existence: "We have an eye-democracy: the photo-mechanical. The same picture for the millions of readers of magazines, for the millions of visitors to the cinema. A class-less see-culture, much more: see-habit. The collective-optic. The standard-seeing."[29] Photography's focus on the sensory mode of experience of the eye is central to a new system of general equiv-alence, and so as the text develops with some amusement and play—referring to the American "bubblegum" language like *nice* and *wonderful*—the *Augendemokratie* brings democracy into other areas of dwelling and experience: building (*Baudemokratie*), sitting (*Sitzfleischdemokratie*), cooking (*Kochtopfdemokratie*), and even the curing of calluses. But the essay takes a more cynical turn toward the end, throwing a sinister light on what at first seemed to be an unblemished espousal of the eye. Kállai notes: "Against it: hunger-democracy. Not only for hungry artists, everyone may be hungry. Also the unemployed. We have a poisonous gas-democracy: the same poisonous gas for the military and citizens, for grownups and for children."[30] The "boom times" argument two issues later, though ascerbic, would not come close to the pessimism of this cri-tique of photography and the new "see-culture."

The invocation of facture was often deployed to set the bal-ance right—though it provoked more anxieties than clear conclu-sions.[31] Even the definition of *facture* would come under scrutiny in the photographic debates. Kállai defines it in the 1927 issue of *i10* as the visual characteristics of a material's texture, or "the visu-ally perceptible tension between the image and the [tactile values of] the picture material."[32] Moholy-Nagy takes issue with Kállai's definition, making the point that *facture* did not simply refer to the material's texture or "tactile value," but also to "the way in which something . . . produced shows itself in the finished product."[33] "Surface aspect," as Moholy-Nagy explained, is equivalent to fac-ture and has a very precise definition: "The sensorily perceptible result (the effect) of a working process as shown by any given treat-ment of a material [smoothness, for instance]. . . . Surface aspects may be due to elemental causes, such as the influence of nature, or to mechanical causes, such as machine treatment."[34] Moreover, Moholy-Nagy responds to Kállai, arguing that in his "veiled attempt to rescue craftsmanly, representational painting," Kállai's definition sees *facture* as "an end in itself," and it "simply turns into ornament."[35] Drawing on his constructivist background, Moholy-Nagy defines *facture* as a by-product of production, while in the illustrations found in his books he makes the case that facture is indeed visible in (and central to) the light and dark of photographic form. Still, for Kállai, the problem with photography is that it lacks the capacity to have *its own* facture—a tension between the material and the image. There is a complete "optical neutrality" of the photographic surface.

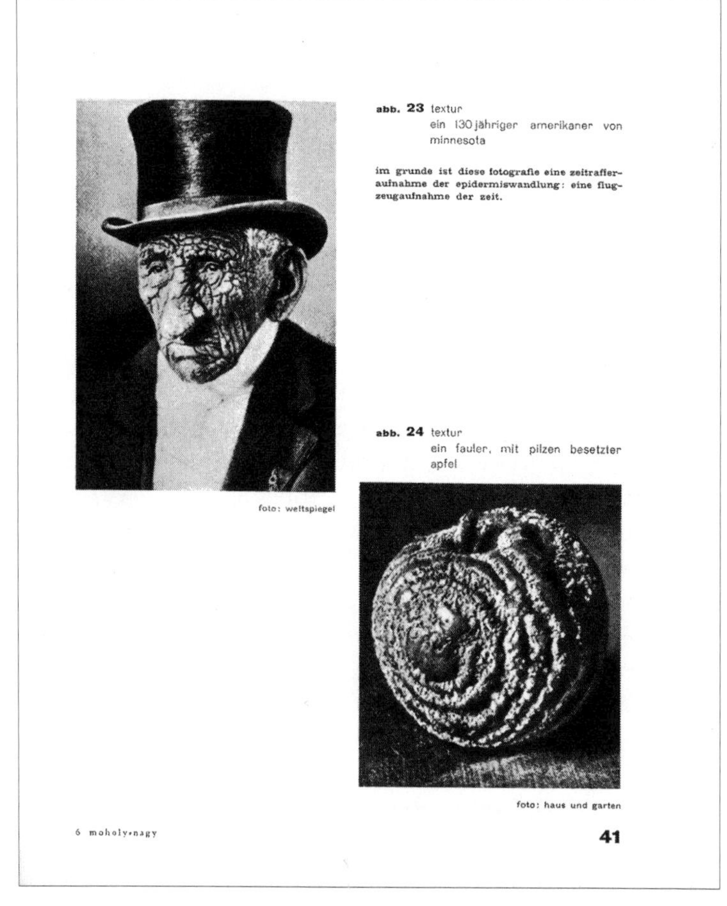

Page from László Moholy-Nagy, *Von Material zu Architektur, Bauhausbücher Nr. 14* (Munich: Albert Langen Verlag, 1929), 41.

So while it appeared that Moholy-Nagy was defending a condition of "pure optics," he was also committed to the question of facture and texture at every turn. Indeed, to make his case for photographic abstraction, he found it necessary to emphasize an underpinning condition of "texture." For two essays written in 1927, "Unprecedented Photography" and "Photography in Advertising," the artist-photographer addressed the subtlety of textures seen through the lens.[36] In the second, he listed nine areas of experimentation with visual phenomena and aspects of the photographic medium, being sure to detail in item three the "use of the texture and structure (facture) of various materials."[37] Despite his advocacy of photography as an "optical" apparatus that could create abstracted, auratic visions in photograms of household items—the direct, material impression of nails, coins, or wire mesh—Moholy-Nagy found texture and materiality to be fundamental to the darkroom medium's subtle capture of light-dark forms.

Tactile Education

This tension between optics and haptics in Moholy-Nagy's thought should come as no surprise. The Bauhaus, with its history of attention to craft in the workshops, was (at least initially) based on the idea that "contact with the material" was integral to artistic and technological developments.[38] But as Rainer Wick points out, more than any other teacher there, Moholy-Nagy emphasized the "haptic" sense.[39] He recognized that modernity's favor of an "eye democracy" over other senses ultimately "neglected our tactile education."[40] Thus in 1927, the Bauhaus form master developed an analysis of materiality and texture for his *Vorkurs* curriculum, which he recorded in his book *Von Material zu Architektur* (From Material to Architecture) published in 1928. Drawing on Riegl's argument, Moholy-Nagy posits the tactile sense as the necessary ground of sensory experience. The form master thus advocated teaching this sensory mode through the development of tactile exercises (*Tastübungen*) in part because "the sense of 'touch,' more than any other, may be divided into a number of separately sensed qualities, such as pressure, pricking, rubbing, pain, temperature, and vibration."[41] He thus established the reasoning for a group of exercises performed by students Willy Zierath and Otti Berger.

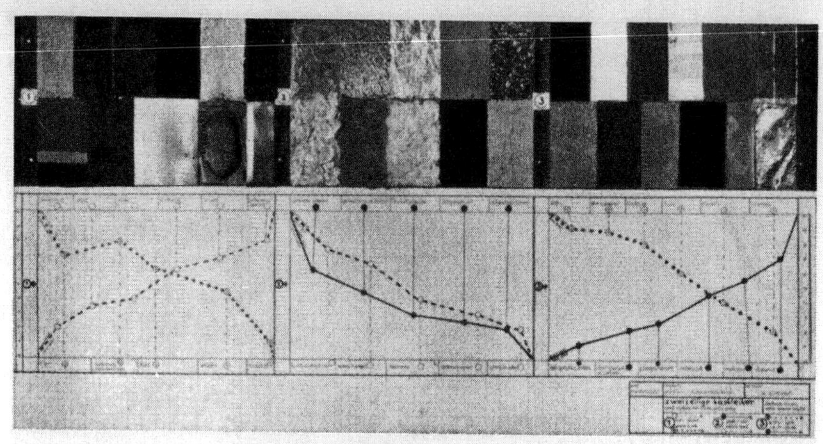

Page from László Moholy-Nagy, *Von Material zu Architektur, Bauhausbucher Nr. 14* (Munich: Albert Langen Verlag, 1929), 26. W. Ziereth, "Zweizeilige Tasttafel und Versuch zu ihrer grafischen Übersetzung," from Moholy-Nagy's Preliminary Course, winter semester, 1927/28.

Later photographed for his book, these experiments initiated an investigation of the limits of touch and vision, first by analytically piecing them out and then by setting them into conversation.

Zierath developed a particularly clever version—what he described in the object's key as a "Zweizeilige Tastleiter und optische Übersetzung" (Two-tiered Touch Scale and Optical Translation)—during the winter semester of 1927–1928. Here, rectangular samples are spread across three sets of horizontal scales, each made up of two rows, to display different tactile properties. Man-made materials are set against natural ones, and fabricated (or woven) samples are juxtaposed with raw states of wool or cotton and various metals. Below the double-tiered sampling of materials, three ink diagrams translate this touch scale into a visual model, exhibiting the properties of smooth to rough in systematically measured calculations according to the different sensory stimuli generated by each tactile sample.

Soon-to-be weaver Otti Berger's "Tasttafel" (touch panel), also created for Moholy-Nagy's course, executes the relationship between optical and tactile differently. On a long piece of metal screen that acts as both background and pedestal sits a raised layer of threads woven into triangular forms. With threads of different textures and thickness situated on a rough but pliable metal ground, Berger's "Tasttafel" attests to her early interest in the role of touch and her desire to explore the specific properties of different materials: silk, rayon, velvet, wool, organic and chemically treated cotton, and metal twisted through various threads (see Plate 7). The colors of the threads are mostly raw or neutral, but more brilliant tones enter the composition through the placement of orange, red, yellow, green, and purple squares inside the woven triangular pockets.

Perhaps the work is not a pure touch diagram like Zierath's (it is not so "scientific" in its approach), but Berger presents a composition of colors and materials in order to explore the specific convergence of optical properties (such as color and composition) with tactile ones (such as smoothness or roughness) in a single piece. These two apparently distinct sensory modes occupy the same surface, where color literally saturates the materials. While the squared sheets of colored paper seem at first divided from the tactile qualities of the threads for the purpose of the exercise, they also join within the structure of the panel. The optical shimmering effect of the silk is juxtaposed against the matte effect of the cotton, and as one looks at the work from different angles, one is able to see the ridges and bumps of texture from the various materials. Through her juxtaposition of material against color, or different visible textures, Berger reminds the viewer that the sense of touch is often used in concert with vision. They overlap—indeed, are fused—on the same surface.

Thus Berger's touch panel poses the questions: to what degree is it possible to "translate" or "represent" one sense into another? And to what extent can the senses be juxtaposed productively if they ultimately move in and out of each other? Her touch panel is a model of the ideas that Berger would later address in her theory of weaving, just as photographers would begin to explore the translation of material texture into the slick surface of the gelatin print.[42]

Tactile Theory for Fabric

Although Moholy-Nagy had left his post at the Bauhaus two years before Berger published her essay "Stoffe im Raum," he had clearly played a central role in her formation as a student. No other member of the weaving workshop would address the question of tactility with the same force or consistency.[43] Though other weavers such as Gunta Stölzl or Helene Schmidt-Nonné had spoken of the functional utility of fabric and focused on weaving's objective material properties, Berger's theoretical texts emphasized the tactile as the primary quality and experience of cloth.

The young weaver from Yugoslavia entered the Bauhaus in January 1927 and completed her studies quickly, receiving her diploma in November 1930.[44] After a six-month teaching residency in Stockholm following her coursework in 1930, Berger taught weaving technique (alongside Albers) while the Werkbund designer Lilly Reich (appointed by Ludwig Mies van der Rohe, the third Bauhaus director) acted as the nominal master of an integrated interior design workshop.[45] During her teaching stint at the Bauhaus, Berger also developed and taught her own theory of materials, color, and the role of fabrics in space. In 1932, when the Bauhaus closed in Dessau, she established her own fabric design studio in Berlin, Otti Berger Atelier für Textilien. Berger had ambitions to innovate fabric structures and weaving techniques and would ultimately gain a reputation for her patented textiles for industry.[46]

The language of perceptual self-evidence that dominates "Stoffe im Raum" yields a series of shorthand notes. Berger analyzes weaving's properties and the role of fabric in space, beginning with a typical Bauhaus, manifesto-like statement: "In interior decorating, textiles command a small, but important area. In order to fulfill the demand of a living construction, we must make clear to ourselves what fabric is and further: what fabric in space is."[47] Just as Stölzl did in 1926, Berger signals her ambition to specify the identity and function of cloth as a structural and functional entity.[48] But Berger goes one step further. In addition to arguing that the "first principle" of weaving is the discovery of "the harmony . . . of materials" (thick or thin, soft or stiff), Berger stresses the importance of recognizing fabric's tactile identity within space. The order of principles, she insists, begins with the material (texture) and only afterward the structure or color of the cloth. The *Haltbarkeit* (durability, but also "hold-ability") of the object must be taken into consideration at every stage. As such, she argues, this undervalued sensory faculty is necessary in order to truly "grasp" and "recognize" a fabric:

Most important in cloth is its tactility. The tactile in cloth is primary. A cloth should be grasped (*gegriffen*). One must be able to "grasp" (*begreifen*) [its structure] with the hands. The value of a fabric should above all be recognized tactilely, through the sense of touch. The understanding (*Begreifen*) of a cloth can just as well be felt with the hands, as a color can be with the eyes, or a sound can be in the ear.[49]

In her use of repetition Berger's style is unrelenting—indeed, filled with a bursting energy regarding her observations. Short, choppy sentences are insistent and redundant. The parallel between Berger's essay and Moholy-Nagy's pedagogy is noted by Regina Lösel: "This formulation recalls the foundational teachings of Moholy-Nagy, who spoke to the large role of the sense of touch." But as Lösel also remarks, "the intensity with which Otti Berger emphasized the sensual-tactile is specific to her own writing and theory."[50] More is at stake in Berger's writing style with the variations on the verb *greifen*. Through her verbal play with the word *begreifen*, which she sets off in quotation marks, Berger demands an attention to its different meanings: to grasp physically (with the hands, for instance), and to comprehend or to understand. She continues the play on *begreifen* by setting up an analogy with other media: *das Begreifen* can be felt (*empfunden*) with the hands just as a color can be sensed by the eyes or a sound can be heard by the ears. Although the process by which the modality of touch apprehends objects is in part coincident with vision for obtaining information about the spatial properties of objects, Berger makes clear that touch is nevertheless very specific.[51]

Berger's reference to other senses recalls the lessons learned in Kandinsky's theory courses, where the concept of synesthesia—one sense being activated by the stimulus of another—was central to his theory of color.[52] For Kandinsky, synesthesia "forms a bridge to the inner pulsation of a work of art." Kandinsky's way of explaining synesthesia was, according to historian Clark Poling,

through a generalized metaphor, that the impression provided by one sense is communicated to the organ of another sense as in the case of sympathetic vibrations in music—one instrument echoing another without itself being touched, or one part of an instrument causing the other parts to reverberate. . . . [Kandinsky] explicitly compared the nerves with the strings of the piano, so that a visual impression can cause the "cords" of other senses to vibrate.[53]

When Kandinsky refers to the tactile feelings aroused by certain colors, he finds yellow to be "hard, resistant, sharp, and prickly," whereas blue is "soft, unresistant, and velvety."

Thus on the first page of Berger's notes from a Kandinsky class, she writes: "The value of a color can be noticed not only with the eyes but also with all other senses."[54] As the first sentence of her lesson, this idea was clearly significant to Berger, who was attempting to understand her own medium and its sensory parameters. While Kandinsky's lesson went on to discuss the *Hören* (hearing), *musikalische* (musical), and *sprachliche* (lingual/vocal) qualities of colors, the faculty of touch would become the model through which Berger explores the question of sensory perception in general, thus she uses the verb "to feel" (*empfinden*), not "to see" or "to hear," when referring to both colors and sound.[55]

For Berger, different sensual properties overlap, or are of the same substance, within a woven fabric. Several years later, in response to a growing frustration she experienced trying to design textiles with the limitations of color, material, and cost set by the manufacturer, Berger would call for the "free" exploration[56] of these relationships:

We are searching for the relationships in cloth between color and material, between color and structure, and we see that the possibilities with these means toward cloth are endless. He who knows these relationships has endless possibilities before him. He is attentive to the way the . . . material changes itself through structure, color changes itself through material and structure. Silk works differently in a raw or smooth structure. Smooth structures reflect light, but raw structures suck up the light nearby and create shadows.[57]

This understanding evidently came from her practical experience weaving materials, just as it had begun to develop in her "Tast-tafel." Berger's woven experiments would determine her thoughts on the matter—revealing a consistent engagement with the visual properties of color in their combination with the tactile character of materials. So we see in Berger's experiments a concern, say, with the relationship between light-reflective synthetic fibers and matte cotton or wool. In her *Bindungslehre* (a book of her teaching methods developed while at the Bauhaus and in Stockholm between 1930 and 1931), samples juxtaposed against draft notations demonstrate how certain materials interact with different colors and structures—some drawing on the fluid character of rayon (*Kunstseide*) in pastel pink and white, others on the stiffer properties of wool in bright blues and reds.

Later she would continue to experiment with the interactions of materials: one textile from 1932 uses cellophane, a paper-like brittle material; another, a drapery fabric from 1933 (manufactured for the south-facing windows of the Landhaus Schminke in Löbau/Sachsen by architect Hans Scharoun), contrasts kapok and chenille threads.[58] The crossing of these threads in a loosely woven fabric combines the tactile feeling of scratchiness and softness but also lends the work a shimmering optical effect. In samples of her textile designs that were patented in 1934 and sold by the Schriever textile firm under the label Rosshaar Doppelgewebe, a plastic-like material known at the time as artificial horsehair (*künstliches Rosshaar*)—shiny, hard, and sharp at its edges—is double woven with softer rayon (*Kunstseide*) and cotton threads. The sets of colors alternate in each sample, with variations on the contrast between greens and red tones in one, and greens and purple tones in the other. Each plays with the two-sided, double layers of colors and materials. Seen (or photographed) from different angles and under different light conditions, the verso layer of red shows through the recto layer of green with greater or lesser intensity depending on the degree of reflection off the shining threads.

Through discussions about spatial fabrics and tactility further into the 1930s in several unpublished manuscripts and articles published in such textile journals as *Der Konfektionär* and *International Textiles,* she sets up a paradigm in which touch is a distinguished sense only to reveal how much this sensory modality is implicated in the terrain of visual experience and optical media.[59] The notion of tactility in Berger's theory is not simply posed as "fact," nor is it simply an appreciation of how tactile properties overlap with optical ones in a woven entity. Indeed, her argument for tactility becomes more complex toward the end of her 1930 essay in *ReD* when she addresses the problem of fabrics in space. And in two unpublished essays, titled "Weberei und Raumgestaltung" (Weaving and the Design of Space) and "Stoffe und neues Bauen" (Fabric and the New Architecture), both from the early thirties, Berger becomes increasingly convinced that the central concern of textiles in the modern world rests not on their visual properties but on their role within the design of haptic, spatial environments. Indeed, what begins as an argument against the optical becomes an argument for a haptic understanding of fabrics in the design of space.

In "Weberei und Raumgestaltung," Berger makes the thrust of her argument about tactility quite forceful: "A textile is not only an optical object. We come into perpetual contact with it, so it is recognized through our tactile sense. A material, therefore, also has a 'grip' ["*Griff*"]."[60] Despite her seeming matter-of-factness and straight-to-the-point style, Berger employs a single word to designate multiple ideas—*Griff,* which is set off in quotation marks and can be translated as "handle" but also means something like the texture or friction of a cloth felt to the touch and evokes the ineffable sensation of contact with an object. Moreover, by calling attention to this *Griff,* Berger acknowledges the precarious role of tactile sense perception, insofar as this contact is "perpetual" and without definite temporal boundaries. This brings to mind what Berger wrote in "Stoffe im Raum": "One must grasp the structure not only with one's brain but also feel it out with the subconscious (*Unterbewußtsein*). Then one will know about the particularity of silk, which is warmth, or of artificial silk, which is called cold."[61] In other words, through "perpetual" or mobile "contact" with textiles, as one traverses an interior space, sits down in a chair, or pulls aside a curtain, one "instinctively," even unconsciously, grasps their structures and their material properties. As Lösel notes regarding

Berger's theory, her "interest in tactile experience applied not only to the physical, but also to the *psychical* sense of touch."[62]

Despite the manifesto-like quality of her writing, Berger's texts allude to something more esoteric, as indicated by her reference to Paul Klee: "Here one could say with the painter Klee: Intuition is still a good thing!—for one must listen to the fabric's secrets, track down the sounds of materials."[63] Her use of the word *erfühlen,* which means to feel or grasp instinctively (*gefühlsmässige Erfassen*), further draws out her word play on the relationship between sensing, touching, grasping, and understanding. And in the use of *erfühlen,* which she also aligns with touch, Berger differentiates instinctive feeling from the grasping (*erfassen*) of a structure with the brain, which works at a cognitive level. Berger shows that without the more intuitive—what she refers to as "subconscious"—sense of textiles, one could not know the difference between silk (*Seide*) and viscose rayon (*Kunstseide*), which look more or less the same but through physical contact conduct different sensations of heat.[64] Thus Berger recognizes that there is more to her object than meets the eye. The visual pattern produced by the structure and colors of the woven field or the print often eclipses the perception of a fabric's texture, and the tactile contact with the surface is not always, necessarily, consciously recognized. The subject (be it the weaver or the user) may sense the cloth's *Griff,* yet within the habitual realm of contact this texture can go more or less unnoticed. "Perpetual contact" thus suggests that one approaches the object not simply through visual, conscious perception, which leads to the recognition of textiles as objects, but also through tactile (unconscious) perception, which contributes to one's overall physical experience of an environment.

Otti Berger's idea of *Unterbewußtsein erfühlen* resonates in a particular drapery fabric prototype from 1927, identified as #471 in the Bauhaus archive and attributed to the weaving workshop master Gunta Stölzl. The design draws out Berger's particular concern with *Raumgestaltung.* When hung against a window, spacing between the threads allows light to shine through, emphasizing the light-reflective quality of the rayon. As drapery, the material works with the optical effects of light, but these effects do not always appeal to vision's sense of recognition; rather, they function within the space to let light in or to protect the inhabitant from being seen from outside. Berger writes: "A curtain fabric serves different purposes and must be constructed accordingly. Either it regulates the light by day (sun-curtain) or it should hinder the view into the living space (drapery) or it is used to darken the space."[65] Alternatively, a wall covering made of cellophane works to reflect and give the impression of more light within otherwise dark rooms but also helps to warm the space during cold German winters. Anni Albers's earlier design for soundproofing fabric using cellophane with cotton chenille similarly functions to insulate the interior of the architectural space, in effect cloaking the body in a silent vacuum-like environment. The textiles appeal to the entire body's inhabitation of space. Thus even the effect of light through the fabric is registered or experienced haptically.

We can make a distinction between the terms *haptic* and *tactile* by noting that a haptic experience of space has already broken down any opposition between tactile and optical. Though "necessarily linked to the purely cutaneous perceptions generated by skin contact," writes psychologist Yvette Hatwell, the "indissociable whole labeled 'haptic' (or tactilo-kinesthetic, or active-touch) perception," is formed by "the kinesthetic perceptions resulting from [bodily] movements."[66] And these bodily movements through space are, for sighted (nonblind) experience, at once bound up in vision and touch. Blankets, curtains, pillow coverings, upholstery, wall and floor coverings (*Wand-Bespannstoff*)—all textiles occupying the interior spaces of architecture, trains, automobiles, and so on—are grasped by the subject through a combination of touch, movement, and vision.

Fabric is for Berger an integral part of the modern architectural envelope: "First it should be pointed out that these fabrics are necessarily elements and are thus to be arranged within the totality of the space."[67] Thus in "Weberei und Raumgestaltung," Berger writes several paragraphs on the function of various types of curtains:

The Sun-curtain should diffuse sunrays, without darkening the room. Generally, it will be relatively colorless, although it may also be colored, especially if the effect of colored reflections in the space is desired. . . . The darkening-curtain should fully isolate the room from the outside world. Aside from the thickness of the material, this is achieved by the suitably chosen colors. A partitioning-curtain should at once be sound-insulating and two-sided, for it hangs between two spaces, from which both sides are seen.... Important for all curtains is that they hang well, that the structure of the fabrics makes this possible.... Also there is the fall of the folds and shadows to consider.[68]

Berger argues that colorless textiles are best for curtains, unless there is an interest in changing the color of the entire room through reflections and filtering. Thus color and light have more to do with the needs of space than with a purely optical experience, as they might in ornamental designs. Moreover, the sculptural quality of the object (the falling and folds of the curtain) within the interior design of the space contributes to the working of shadows—ones that move with the weight of the curtain's material. Folds are at once tactile and visual: they are produced out of a specific material thickness but also yield shadows, plays of light and dark. Berger notes further that wall fabric, when used in place of wallpaper, should address multiple sensory concerns beyond the visual attributes of space: "When wall-fabrics are well developed, they must not only achieve for the space an appropriate optical effect, but also under certain circumstances insulate sound and temperature."[69]

Indeed, for Berger a fabric must always address the needs of the architectural interior—particularly as that space is not a purely formal entity but one that is experienced haptically by a subject. She would reiterate her attack on textile designs based on purely formal ideas—which she aligns with "sketches on paper"—in the essay "Stoffe und neues Bauen" from about 1933, when she was beginning to work for the interior design company Wohnbedarf AG. Developing a historical overview of textile production from hand to mechanical weaving and from wall tapestries to clothing and interior fabrics, Berger warns against pictorial weaving and printed fabrics and once again stresses the importance of the tactile:

Sketches for pictorial weavings and printed fabrics inevitably come into being (develop) on paper. The tactile character thereby is almost completely lost [in the final product], which the sketcher, worse still, [seems to have] intended. The persons working on these cloths through the hundred-year-long constraint of paper work missed the tactile feeling almost completely.

These kinds of fabrics are unfortunately still manufactured today, but they are essentially foreign to the new architecture. In order to fulfill the demands of a *living interrelation* between the new building and fabric, we must first of all make clear to ourselves their purpose in architecture.[70]

If pictorial weaving and printed fabrics are most troublesome for Berger, it is because they do not succeed in fully connecting the weaver to the process of production. So too, then, the woven object fails to have a relationship to the space in which subjects experience that textile. What we need for architecture today, Berger declares (clearly drawing on the discourse around the Neues Bauen), is a living relationship between the new building and cloth—a connection that is conceived as a necessary interrelation. Whether the design process acknowledges and meets the conditions of tactility and function in textiles determines the capability for those fabrics to have a "living interrelation" with the new building, but also with the subject that experiences that space through touch.

That Berger should have made an argument about tactility for fabrics in space and architecture is not strange, but that she should do so with such a strong invocation of photography's language of the optical perhaps is, suggesting that the immaterial aspect of the photograph (along with its subtle attention to texture) on some level *requires* a theorization of the textile medium's haptic identity for the architectural environment. Indeed, it was photography more than architecture that had Berger thinking differently about the optical and the tactile within *Raumgestaltung*, much in the way that Walter Benjamin's comments on the technical reproducibility of photographs and film led to his discussion of habit and haptic perception in architecture.[71] Consequently, Berger's writing provides a critical perspective on the studies of sense perception at this moment, particularly as they surfaced in the photograph and as they linked different media to the modern medium of photography.

The Photographic Mediation of Textiles:
The Optical Mediation of Tactility

So we return to photography, which is what sparked the discussion. Berger's burgeoning concern with tactility had everything to do with a trend toward photography in and around the Bauhaus, as cameras generated images for a market increasingly hungry for pictorial reproductions of products for sale. Design magazines like *bauhaus* and *Die Form,* published by the German Werkbund, appealed to a professional and design-curious population through beautifully conceived photographic prints and layouts. Under the impact of Moholy-Nagy's experimental photographs and photograms, as well as the intention of Peterhans to establish a photography workshop at the Bauhaus specifically with the idea of "precisely" imaging objects for brochures, *bauhaus* magazine became a site of photographic display.[72] Sprinkled through the pages of the first issue of *bauhaus* in 1926 and juxtaposed against architectural drawings or artist sketches, photographs quickly came to dominate the magazine's overall aesthetic, almost eclipsing the boldly designed and modern typeface.

Compare two covers from 1926 and 1928. On the cover of the first issue of 1926, an aerial photograph of the Bauhaus school in Dessau is stacked on top of another view taken from the ground. Each is then set over plans of the lower and upper floors. The photographs, like the text to the right and the blueprints below, function merely to describe or illustrate the architectural design. The 1928 cover, however, brought significant changes to the look and format of the magazine, including a different vision of photography. Here, a photograph presents the graphic design process as a kind of still life, where a sphere, cone, cube, pencil, and drafting triangle cast shadows over a folded version of issue number 2 from 1927. The difference between the two covers is reflected in the way photographs grace the pages of each issue. In the 1926 issue, photography, used somewhat sparingly, performs the function of witness, reporting the existence of architecture and industrial objects. For the 1928 issue, photographs and photograms by Moholy-Nagy and students Ulrich Klavun, Erich Consemüller, Albert Braun, Lotte Beese, and Irene Bayer-Hecht are carefully composed, printed in high contrast, and reveal formal experiments with light, shadow, mirrors, reflections, and, significantly, rippled, bumpy, and grainy textures produced through suble contrasts in light.

Another juxtaposition found in some depictions of fabrics makes the use of texture in photographic technique even more evident. Within the pages of *bauhaus,* an attention to photography's potential for detail evolved over the span of a few years from

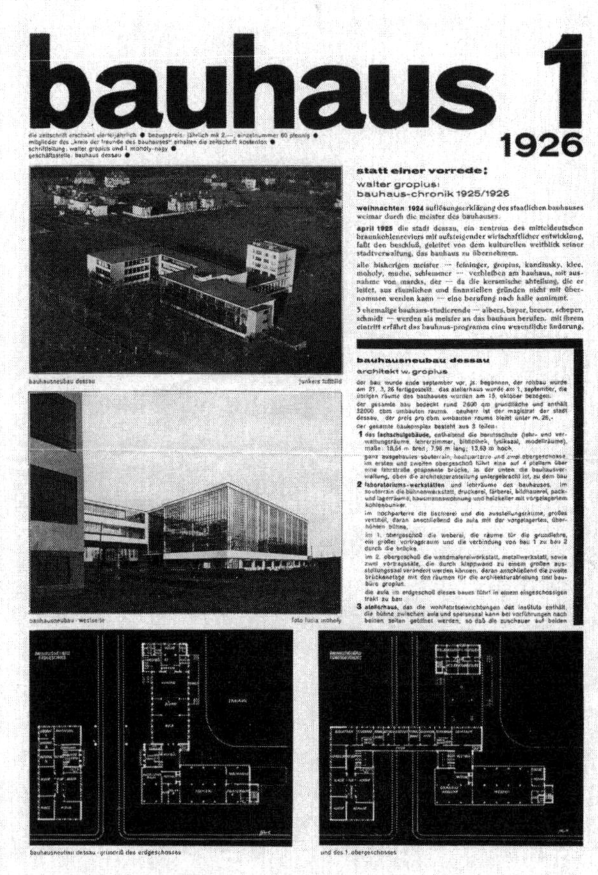

Cover of *bauhaus zeitschrift für bau und gestaltung*, vol. 1, no. 1 (1926). Issue design by László Moholy-Nagy. Bauhaus-Archiv Berlin.

simply presenting woven objects as flat *structures* to giving a sense of *textural* depth within the surface. First, on the cover of issue 4 from 1927, two textile samples, exhibited one over the other, give the audience a glimpse of the workshop's experiments. The photographs in this case present the samples of fabric as structures or diagrams, similar to the text at the left used to detail the amount of warp and weft, and the types of material, as well as their color, in each textile prototype. Both the text and the images act as documents of the design conception. A grid likewise relativizes the

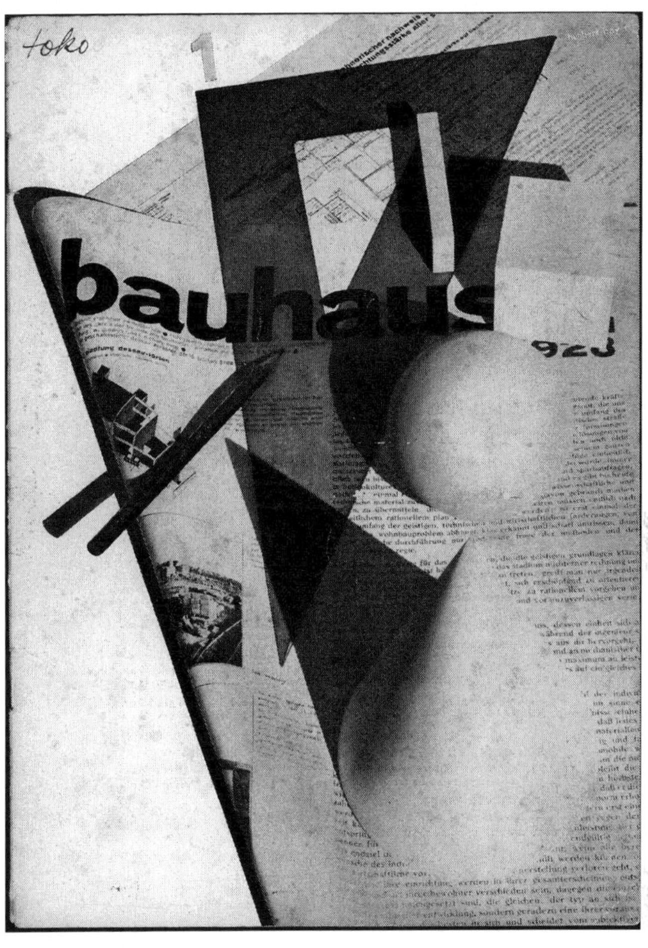

Cover of *bauhaus zeitschrift für bau und gestaltung,* vol. 2, no. 1 (1928).
Issue design by Herbert Bayer. Bauhaus-Archiv Berlin.

images, each of which is seen to be just one among several objects and blocks of text functionally spread across each page.

In the 1931 special issue on the weaving workshop, by contrast, three full-page spreads of close-ups of textile samples are presented in monumental form, each photograph conveying a sense of the uniqueness and variety of the weavers' products. A close-up of a sample of "drehergewebe Noppenstoff," by Margaret Leischner, set flat, fills the cover (see the figure early in this chapter). The white cotton threads are not evenly spun, so bulbs form along the length, making the surface of the fabric appear to undulate in waves. In the abstract field of loosely woven weft threads against a contrasting black ground lie three smoother gray cords and, for the warp, even thinner strands of linen. The photograph imparts a sense of the fabric's warm softness—the way that the cocoon-like and fraying cotton bulbs, rayon cord, and finer linen together create the particular texture of the cloth. The next image in the issue, opposite a text by Stölzl, also covers the page and imparts an entirely different kind of texture. A flat "Wandbespannung" (wall covering) is photographed as though the three kinds of cellophane—black, silver, and white—are in the process of being woven (or unraveling). Here, the fabric's stiffness and fragility are made apparent under the glaring bright light; it seems ready to crackle under even the most delicate contact with a finger.

These photographs of fabrics appealed to the (consumerist) desire to take hold of the object. Indeed, while Moholy-Nagy's experimental and Peterhans's advertisement photographs were seen to be in conflict (the first concerned with experiment, the latter with fact), they also worked in tandem, each to the benefit of the other. Parallel to presenting its own autonomous, formal dimensions, photography advertised industrial goods in newly aestheticized form.[73] Moholy-Nagy considered the tactile-textural elements foundational to an investigation of the "non-illusionistic," or nonrepresentational "light-dark" properties specific to photography's formal potential. So where a Moholy-Nagy photograph of a puddle from *Von Material zu Architektur* showed, according to the caption, the "Häufung von Wasserfakturen" (accumulation of water facture), by highlighting reflective surfaces in an entirely experimental work Peterhans, for an advertisement shown on the back cover of the 1931 weaving issue, used soft lighting to project the subtlety of tonal gradations and textures of different layers of threads.[74] Paradoxically, Peterhans took up Moholy-Nagy's edict of conveying photography's "specific" formal characteristics—its depiction of "pure light and shadow," or the use of a lens to gain a fuller view of the texture of a surface—in order to represent textiles within advertisements, such as the one for the back cover of *bauhaus*'s special weaving issue, which displayed a loosely woven grid of white yarn sharply lit against a black ground. The photographic advertisements of textiles at once glossed over the textured surface

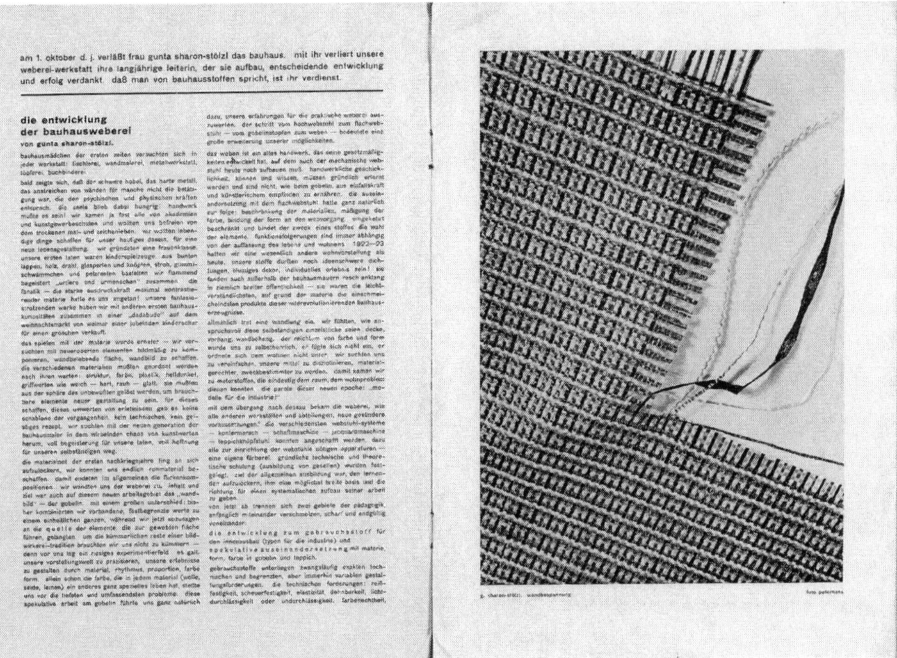

am 1. oktober d. j. verläßt frau gunta sharon-stölzl das bauhaus. mit ihr verliert unsere weberei-werkstatt ihre langjährige leiterin, der sie aufbau, entscheidende entwicklung und erfolg verdankt. daß man von bauhausstoffen spricht, ist ihr verdienst.

**die entwicklung
der bauhausweberei**

von gunta sharon-stölzl.

bauhausmädchen der ersten zeiten versuchten sich in jeder werkstatt: tischlerei, wandmalerei, metallwerkstatt, töpferei, buchbinderei.

bald zeigte sich, daß der schwere hobel, das harte metall, das anstreichen von wänden für manche nicht die betätigung war, die den psychischen und physischen kräften entsprach. die seele blieb dabei hungrig: handwerk mußte es sein! wir kamen ja fast alle von akademien und kunstgewerbeschulen und wollten uns befreien von […]

dazu, unsere erfahrungen für die praktische weberei auszuwerten. der schritt vom hochwebstuhl zum flachwebstuhl — vom gobelinstopfen zum weben — bedeutete eine große erweiterung unserer möglichkeiten.

das weben ist ein altes handwerk, das seine gesetzmäßigkeiten entwickelt hat, auf dem auch der mechanische webstuhl heute noch aufbauen muß. handwerkliche geschicklichkeit, können und wissen, müssen gründlich erlernt werden und sind nicht, wie beim gobelin, aus einfallskraft und künstlerischem empfinden zu ernähren. die auseinandersetzung mit dem flachwebstuhl hatte ganz natürlich zur folge: beschränkung der materialien, mäßigung der farbe, bindung der form an den webvorgang. umgekehrt beschränkt und bindet der zweck eines stoffes die wahl […]

g. sharon-stölzl. wandbespannung   foto petermans

Page spread from *bauhaus zeitschrift für gestaltung*, no. 2 (July 1931). Textile by Gunta Stölzl, "Wandbespannung." Issue design by Josef Albers. Photograph by Walter Peterhans. Bauhaus-Archiv Berlin.

of the fabrics, rendering them flat, and also made that texture evident, or brought it into view.

Where tactility was the precursor to an optical *Kunstwollen* within Riegl's teleology, the *visual* perception of texture, through photographs of textiles, became a precursor to the recognition of the tactility of fabrics. Photography acted as the lens through which texture could (literally) be seen, and through which weaving at the Bauhaus came to be recognized and sold. Fabric was mediated by the optical view presented by the photograph, and weaving at once asserted its status as an inherently tactile art and sutured itself to magazine pages, becoming an image—a shiny, flat, black-and-white rectangle. Still missing in the photograph, of course, was any actual physical sense of the intricacy of the sensory differences activated by each piece to the touch (not to mention the color), but the textures became visible, set as they were under strong lights and against a clearly contrasting ground. In other words, the terms of tactile and optical, as exhibited in this instance of photography, served as preconditions to each other. The overlapping of visual and tactile texture in the photographs in *bauhaus* magazine points to the larger debate going on at the time about the interdependence of optical and tactile perception.

At the same time that critics debated photography's purity as an optical medium, the tactility of textiles and objects in the world was dialectically making itself felt within the photographic (and architectural) frame. By saying that a "textile is *not only* an optical object," Berger situated her argument about textiles squarely in the frame of contemporaneous debates about vision, only to reveal how tactility was necessarily entwined in that discussion. Vision cannot be distinguished from touch and even less so from texture. Berger observed that tactile contact with the surface of a textile is not always consciously recognized, but she wished to prevent the perceptual forgetting—one that Riegl's earlier discussion of "tactile memory" in the visual perception of space both acknowledged and required. So the weaver emphasized the way that certain aspects of fabric are not only felt by the hand but also sensed unconsciously. But the discussion of the tactile and the optical in photography was never uniform, and it often performed acrobatic feats, one side flipping into or before the other. So where tactility was the precursor to an optical *Kunstwollen* within Riegl's teleology, the *visual* perception of facture, through photographs of textiles, became a precursor to the recognition of the tactility of fabrics. And at the same time that Bauhaus textiles were moving into the optical public image bank, the discourse of photography had to acknowledge the centrality of the tactile to its project of visual form, especially as it helped push the medium toward commercial goals. With sensual images of textile surfaces and a good marketing strategy for their products, the weaving workshop gained a contract for the mass manufacture of their products with the Polytex-Textil company.

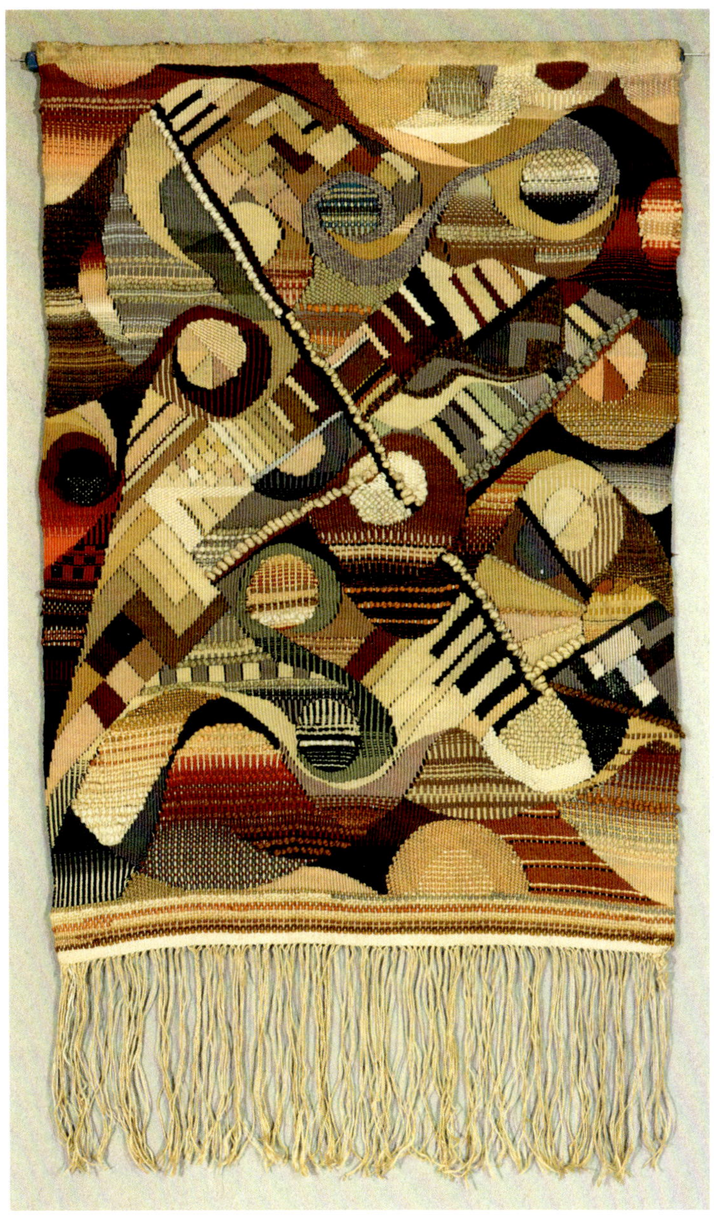

Plate 1. Hedwig Jungnik, Gobelin wall hanging, 1921–22. Wool, linen, cotton, chenille, rayon, and silver thread. Klassik Stiftung Weimar.

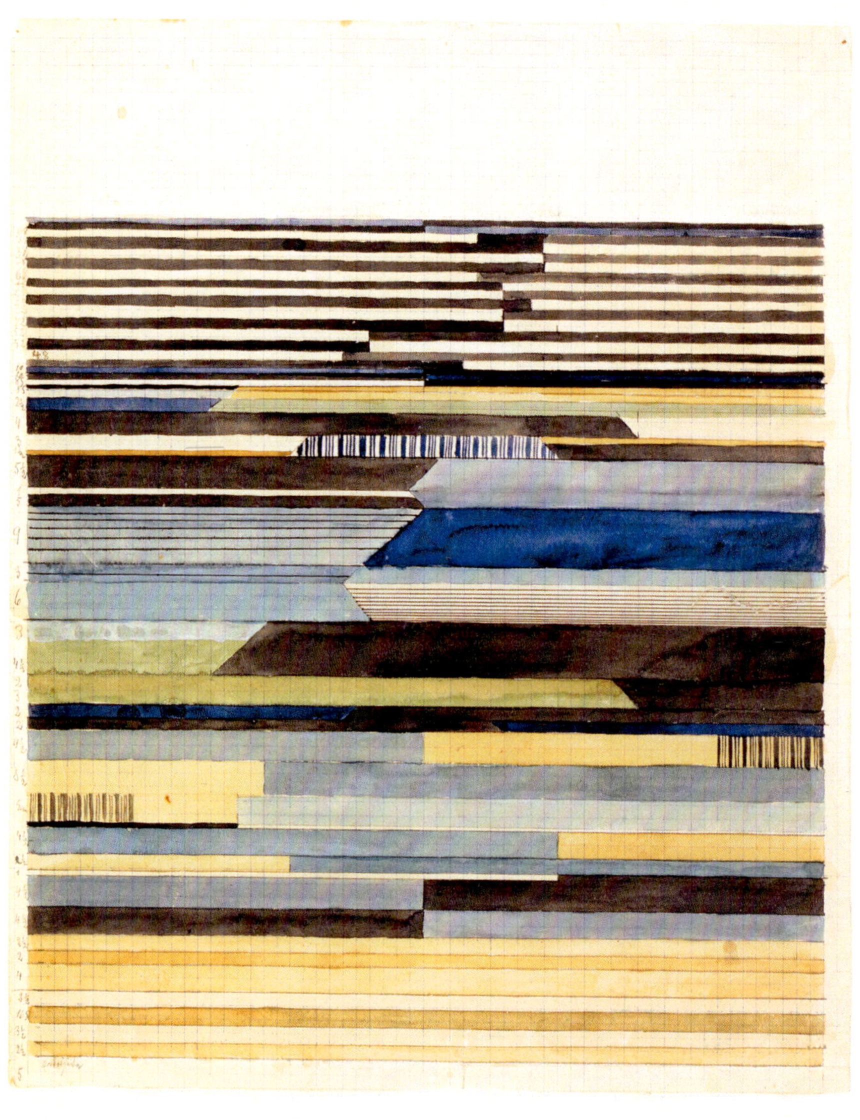

Plate 2. Gunta Stölzl, design for *Wall Hanging*, 1923. Watercolor over pencil on grid paper. Photograph by Atelier Schneider. Bauhaus-Archiv Berlin. Copyright 2013 Artists Rights Society (ARS), New York / VG Bild-Kunst, Bonn.

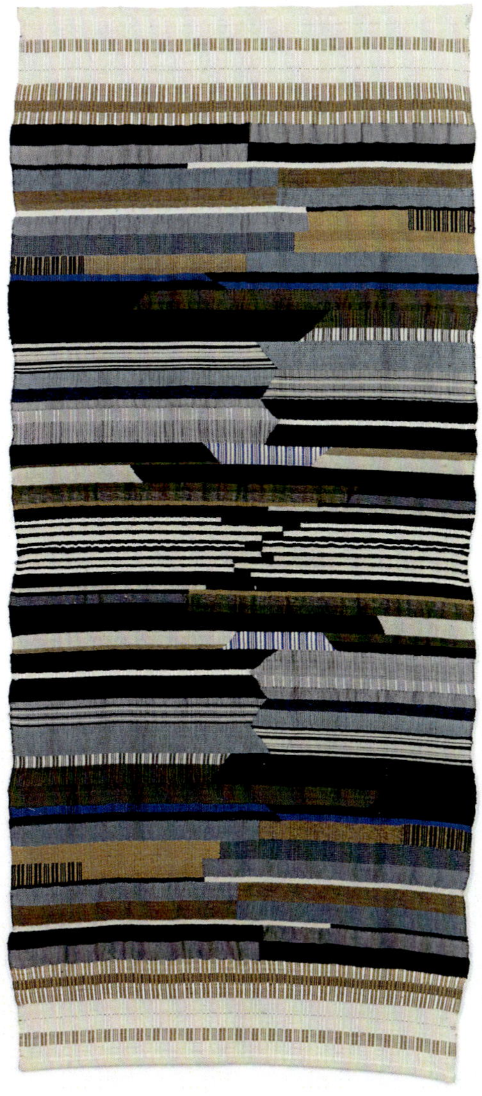

Plate 3. Gunta Stölzl, *Wall Hanging*, 1923. Cotton, wool, and viscose. Museum für Gestaltung, Basel, Switzerland. Copyright 2013 Artists Rights Society (ARS), New York / VG Bild-Kunst, Bonn.

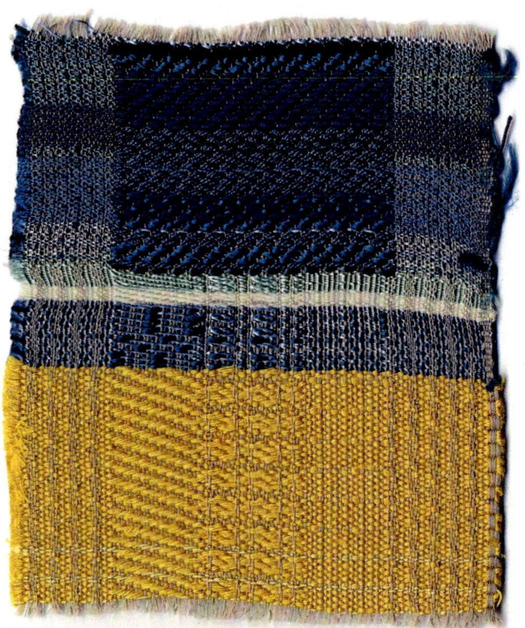

Plate 4. Gertrud Arndt, blue–yellow prototype, experimental textile sample, weaving workshop in Bauhaus Dessau, n.d. Inventory number 1999/88. Bauhaus-Archiv Berlin. Copyright 2013 Artists Rights Society (ARS), New York / VG Bild-Kunst, Bonn.

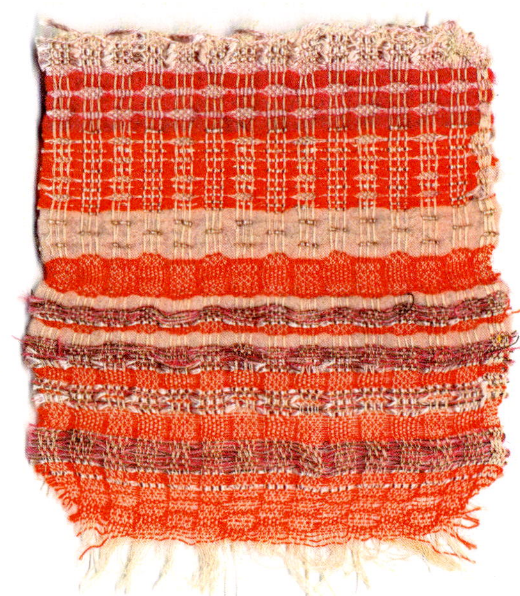

Plate 5. Gertrud Arndt, orange prototype, experimental textile sample, weaving workshop in Bauhaus Dessau, n.d. Inventory number 353a. Bauhaus-Archiv Berlin. Copyright 2013 Artists Rights Society (ARS), New York / VG Bild-Kunst, Bonn.

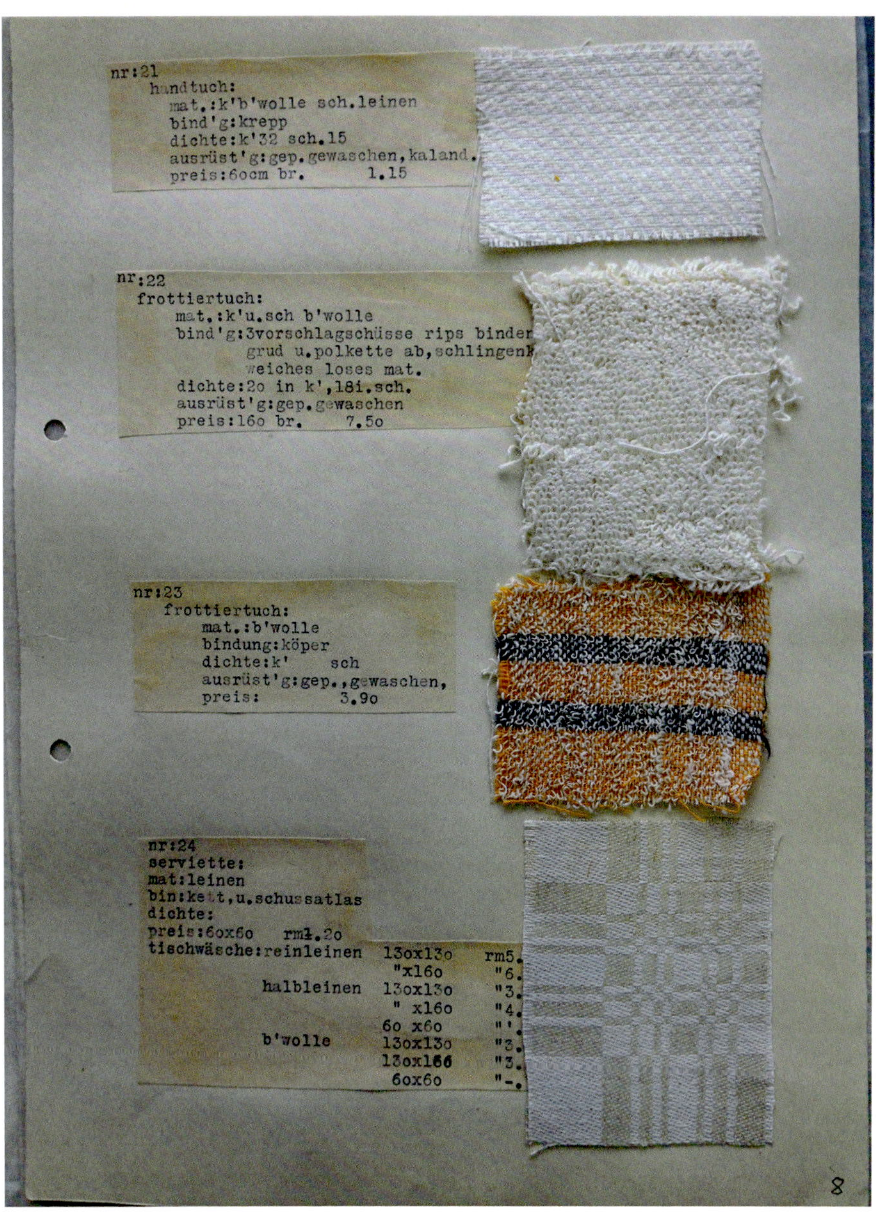

8

Plate 6. Gunta Stölzl, *Unterrichtsmaterial*, after 1925 (detail). Bauhaus-Archiv Berlin.
Copyright 2013 Artists Rights Society (ARS), New York / VG Bild-Kunst, Bonn.

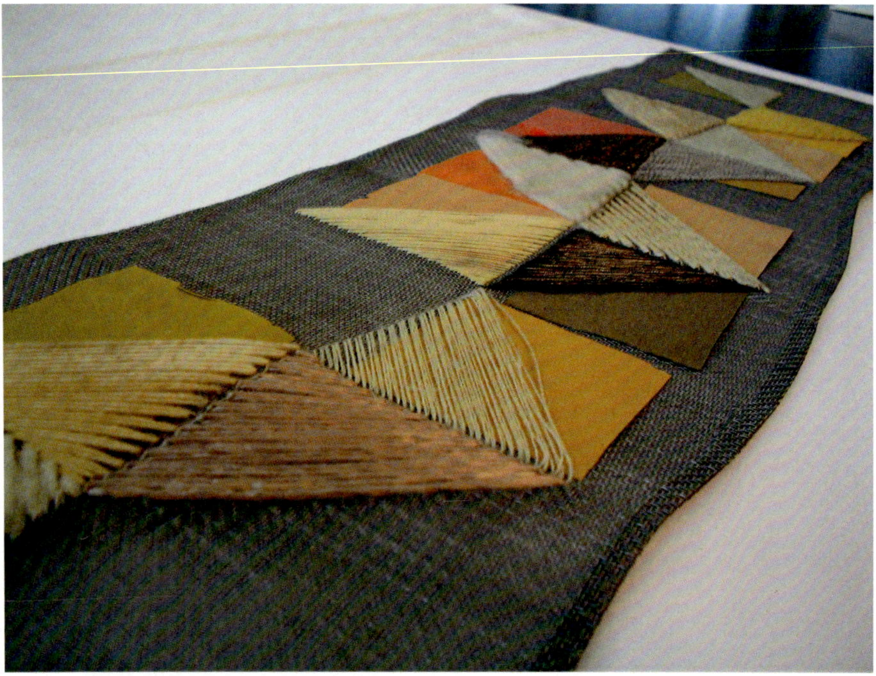

Plate 7. Otti Berger, "Tasttafel," from Moholy-Nagy's Preliminary Course, winter semester 1927/28.

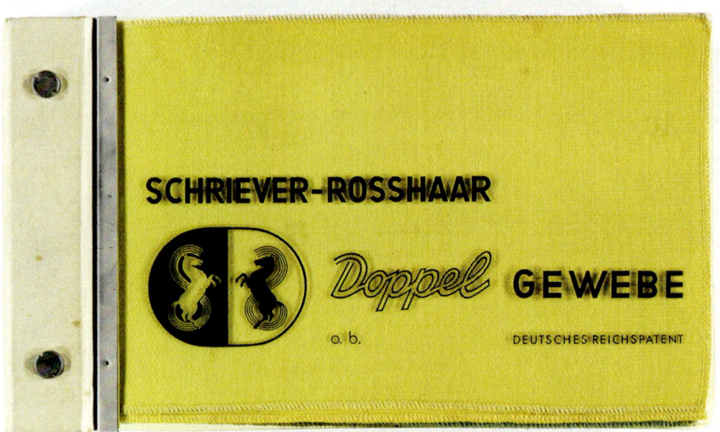

Plate 8. Cover of Schriever-Rosshaar textile sample book, 1930s. "Schriever-Rosshaar, Doppel Gewebe, o.b., Deutschesreichstpatent." Bauhaus-Archiv Berlin.

ANNI ALBERS: On Weaving

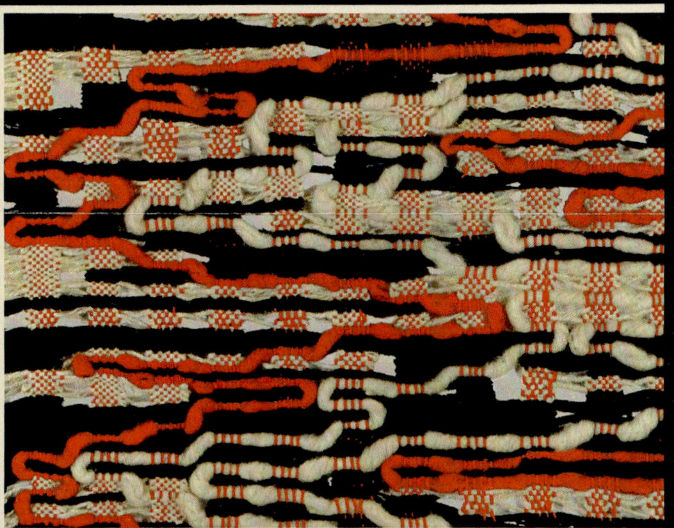

Focusing on the visual and structural side of weaving, Anni Albers discusses textile fundamentals and its underlying principles. Spanning a wide horizon, her analytic approach reaches back into earliest textile history to a pre-ceramic age, deliberates upon the present, and, looking ahead, considers that which may be.

This is a book directed to those thoughtfully involved in the work of weaving and those whose work in other fields encompasses textile problems.

Plate 9. Flyer advertising Anni Albers's book *On Weaving,* circa 1965. Anni Albers Papers, Archives of American Art, Smithsonian Institution.

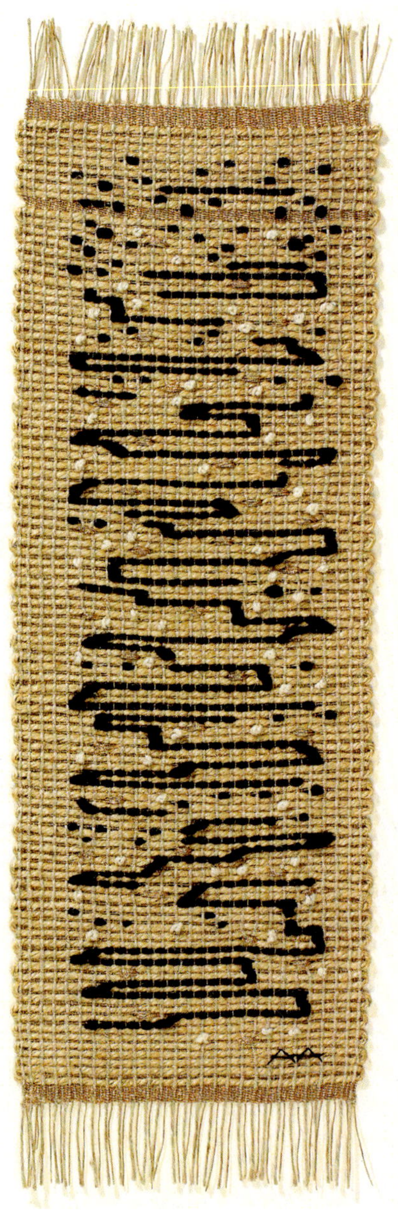

Plate 10. Anni Albers, *Code*, 1962. Cotton, hemp, and metallic thread. Copyright 2013 The Josef and Anni Albers Foundation / Artists Rights Society (ARS), New York.

PATENTING AUTHORSHIP

> The greatest invention of the nineteenth century was the invention of the method of invention. A new method entered into life. In order to understand our epoch, we can neglect all the details of change, such as railways, telegraphs, radios, spinning machines, synthetic dyes. We must concentrate on the method itself; that is the real novelty. . . .

—ALFRED NORTH WHITEHEAD, *SCIENCE AND THE MODERN WORLD*

There are more than one thousand samples of the Bauhaus weaver Otti Berger's textiles in the Busch-Reisinger archive at Harvard University, many of which are variations on the same basic design, including a sample book from a series of textiles based on her patent "Möbelstoff-Doppelgewebe," which she applied for in 1932 and received in 1934.[1] With the words *Schriever—Rosshaar Doppel Gewebe, o.b., Deutsches Reichspatent* and a logo bearing two mirrored horses emblazoned across its bright yellow cover, the sample book opens to fifty or so swatches based on three distinct textile patterns made of nylon, each in various colors.[2] Having patented her invention, Berger signed over production rights to the Schriever corporation with the condition that her initials be imprinted on the book and all samples, so a simple "o.b." appears on the cover and within the Schriever trademark (see Plate 8).

In the example of "o.b" we find that a new kind of author was born—or rather, invented. Berger was not the typically creative author-artist—at least insofar as that would have signaled the deep recesses of her inner life, the projection of her soul onto her work. But neither was she the anonymous factory laborer. She did manage to achieve the status of an individual inventor during her brief, though immensely prolific career. Otti, as many of her friends and colleagues often referred to her (not Fräulein Berger—as she was addressed more formally by the Reich Chamber of Culture), was foreign born—a "wandering Jew" from Yugoslavia—but diligently carved out a space of her own in the burgeoning German and Swiss design world of the 1930s.

After a year spent teaching weaving technique at the Bauhaus's interior design workshop headed by Lilly Reich, Berger left in the summer of 1932 and quickly opened a textile design studio, otti berger atelier für textilien, in her apartment in Berlin, Charlottenburg. There she analyzed materials and woven structures with the objective of making advanced fabrics. She pursued a number of contracts with, among other firms, the Swiss interior design company Wohnbedarf AG, for which she designed curtains and upholstery for a movie theater in Zurich.[3] Throughout the mid-1930s, Berger published both articles and images of her designs, creating something of a brand name (o.b.) in what the magazine editors often contrasted with "the otherwise anonymous field" of textile production. And between 1932 and 1937 she did something that no other weaver from the Bauhaus would ever bother to do: she applied to patent three of her textile designs or, rather, inventions.[4] Though her third application was rejected, two patents were ultimately granted: one in Germany in 1934 and another in London in 1937.

Through the act of naming her work in a patent, and branding it with her lowercase initials—a sufficient mark without being immodest in an otherwise signature-free industrial field—she established herself as a new kind of textile author, an inventor, for the modern synthetic world.

Inventing Authorship

So what is the model of authorship at stake in the invention, the patented textile? What kind of author is Otti Berger in the 1930s, if we can call her an "author" at all? As differentiated from an earlier Bauhaus model of the expressionist painter—typified, for instance by the school's form and color theory masters Kandinsky and Itten—this new author (the inventor) is neither defined nor driven by deep, personal intentions. Instead, she is defined by the patent text, by the rhetoric of legal loopholes and the details of the invention system. The inventor is part of the machinery of industry and "advancement" in technology—not so that her individual subjectivity can "express itself" (or an inner "spirit") but so that her innovation and intellectual property can be reproduced with proper credit. The artist sells his painting (a specific commodity) to a collector who cherishes that work. The individual or corporate author of a patent or design prototype sells rights to the reproduction of that entity for sale on the market, where it may be bought by any number of anonymous consumers.

The descriptive text of Berger's patent certainly provides insight into the parameters of the nature of the object and its consumer. The material used as the warp and called in German patent #594075 "künsthliches Rosshaar" (artificial horsehair) is strong and sharp, a plastic-like thread that produces a smoothly textured surface resistant to both wear-and-tear and water.[5] Though generated from cellulose, kunstliches Rosshaar resembles certain kinds of strong polymers, so the fabric is not entirely stiff—it's flexible—but it does not fold easily; no creases enter into the space of cloth and its surface remains smooth. On the face side of this fabric intended for upholstery, the Rosshaar warp is visible as a shiny, Plexiglas-like barrier that shields the thinner, colored weft threads beneath.[6] An additional warp, seen from the back but not from the front, is made of a white cotton fiber. This forms a double layer, which works to increase the fabric's durability—to effectively cover and protect the seats and walls of railway cars and automobiles (as specified by the patent text, which we will get to in a moment). With no comfortable, deep folds to cushion an occupant bent on dwelling, or at least staying awhile, Berger's patented fabric sets a boundary, a kind of distance between the space and the transient individual. Covered with this dirt-repellent, water-resistant, and easily washable artificial material, the modern train interior likewise helps the passenger maintain distance from all the other passengers who formerly sat in that seat; the textile's glaze-like surface perfectly suits the anonymous subject of railway cars and chilly train stations. So in spite of the crowded proximity of the train interior, there is another kind of distance; the textile is the perfect mirror for this smooth, texture-less subject.

But if Berger's textile mirrors the person intended to use it,

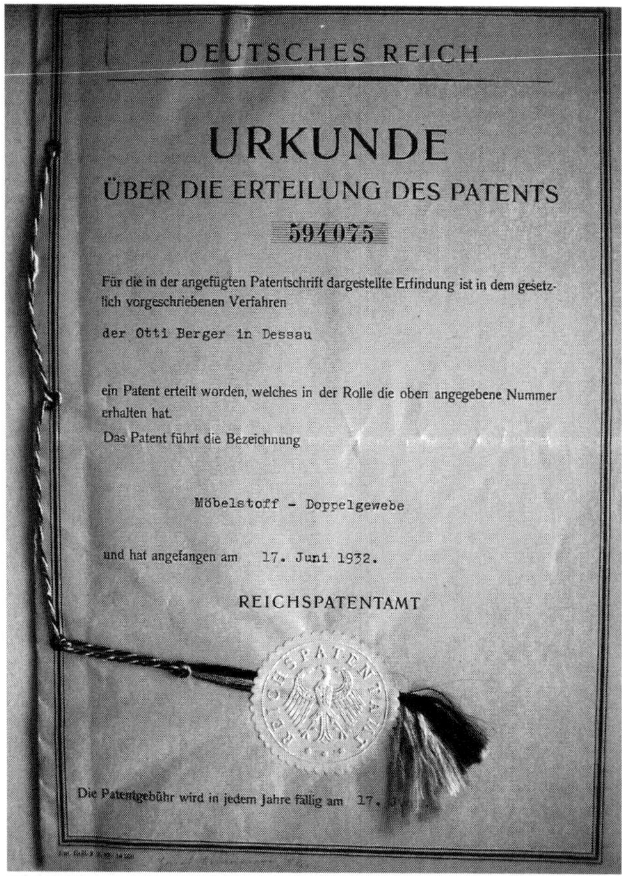

Document for Issuance of Patent 594075: Otti Berger, "Möbelstoff-Doppelgewebe," registered June 17, 1932. Bauhaus-Archiv Berlin.

it also gives some sense of the person who made it; the object at once indicates a redefined user and maker. The branded fabric indeed reflects—conceptually and metaphorically—a specific kind of author: one raised in the technological culture of engineered inventions and legal documents in the 1920s and 1930s.

To better understand this new author's outline, its shape, it helps first to juxtapose it with another, obsolete model related to the occupant of Wilhelmine- or Empire-style plush dwellings. In "I: The Interior, The Trace," alongside disjointed quotations and aphoristic comments about the nineteenth-century architectural interior, Walter Benjamin conjures up a different kind of interior—that of the bourgeois subject's psychology. To live in such a space, Benjamin notes, "was to have woven a dense fabric about oneself, to have secluded oneself within a spider's web."[7] In this interior, there is a lack of distance between the dweller and the dwelled-in space, and this is especially evident, Benjamin implies, in the literary form of that era. Just as a novel by Balzac may be conceived as a kind of dwelling ("A novel is not a place one passes through, it is a space one inhabits"), so too the novel's "mood" imprints itself on the "atmosphere" of that era's domestic spaces.[8] Reading such texts is like entering a space of "dense fabric" in which the inhabitant is encased "with all his appurtenances so deeply in the dwelling's interior that one might be reminded of the inside of a compass case, where the instrument with all its accessories lies embedded in deep, usually violet folds of velvet."[9] Benjamin understands the domestic interior's "etuis, dust covers, and sheaths" as those which "capture and preserve traces" of the bourgeois subject's moods. We might extrapolate further: the nineteenth-century dweller-as-author becomes the signature embossed on the first page of novels or embedded in the facture of paint.

By contrast, and more appropriate to the consumer and inventor of Berger's patented fabric, there is what Weimar historian Helmut Lethen describes as the "cool persona" of Neue Sachlichkeit culture, found in the literature and social discourse of the era of mechanical reproduction, who only ever "passes through."[10] This modern persona lacks the sense of depth found in its nineteenth-century counterpart: "Free of the complexity of deep psychological structures, characters with simple contours appear as 'metallized bodies,' innocent of organic frailty. . . . They strive for the greatest possible mobility and are constantly alert, 'as if they had an electric bell going off nonstop inside them.'"[11]

This new persona, according to Lethen, corresponds to a particular topos: the domain of traffic, which circumnavigates an "empty center" (an ego) and allows the senses to focus on circulation itself.[12] Space is not occupied but rather traversed, as "points of rest are provisional: the waiting room, foyer, railway compartment, subway, elevator, bus stop, reloading depot, planning office." And so this ego gravitates, or drifts, toward a specific kind of design object: like Bauhaus designer Marcel Breuer's tubular steel chair, which "is both [the] reflection of and stimulus for the distracted urbanite . . . who regularly spends many hours of his life on the train, in the streetcar, automobile, or on a bicycle."[13] As Weimar architectural critic Albert Sigrist comments, "the only sort of person who would feel comfortable in this chair is one for whom the constant tension of modern life and the taut sense of high-speed energy have become necessities even in relaxation."[14] So just as "dwelling in the old sense," as Benjamin says, is replaced in the early twentieth century by an "architecture of transparency," and obsolete plush fabrics are replaced with hygienic, easily washable, and durable ones, so too the model of authorship and subjectivity— now the engineer or the modern consumer—is uprooted, roving from place to place.[15]

The description for Berger's second patent, originally named "Gewebe (Lamé-plume)," sealed in London as #476,966, and given the title of "Improvements in or Relating to Textile Fabrics Made of Ramie Fibers," again details the parameters of her medium's new identity and, with it, the model of its author. According to the patent, the innovation of the textile was a "new method of crossing or interlacing the threads" that "gives the fabric remarkable tensile strength, combined with pliability."[16] In this invention,

the "Lamé-plume" strips are individually twisted and such twisted strips are then woven into a fabric, or two or more of such twisted strips are twisted or doubled together and such doubled strips are then woven into a fabric. . . . In order to obtain a sufficiently close weave and avoid splitting, the "Lamé-plume is moistened during the preparatory work and also during the weaving. . . . [It] is therefore suitable for upholstering automobiles and railway carriages . . . or covering steel furniture . . . [and] also advantageous for floor coverings, because dirt cannot penetrate into [its] fibers.[17]

The "tensile strength" and "pliability" of the fabric, combined with Berger's "preparatory work," became the terms of her innovation. The threads themselves (the ramie) were already known, but Berger's patented invention introduced a new process, developed through experimentation and analysis in her laboratory-atelier on a nonmechanical loom.[18] By moistening the threads during the weaving process, a weaver could interlace the otherwise brittle material with threads of its kind or with other materials. Moreover, the fabric could be used in any number of modern transitory spaces, from railway carriages to automobiles, or in modern spaces that were furnished with steel.

Berger's object is rendered in a precise terminology that at once absorbs earlier Bauhaus theories about the specific properties of textiles and also places this rhetoric within the domain of patent protection. In the patent (another apparatus), her identity as an author-inventor finds its perfect script. A state of artificiality, or "mediated immediacy" as Weimar anthropologist Helmuth Plessner puts it, is integral to man's social interactions in modern society.[19] Leaving behind the deep folds of an "inner self" who occupies the privatized, domestic interior and creates (or dwells in) novels or paintings, this new author-inventor is mediated by the "cool" public spaces of modernity and the language of legal speak that encourages her to rephrase her object's description (its structure and function in transit spaces) in order best to justify a patent. Berger thus invents new processes of weaving synthetic materials (and a new way of envisioning the medium), just as her identity as an author is synthetically refashioned (or reinvented) out of legal briefs, patent proposals, and logos.[20]

In the years Berger was seeking her patents, Walter Benjamin was formulating a name for another kind of author for that moment in Germany. The "author as producer" emerged in the montage work done by John Heartfield for newspapers or in the Epic Theater of Bertolt Brecht, who drew on the technological culture of radio and film rather than the obsolete plots of novels.[21] Benjamin's model and the Bauhaus designer's practice are part of the same technological and social condition, but while the two are not quite at odds, they are still very different—and the differences are instructive. Benjamin's "author as producer" has a political agenda—to produce a "functional transformation" (or *Umfunktionierung*) through the devices of interruption and alienation, and to awaken the audience to the social relations of production and to revolutionary goals. The inventor is different. There is very little in the way of "critical distance" or revolutionary ambition for Otti Berger, the author of patents. Berger was concerned with inventing new processes of weaving new materials, and with procuring and protecting her identity and the identity of her inventions. Just as her inventor model of authorship was entwined with legal practice and theory, so too was the language that cohered her medium's parameters, its identity as an object. The formula that binds authorship and ownership at this moment is brought to a head in Berger's patent descriptions, which function both to define her as a patent author and to provide a formal theory of her (invented) medium's domain. This author-inventor's subjectivity is not so much a "producer" as she is "produced," a product of her anxiety. As revealed in diary entries and letters to her attorney, Berger was filled with unease over the status and recognition of her work in the male-dominated sphere of industrial design.

Productive Anxiety, the Anonymity Problem

This anxiety is especially manifest in the correspondence between Berger and her lawyer leading up to her London patent, which documents the trouble facing the weaver over rights for her design.[22] The path toward patenting her invention was not easy, for although she eventually acquired the patent in England, the success was not immediate. According to the English patent office representative, her original application in 1936 was not specific enough to warrant an invention title:

Since the material itself is not novel, and the purposes for which the fabric is to be used are in no sense new, there is no patentable invention disclosed at all, according to English law, unless there is something novel in the manner in which the fabric is woven. The mere suggestion that a known kind of thread should be woven into a fabric and used for specified purposes cannot be patented in this country.[23]

A month later the examiner of the patent again insisted: "There is no new manufacture in the sense that the material was known at the date of application . . . and that the weaving of a known material does not [c]onstitute a new invention."[24] In this case, the patent office was uncertain about the specific innovation in the realm of weaving, as they found its invention difficult to measure. Thus her individual rights to the textile experiment were put in question. Berger later rewrote her application and achieved the patent, but the confrontation on the matter of her right to specify the textile as an invention only confirmed a longstanding fear Berger had about the protection of her designs, particularly since 1932, when she was first compelled to register for a patent on the design of her "Möbelstoff-Doppelgewebe." That was also the year she parted ways with the Bauhaus and requested that they overturn a provision of her contract, which had stated—as per usual Bauhaus policy—that all work she developed while in tenure at the school was the legal property of Bauhaus GmbH. In correspondence with the Bauhaus *Sekretariat*, Berger asked that she be given the sanction to protect her designs. She was beginning to gain contracts with a number of textile designs firms, as well as with the architect Hans Scharoun, and she was anxious to have her inventions properly accredited to her, not them.

Another, tangentially related example is telling. For a Christmas greeting Berger developed while in London, she wove a sample, four by six inches in size, with a fringe of warp threads left at the bottom and top, making it appear like a miniature carpet.[25] Four sets of nine single-thread blue horizontal stripes are woven into a heathered ground of light brown weft through white warp, turning the fabric's surface into what looks like music composition paper. Text spanning the three sections marked by the blue stripes reads, "a merry christmas and . . . a happy new year . . . otti berger / 8 gordon st / london wc1." At the top left corner a conspicuous mark, a set of red-ink o's, 1's, and = symbols, form what appears to be a weaving pattern code but also a rudimentary logo, imprinted through the use of a typewriter:

```
—o
oo=
  oo=
  11
```

The use of a logo on such an item, in addition to the imprint of her name and address, seems significant. It is as though Berger's simultaneous venture in patenting during her stay in London compelled Berger to sign, even trademark her textile Christmas greeting. The difficulties she encountered in the arena of patenting her textile designs, both in London and Germany, gave Berger the wherewithal to sign, or (quite literally) stamp, even her more peripheral creations.

In an undated diary entry from the early 1930s, Berger commented on the problem of working in the otherwise masculine field of design, where the textile medium's existence in space was more "unconsciously" perceived than monumentally visible. Although she sought to create textiles "that don't every time [one enters the space] cry out 'Hurrah, look at me,'" she recognized that her "simple" and functional fabrics for architectural space paradoxically worked against her recognition as a designer.[26] The ideas on weaving that she and other Bauhaus weavers promoted in the interest of promoting their work—especially as they aligned their work with architecture—only affirmed their status as being in the background. The nearly invisible condition of her textile products coincided with her gendered identity.

Many of the troubles Berger faced with the design firm Wohnbedarf AG indeed centered on the issue of recognition. After developing a series of textiles for a movie theater interior, she went on to produce sample prototypes for the firm. But she feared that an alignment with that famous firm would mean giving up her name. Thus she wrote in 1932 to Sigfried Giedion, then head of the firm, requiring that the name "Otti Berger-Stoffe" be added to her prototypes, for it was "impossible to work anonymously anymore."[27] Regina Lösel notes that a "large part of the correspondence between Otti Berger and Wohnbedarf AG involved negotiations over the . . . financial settlement to her as a designer."[28] Berger commented that the difference in price paid for a piece of furniture and a couple meters of curtain fabric was a significant problem. Even if she put just as much analysis, work, and time into that textile design, her work did not receive adequate compensation by comparison. Moreover, Berger noted that the names of architects for Wohnbedarf were acknowledged, and so she too wanted the same privilege.[29] She eventually won this battle, and the title caption for a Wohnbedarf advertisement from 1933 added her name and logo. Berger's anxieties over the monetary compensation and crediting of her textiles thus informed her decision to seek a patent. She needed to establish her identity as a designer but also knew that it would have to be a different kind of name, a new kind of author. In the interest of self-preservation, Berger sought a patent in order to have her work credited and identified, and to ensure that she would be paid properly for her ideas. The authorship of a patent—the title of inventor—became for Berger the means to counteract the anonymity of a field otherwise dominated by companies whose authorship of patents amounted solely to a form of ownership.

Even so, Berger's ambition needs to be contextualized. Her wherewithal to pursue patents for her weaving work did not come like a stroke of genius on a clear afternoon, nor was it simply the result of personal anxiety. Debates about textile protection were prevalent throughout writings on textile design at this moment in the late twenties and early thirties. In 1927, a contributor to *Die Form* magazine, Dr. Else Meißner from Dresden, contributed an article on the history and problem of "artistic protection for textile designs." Referring to the Bauhaus weaving workshop, Meißner argues that explorations of artistic abstraction at places like the Bauhaus reveal how much some textile designers engage artistic questions, and therefore their designs should be protected as such.[30] Such an argument was, however, hardly congruous with what was going on in that workshop in the late 1920s and early 1930s, where student designers, and particularly the weavers, had shifted from making "unique" wall tapestries, had harnessed functionalist discourse to their theories of weaving practice, and began making prototypes for mass production. Meißner's argument in 1927, insofar as it was focused on the visual compositional form, was already slightly out of date. The copyrighting of patterns was no longer adequate to the weaving workshop's structural project.

At this point, the workshop's textile designs were increasingly submitted to the anonymous status of the textile industry. In fact, probably more than any other utilitarian object design to come out of the Bauhaus, the textile prototypes test the limits of recognition, and these objects are often left unattributed.[31] Differences among various fabrics exist in the intricate and often subtle relationships among the materials, woven structures, and functions, not in their more apparent visual or compositional properties, as would be the case with a painting, say, or even a lamp. So what made textiles functional (and neutral) also made them anonymous, unconnected to an author. As Bauhaus scholar Magdalena Droste suggests, anonymity is endemic to the field.[32] A proper name is often difficult to pin down.

Several prototypes developed by the Bauhaus weaving workshop in 1930 and later manufactured by the Polytex-Textil company in Dresden have been credited by the editors of the *Bauhaus Webt* catalog to an author named "Anonymous."[33] One can see that the designs themselves are relatively unremarkable, particularly when compared with some of the more unusual fabrics using cellophane or the more experimental structures developed by the weavers. The Polytex designs are essentially modifications of a plain weave, with single-spaced warp threads alternately crossed over and under by single weft threads, and of the same material or similar weight. An essentially mutable weave in the gamut of weaves, plain weaves can act as the ground against (or through) which a design can be formed without much in the way of structure to disturb the intentions of composition and color. There are no open spaces made from skipped warp threads, as in a lace weave, or no raised surfaces, as in a corded weave, and the material of the threads is entirely rayon, so there is no significant mixing of materials or textures. The woven designs for the prototypes are, moreover, variations on a tartan plaid, a pattern of repeated stripes, unevenly spaced and of varying widths, crossing at right angles. This Bauhaus plaid is actually far less complex than the Scottish varieties, and more reflective of the most generic Bauhaus grid. The compositional variations on the standard Bauhaus grid put it in the range of what some refer to as a typical Bauhaus style. So the distinctiveness of the woven pattern—if we are to call it distinct in any way—is also precisely what makes the design unexceptional. Furthermore, unlike most of the other designs from the workshop at this time, these prototypes do not specify a function—*Wandbespannung, Vorhangstoff,* or *Möbelstoff*—as many other Bauhaus textiles did. Thus, in keeping with their anonymous status, they could be used in any number of ways to fulfill any purpose.

What is perhaps interesting about these Polytex textiles is that they existed at one point in mass-produced scale, with a non-name, an anonymous designer—perhaps because of (or at least related to) the generic quality of their design. The personal name for these textiles is absent; or rather, there is a placeholder for the author, called "anonymous," in the event that a name is "discovered." The only identifiable author comes with a corporate tag, the Bauhaus-Polytex label, a conglomerate of several identities including designers from the weaving workshop, managers, laborers, and marketers located at the school and the manufacturing company.

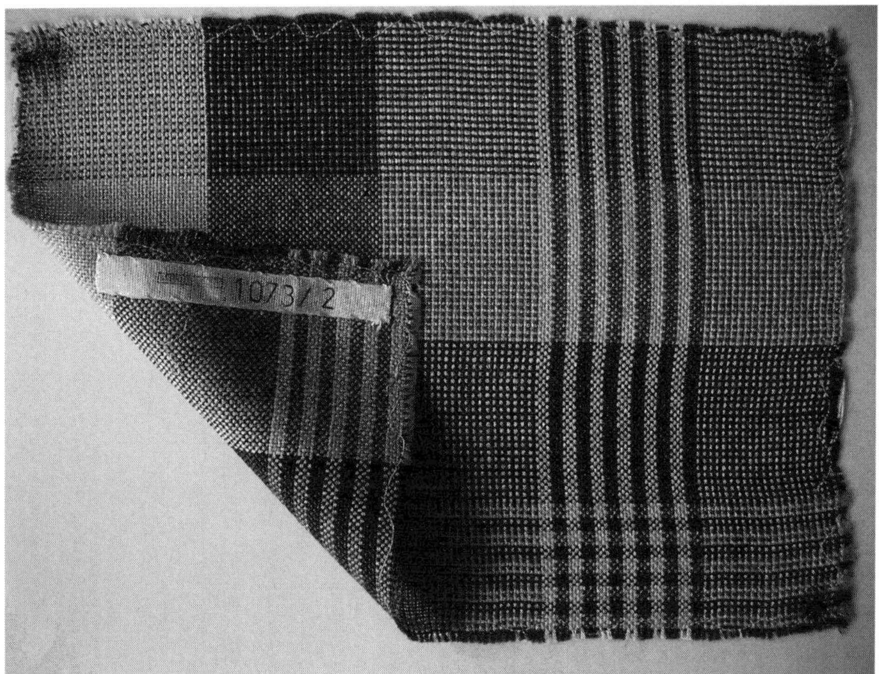

Bauhaus weaving workshop, textile sample, 1930, manufactured by Polytex-Textil GmbH, Dresden, 1930. Photograph by T'ai Smith. Bauhaus-Archiv Berlin.

Another anonymous Bauhaus fabric is slightly more noteworthy from a functionalist vantage point. Developed in 1927 to accompany Marcel Breuer's designs for tubular steel chairs—such as the club armchair also known as the Wassily chair (1925)—the durable fabric was woven out of a material marketed under the name *Eisengarn* (iron yarn) and slung tautly across the space between the sculptured piping to form a back rest, seat, and arm rests. The weave was engineered to support the weight of a relaxed body, floated into the space of a curving steel pipe, and as such meets the demands of the sturdy but formally delicate Breuer armature. But in spite of the weave's engineering feat, the chair's fabric remains relatively unmentioned in the histories of Breuer's design.[34] And the Bauhaus label attached to this woven product indicates no author, or even group of personal authors.[35]

One could say that the difference in status between Breuer's tubular frame and the textile seat is that the former maintains its

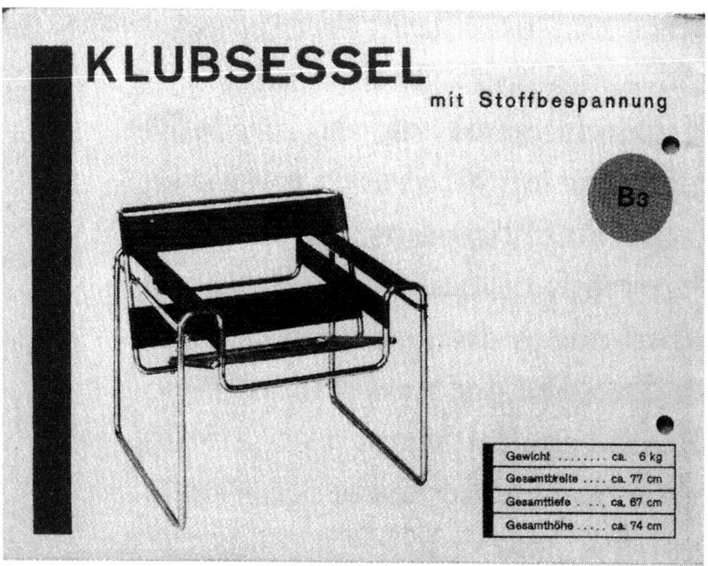

Standard-Möbel / Thonet advertising leaflet, 1928. Marcel Breuer club armchair with fabric B3, 1927–28.

iconic, even sculptural status with an attached author-signifier, whereas the subordinate textile becomes increasingly indistinct in its movement to the periphery of architectural space. No longer hung centered on walls as tapestries, the new fabrics produced by the Bauhaus weaving workshop were to function on the practical margins of the room—as window curtains, furniture fabrics, or wall coverings. In the case of Breuer's club armchair, it seems that the interstitial function (as well as the soft pliancy) of the fabric, draped as it is in the open space of the sculptural chair form, only contributes to its status as peripheral. Such an observation achieves the status of irony in the face of the fact that the Bauhaus at once asserted anonymity as part of its program and simultaneously heralded a specific set of authors.

Indeed, the role and question of anonymity at the Bauhaus are rather twisted. Alternately a school, a prototype production facility, a marketing agent, a corporation (Bauhaus GmbH), and an ethos of experimental creation, the institution at once embraced and eschewed the condition of anonymity that came with the sale of its workshop's designs for industrial manufacturers. Johannes Itten's presence from 1919–21 had mobilized an ethos of individuality and cult of artistic genius with such strength that Gropius's original manifesto for the school—to dissolve the boundaries between fine art and the crafts—almost imploded. After 1923, however, when Itten left and Gropius gave his speech "Art and Technology—A New Unity," an alternative set of values emphasized the role of the anonymous collective machine. According to historian Éva Forgács, "the processes that took place in the Bauhaus after 1923 became increasingly crystallized around the ideal of the 'perfect technician,'" and "closely related to the new worldview and value system emerging at the Bauhaus," collectivity took the place of "the word *individuum*."[36] For a brief written in 1924, a few months after his lecture, Gropius wrote: "In order to achieve precision [in design], we must consciously seek to make the personal factor more objective." Although "every work of art carries the signature of its creator,"[37] the work of design, for Gropius, indexed a collective agent, communal intellectual property (the property of Bauhaus GmbH),[38] and, with that, the integrity of the Bauhaus "idea."

The designation of an "anonymous history," particularly in German and American modernism, would later be discussed by Sigfried Giedion in *Mechanization Takes Command*. Two decades after the Bauhaus closed, Giedion celebrated the anonymous engineer, whom he saw, along with the patent, as a product of mechanization in the advancements of modern society. Similarly, the anonymity of the inventor or engineer (or the work of the housewife) was, according to Giedion, the preferred model for the modern architect or designer.[39] But while the theme of anonymity is continuously acknowledged in the aftermath of the Bauhaus and was a topic central to Weimar discourse, it is rarely addressed in the secondary literature on the school.[40]

The Bauhaus applied for and gained corporate status in 1923 and again in 1925. As a company, the Bauhaus didn't have enough capital to mass-produce its products, so the second corporate title, formed with the move to Dessau in 1925, allowed private industries to finance, buy, and manufacture its prototypes. The introduction of a seal—a kind of corporate logo—designed by Oskar Schlemmer in 1921 aided in giving a sense of unity and professionalism to the products developed at the institution. After 1923, a version of the logo came affixed to the Bauhaus's workshop products and stationary, so when the prototypes were manufactured by other companies, the seal functioned to market both the prototypes and the institution as an entity.[41] The Bauhaus trademark helped to ensure a kind of loyalty from the products' consumers, even while other manufacturers produced and distributed its products. But it also worked to give a sense to companies that the experimental prototypes they funded through contracts for options were worth the investment—as they were "approved" by the master of the workshop in which they were produced. The logo most of all, however, represented the school's technological ethos, one that was intended to eclipse the role of the proper name and signature. As the ethos of technology met the ethos of collaborative, collective production and living, the corporate title *Bauhaus* replaced the name of the individual artist.

There continued, of course, to be disagreement over the matter of the anonymous collective from within the institution's walls. Even where it seemed that the Bauhaus had completely dispensed with any kind of author recognition in favor of a collective, anonymous means of production—particularly in the work of the students—anxieties about having their work recognized continued to percolate among the school's journeymen, and the issue was brought before Gropius and the council on a few occasions.[42] Breuer eventually patented his design for tubular furniture under his own name, as his own intellectual property. He sought to manufacture

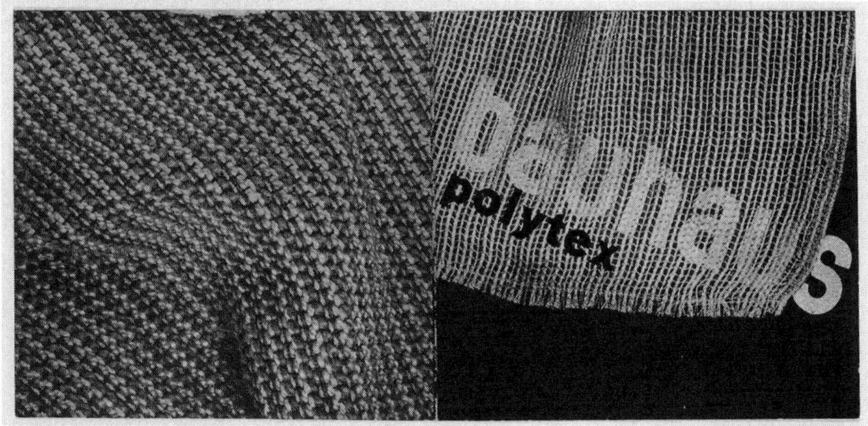

Stefan Schwarz, Bauhaus-Polytex, advertising card, 1930. Offset print on cardboard. Bauhaus-Archiv Berlin.

and distribute his furniture as an independent design through a company, Standard Möbel, which he founded in 1927 with a fellow Hungarian architect, Kalman Lengel, rather than as "a Bauhaus product designed by him."[43] Breuer's decision to create his own manufacturing company in order to market these products at first disappointed Gropius, who expected that all objects designed at the school should profit the institution collectively, not just the individual designer, and should further cohere the Bauhaus identity. When asked to justify his action, Breuer reverted to an analogy between his invention and the unique painting: "The chair was not a Bauhaus product in the sense that a painting by Paul Klee was not a Bauhaus product. [Klee's painting] was done on his own time and with his own money, in his own workshop. To that extent it was not a Bauhaus product."[44] Breuer's alignment of his authorship and that of Klee's status as an artist effectively challenged Gropius's expectations regarding the anonymous nature of design. A fear about his own implied anonymity within the Bauhaus collective and a desire not to have his furniture seen as a mere Bauhaus product (not to mention the wish to gain a higher percentage of the profits) propelled his actions. Moreover, Breuer's act suggested that a redefinition of authorship was at stake—that a kinship with Klee might serve its purpose temporarily in this dispute, but it could not account for the specificity of intellectual property as a legal category.[45] The specific model of the designer who sells his plans/ideas to a manufacturer—or establishes a company—that produces and reproduces them for sale to a wide, anonymous customer base could never correspond with the author of the unique painting, where even the buyer, marked through provenance, has a name.

Gropius's ideas in 1924, however, did not directly correspond with the arguments he had promoted at an earlier date, when he was still at the Deutscher Werkbund and working under Peter Behrens, and when his own name was still less known. The young architect's essay of 1913, "Die Entwicklung moderner Industriebaukunst" (The Development of Modern Architecture), in fact, claimed industrial architecture was an "art," in contradistinction to engineering.[46] So while Gropius promoted the anonymity of design, he nevertheless argued on behalf of the architect's signature.[47] It was perhaps this fundamental contradiction in Gropius's outlook that Breuer found most infuriating.[48]

When Gropius left the school to further his own practice in 1928, the new director, Hannes Meyer, only increased the emphasis on the communal and economic benefit of the institution as a corporate entity. Meyer called on the workshops to foreground industry and function above any concern with individual creativity. His abhorrence of art came out of his own version of the "death of the author": "In the age of cinema and photography [painting and sculpture] are a sheer waste of energy. . . . The creative opus as an 'autonomous entity,' as 'art for art's sake' is dead: our communal conscience will not tolerate any individualistic disruption of order."[49] The artists of course flat-out rejected Meyer's call for the total death of art (and its author), and Kandinsky and Klee nearly left the school over the matter during Meyer's tenure, as they expressed increasing frustration with the degraded place of art (and individuality) in the school's agenda. Yet individuality and collective anonymity, as Georg Simmel had already explained in his sociology of the modern subject, are part of the same dialectical bind. As modern economies and societies expand, they produce the very category of individuality in social existence: "Individuality in being and action generally increases to the degree that the social circle encompassing the individual expands."[50] Thus precisely at the moment that the Bauhaus achieved, during Meyer's tenure, the most explicitly functionalist agenda, and the drive toward collectivity hit its peak, the desire for a new kind of signature grew up in the field of design and patent protection.[51] The dialectic of authorship and anonymity seemed to tip in favor of one model only to simultaneously yield the other.

Anonymity–Femininity

It is perhaps obvious at this point but nevertheless needs saying: the question of anonymity was never a "neutral" problem within modernism. It had profound political ramifications and concrete ties to gendered and national identities. For example, the Bauhaus weavers' struggle to gain recognition involves a connected debate about the feminine gender of the anonymous textile industry.[52]

In *The Gendered World of the Bauhaus*, Anja Baumhoff describes how Meyer's concept of collectivity and anonymity "seemed to promise gender neutrality" for the Bauhaus weaving workshop's products:

Meyer strongly opposed aesthetics as a program and liked to sign his works as "co-op," short for "cooperative." According to this model the workshops would function as cooperatives or collectives, whose individual members would remain anonymous. During Meyer's tenure, one third of the entire student body were communists, a development that corresponded to the increased radicalization of the Weimar Republic in the late 1920s. . . . Collectivism seemed to promise gender neutrality, but for the women weavers it implied a new kind of submission [to architecture] in the name of socialist utopia. Now the producers of hand-woven fabrics were asked to subordinate themselves fully to the intentions of the architects.[53]

The socialist utopia came at a cost, Baumhoff argues, insofar as it subordinated the weavers to the "ideology of architecture." Architecture, she suggests, was the model and therefore the primary cause for the anonymity of textiles. But the condition of anonymity does not belong to architecture per se, for it has an equally sustained history within the weavers' own medium, though it is technically outside their area of expertise, in the language and metaphors that surrounded the textile industry, with its hordes of factory women. The specific condition of anonymity surrounding industrial textiles evolves from a historical matrix dating back to the middle of the nineteenth century and was moreover entwined with a set of anxieties about the "femininization" of industrial labor. Furthermore, as the history of nineteenth-century textile manufacture in Germany shows, the term *feminization* with respect to weaving and industry is much more complex than any unimpeded association with a social subject called *woman*. The spectrum of gender associations, from masculine to feminine, from feminized to defeminized is dizzying.

According to labor historian Kathleen Canning in *Languages of Labor and Gender*, the feminization of textile work by nineteenth-century writers came out of critiques of and anxieties about the mechanization of textile manufacture: "Female factory labor came to represent an urgent social problem in Germany, a profound rupture in the relations between the sexes, between social order and sexual order."[54] Concerning the contradictory associations, she writes:

As the first German industry to move production from household to factory, textiles became an emblem of modernization, of the transformation of technologies and tools, families, communities, and divisions of labor. . . . The textile industry posed unique dangers to masculine identity, . . . for in the narratives of social reform and weavers' protest, the mechanized textile mills symbolized "the problem of female competition in capitalism": they were the first factories to make male workers superfluous, to "cast the *Familienvater* [fathers of families] into the streets."[55]

Critics in the late nineteenth and early twentieth centuries termed the transition from home to factory production the "'feminization' (*Verweiblichung*) of the textile industry," and this term was also synonymous with mechanization.[56] The male weavers in the Rhineland argued that feminization threatened the integrity of weaving as a craft as well as the society and culture. Thus according to Alfons Thun and Robert Wilbrandt, two social critics who focused on the parallel problems of alienated labor and the feminization of weaving, the movement from a domestic system of weaving run by patriarchal masters to factory production posed a whole network of interrelated cultural problems. Wilbrandt's book *Die Frauenarbeit: Ein Problem des Kapitalismus* (1906) saw women's work as just that, a conditional problem of capitalism. Likewise, in 1879 Thun wrote:

The old masters, who lived in the country, found themselves *expropriated* without compensation and had to leave their native soil. . . . the health of the population has been attacked in a most deadly fashion, and the spiritual development of the people has been thoroughly thwarted. The girls who were to become mothers of German men, the children we once thought would grow up to thrive, have been made cripples, have become dull and untamed.[57]

Canning further notes that the feminization of the textile factory workforce was seen to run concurrent with a parallel process, *Entweiblichung*, or defeminization. The term *feminization* therefore not only referred to the expropriation of male labor—a leveling of the weaving master's identity through the proliferation of *anonymous* female workers—but also expressed a fear of sexual and social transgressions. Thun depicts a sea of factory women and children at once "dull" or insipid and unseemly or licentious—as though the tastelessness of anonymous factory products was due to the tastelessness of sexual transgression.[58] "With the mass of single girls living in the city, separated from the isolation of their homes in the country," writes Canning, "came the Catholic reformers' visions of *Sumpf und Trunk* (gutter and drink), of 'complete social and economic decay,' of 'sexual excesses, of earnings squandered on fashion, dance, games, and alcohol.'"[59]

By 1922, industrially produced textiles and female factory workers had become so pervasive—with women textile workers exceeding men by nearly 40 percent—that the culture lost sight of the industry's historically contradictory gender connotations.[60] The significance of gender within industry would never remain coherent or stable.

So we return for a moment to a discussion of the cool persona, that other product of mechanization: although anonymous, in fact he is decidedly male, in Lethen's account. The cool persona—with its "metallized" body, measure of distance, and codes of conduct—is apparently not possible for the other sex. According to the anthropologist Plessner, women are banned from that world, for "they are the preservers of first nature," even "suggestive of chaos or fluidity."[61] Still, there is an artificial young woman: "das kunstseidene Mädchen," the heroine of Irmgard Keun's novel by that name, about a young woman living in Berlin around 1931, who shops for chic hats, watches movies, smokes, and goes on occasional dates.[62] Except that she, unlike her male artificial counterpart, defines herself only "in the mirror of others' perceptions"; she is more a product of her era than its productive subject.[63] The "artificial silk girl" does not invent or preserve boundaries: she consumes.[64] The cool persona and the artificial silk girl are not isomorphic. The contradiction of simultaneous feminization and defeminization evident in the language that surrounded textile factory labor fifty years before—the woman who was sexually excessive but also cold, licentious but also dull—now resounds in the image of the New

Woman who wears artificial silk and attends far too many movies, yet also heightens the integral femininity of those capitalist spaces of distraction.[65]

In spite of her gender, in many respects Berger fits the model of the engineer. By aligning herself with the role of the "cool" inventor, Berger escaped the terrain of anonymity, working doubly hard to neutralize the double-feminine connotations of her practice. Berger's persona as an inventor, a new kind of author, was not only concerned with inventing and producing new types of fabric, weaving techniques, and uses for artificial materials but was a bit of a synthetic individual—synthesized out of legal briefs and patent proposals rather than poetry, novels, and paintings. Berger became the author-inventor, exteriorized in the language of legal jargon and loopholes that encourage her to rephrase and amend her object's description (its structure and function) in order best to justify the patent title.

The debate over the gender of textile work continued as a significant subtext in the theoretical writings of the Bauhaus weavers, who concertedly submitted their work to the language of technology at the same time that they both acquiesced to and rejected the feminine connotations of their medium. The adoption of industrial rhetoric, used to theorize and legitimate the work of the weavers, endowed these textiles with a particular value. Ironically, the loss of femininity associated with "craft" gave rise to another kind of feminine status—one associated with the anonymity of factory labor, or with objects that lack all the markers of a personal author. In and around the Bauhaus in the early thirties, in magazines like *Der Konfektionär* published in Germany, and later *International Textile*, out of Switzerland, weaving as a distinct medium and industrial product increasingly entered the arena of debates about the role of design in modern society.

But with increased competition from a new generation of male weavers in the 1930s within the Deutscher Werkbund and the Bund Deutscher Kunstwerker, the theoretical and practical advancements of the Bauhaus weavers were on occasion attributed to a few men who had reestablished their presence in the field of industrial textile design. In 1933, when the Deutscher Werkbund presented its first issue of *Die Form* dedicated entirely to textile designs for industrial manufacture, the magazine articles, written by men, worked hard to neutralize and shed any of weaving's feminine connotations. And with neutralization, the medium became ripe for pilfering.

Taking on the specific language developed by the Bauhaus weavers to legitimize the medium, *Die Form*'s writers make a case for the relevance of hand weaving to mechanical industry. Although women had written for the other two *Die Form* issues dedicated to tapestry weaving and fashion (in 1926 and 1927), the 1933 issue concerning technology consists of articles written only by men.[66] In the first essay, "Über Gewebte Stoff" (On Woven Material), the author Richard Lisker presents an outline of the medium in which he distinguishes the defining characteristics of woven material between "the types of threads" and "the types of weaves."[67] In language that seems to descend from the Bauhaus's pedagogical program and approach to materials, Lisker describes how the crossing of threads is "naturally" the "basic concept" of weaving.[68] Although less nuanced, Lisker's essay sounds remarkably similar to Stölzl's thoughts on the potentially infinite relationships among structure, color, and texture in weaving.[69]

In the second article, "Handwerk und Maschine in der Weberei" (Handwork and Machines in Weaving), Sigmund von Weech makes a case for the practice of handweaving prototypes for the textile industry, arguing for the various ways in which handwoven prototypes remain useful to the modern machine age.[70] (Here we are reminded of Anni Albers's first essay on Bauhaus weaving published in 1924, although his tone suggests he is arguing for an entirely new approach.)[71] Von Weech's work with textiles had previously focused on printed fabrics, and he subsequently designed fabrics with printed eagle crests for Nazi public buildings and homes, but in this essay he advocates handwoven experiments with new material, pointing to the potential of cellophane—a modern material with which the Bauhaus workshop had experimented since 1927.

In the files of the Bauhaus weaver Margaret Leischner at the Bauhaus-Archiv in Berlin, torn-out pages from this issue reveal another level of borrowing Bauhaus ideas. Under several photographs of textiles throughout the article, the name "Prof. Von Weech," has been crossed out and reattributed (in pencil) to "M. Leischner." On other images, which simply attribute her work to the institution at which von Weech and Leischner both taught, the

Textile and Fashion School of Berlin, her name has been added, suggesting that Leischner herself, or an archivist who knew her work, corrected this apparent mistake on the part of the magazine editors. Whether a simple mistake, or an instance of plagiarism by a competing male weaver, the textile sample's female author seems to be for the editors rather unimportant. A gray area emerges where the condition of anonymity within the discourse masks a theft—the appropriation itself is illegible.

The aim here is not to bemoan apparent instances of pilfering in the field of textile design or to rectify past injustices of attribution. As Droste has commented, the difficulty of attributing textile designs is inevitable, and what has been credited to Bauhaus master weaver Gunta Stölzl, for instance, was often the work of her students. Indeed, one of Leischner's designs for a textile fabric, as seen on a cover of the *bauhaus zeitschrift,* is now attributed in the Busch-Reisinger collection to Stölzl, the more famous of the two. And this case may not be a mistake of attribution. It is unclear whether this textile, though apparently Leischner's design, was not later reproduced by Stölzl, perhaps for pedagogical purposes (to teach subsequent students) or to figure out the structure of the weave and use of materials. The stamp of authorship is not comparable to the kind established by the painting tradition. The weavers had systematically copied one another's "unique" wall hangings in the early Bauhaus years when a commission was made for a wall hanging or carpet based on a particular formal-structural design. So a runner designed by Stölzl was re-created using different tones by the workshop's technical master, Helene Börner. The assumption in the workshop was that textiles did not have the same condition of innate (and integral) uniqueness that painting did, where an exactly painted replica (in different colors) would be considered a travesty.

Interestingly, what made the early work of the weaving workshop "inefficient" and "less profitable" in its Weimar years was an association with mainly female clients who often "asked for highly personalized items"—as in the case of Börner's copy of Stölzl's design, which substituted colors but retained the pattern. A single piece of textile work had to factor into its price the many hours it took a weaver to produce it. While the textile workshop in 1924 was one of the most popular with outside clients for the school, its feminine status (arising from its association with female clients in addition to female producers) was in many ways due to the kind of personalization (for the client) asked of the weavers' work. The move toward the production of textile prototypes thus can be seen as more than an engagement with the school's new ideals for technology. Rather, the move signaled a concerted effort to *depersonalize*, and thereby *defeminize* their work, to produce a neutral terrain of prototypes for mass production. One might note the irony here: in the attempt to draw weaving away from its domestic, amateurish, or personalized-for-female-clients associations, the weavers reproduced another level of feminization—namely, an association with anonymous textile manufacture.

The term *feminization* in the nineteenth-century Rhineland signified a leveling of the weaving masters' authority and identity, just as the proliferation of anonymous female factory workers equaled the expropriation of the male weavers' means of existence. With the increased theorization of the medium and *Die Form*'s special issue came another form of leveling—the neutralization of weaving's supposedly feminine character. (In the first case, feminization equaled the increased anonymity of the practice, whereas in the second anonymity paralleled the neutralization of its feminine associations.) In other words, the complex gendering of textiles involves some unpredictable questions regarding the *conditions* and *significance* of anonymity in and around the Bauhaus, where the emphasis on technology and mass production included an anxiety over the status of authorship. Neither *authorship* nor *anonymity* was a neutral term.

The Patentschrift as a Theory of the Medium

This quest for the late-Weimar model of subjectivity found in the author-as-inventor is critical, for if a new model of authorship is at stake, so too are the parameters that circumscribe the medium, its identity as an object. Upon leaving the Bauhaus and entering the arena of competitively marketed designs, Berger and the many hundreds of pages of legal discussions with her patent attorney are perpetually engaged in defining (and redefining) her object. Just as the author-subject has moved over into a new form—the cool persona—weaving's identity, now found within the *Patentshrift*, has slipped into the rhetoric of intellectual property. In Berger's patent, her medium is rendered in a terminology that at once mimics earlier positivist Bauhaus rhetoric and extends its applications.

Although Berger did additionally register and achieve *Gebrauchsmuster* (utility model) status for all three of her patent applications, she saw her woven prototypes as inventions and pursued their protection as such. As Berger's patent texts reveal, the *process* of its production is the very condition that constitutes her medium in weaving and not the matter of forming patterns on a surface. The invention—and that which signaled her authorship—involves the functional status of the fabric and the way the material is prepared and woven, not the attributes by which one could, among other textiles, recognize it visually.

So we return to the entwined questions of the medium and subjectivity originally raised in chapter 1, where I considered the pictorial wall hangings and carpets made at the early Bauhaus weaving workshop. Those objects were morphologically similar to the work of painters like Kandinsky and Klee, but as such they were merely "applied" renditions. Weaving was "feminine" (reflecting the women who made them), but also (mere) labor, and the woven designs and unique objects were only attributed to an author with difficulty. Part of the problem was that weaving lacked in the early Bauhaus a specific theory of the medium such as painting had. The writing of texts at the Bauhaus, in other words, was at once integral to the identification of the medium's parameters and the identification of its model of subjectivity/authorship, the active agent who uses that medium in the service of some greater idea. In the case of painting, the canvas surface provides, through the paint and the painter's brush (at least according to the form master Johannes Itten), a direct impression of that painter's creative soul, his interiority. The woven object, on the other hand, is depersonalized, built through a laborious, almost mechanical, process on a loom apparatus and thus recalls the mechanical activities of the female factory laborer. The question of the author/model of subjectivity is integral to the understanding of the medium and vice versa.

In this chapter, we again analyze an apparatus but a different sort: the patent. For example, the English patent, mentioned at the beginning of this chapter, is an extremely sharp formal description of Berger's design, a sample of which does not exist. Her patent texts double as a formal theory of her medium and indeed are very similar to earlier articles about fabrics where she stresses the possibilities of her fabric for modern life. In both she mentions the new architectural interiors, the railway cars, and automobiles as some of many new spaces that fabrics must work within and which they must consider. Like her essays of the 1930s for *Der Konfektionär* and *International Textiles* magazines, her patent texts were written to address the needs of her career as an inventor of fabrics for companies such as Wohnbedarf AG. One article from 1932, "Umsatzsteigerung durch Geschmacksveredelung" (Increase of Sales through the Refining of Taste) merges the practical and economic concerns of textiles in a way that established Berger's recognition of financial restraints as well as her wish to achieve financial gain. It is as though the language of theory entered the language of the patent and vice versa.[72] Berger's analyses of her field—as written more directly in magazines or in diary entries and also found in her patent texts—consistently address the functional and structural inventions of her woven products, and all are written to make a case for the recognition of her individual contributions to the textile field. The patent texts become the model for describing the woven object, and also to illuminate the broader context of consumption and authorship under modern capital—the shape of that subject and the mobile sites or short texts that it occupies. Berger's identity as an inventor is thus defined by a newly adapted textual apparatus, a patented theory.

Postscript: The Death of an Author

Still, Berger had a lot of difficulty maintaining her identity as an inventor, even after she achieved certain rights to her designs. Her identity as a woman in the otherwise anonymous field of the textile industry surely did not help her case to begin with, but her identity as a Yugoslav Jew would later muddy the waters even more. Indeed, it seems important as a conclusion, or rather postscript, to describe briefly the place of patent law in Weimar and Nazi Germany and its relevance to the Berger case. Following the introduction of the first patent laws into Germany in 1877, debates between companies and their employed engineers or chemists were central to ensuing definitions of authorship. In the Weimar era, according to patent historian Kees Gispen, as individual inventors fought for legal rights, they harnessed a rhetoric of creativity calling themselves the "poets" of industrial and chemical patents. Indeed, the debate at the time was not only over ownership but over the ways that the identity of the inventor was framed; the pro–inventor advocates often called on a language of genius and artistry in order to justify their arguments against business.[73] Berger might have wished to align herself with the model of the inventor-as-genius during the Weimar era, but as history would prove, the swing toward the inventor would come to Germany at a price. The 1936 Patent Code reforms finally tipped toward the pro–inventor party. The process of reform began with the rise of the Nazi party in 1933 (one year after Berger registered for her first patent) and finally cohered in 1936. Hitler was obsessed with the idea of the modern Aryan hero, the individual inventor as the source of vitality and dynamism in industrial society.[74] Thus Hitler's domestic policy objectives, according to Gispen, involved getting "rid of the Jews and other 'biological undesirables,'" but also building "a more fluid system of equal opportunity and social mobility for the remaining, purified community of true Germans."[75] Or in order to pursue "equal opportunity," "biological undesirables" could not be part of the system—they had to be gotten rid of. Thus the favor of the "Aryan hero" would have left no place for Berger, a Jewish woman from Yugoslavia. (If a female Yugoslav Jew, then not an inventor, so the logic went, regardless of past [legal] definitions.) Moreover, the logic continued at this time, the invention could not be given the jurisdiction of an invention if the author wasn't a legal citizen.[76] (Thus her third patent application was rejected.) Authorship, once again, is historically, culturally, and disciplinarily (as well as nationally) contingent.

The stakes involved in the death of this author are more concrete than a Barthesian "death" would imply. After being driven out of Germany in 1936 by the Nazi government and expelled from her status as *Musterbildnerin* with the Reichskammer für bildenden Kunst on account of her Jewish identity and status as a foreigner, Berger went to London for a year and then returned to her mother's home in Yugoslavia in 1938. In 1937, Berger wrote to László Moholy-Nagy, Naum Gabo, and Walter Gropius in an attempt to gain a visa to teach in the United States, but she never received one. Her letters to friends broke off at the end of 1941.[77] As they later discovered, she had died at the age of thirty-nine, in a concentration camp, only months before the end of the war.

CONCLUSION

ON WEAVING, ON WRITING

The Bauhaus in Berlin closed in 1933 and that year, with the political situation growing increasingly difficult for Jewish citizens and artists in Germany, Anni and Josef Albers left for new faculty positions at Black Mountain College in North Carolina. When the couple traveled by ship to America, under a visa provided with the support of architect Philip Johnson (then director of the Museum of Modern Art's Department of Architecture), they brought with them relatively little in the way of things.[1] They did, however, bear the imprint of a certain field of thought that would carry out in their work as teachers. The internally complex event that was the Bauhaus (an event that became visible as such only after the fact, in its emigration to other contexts) had embedded itself in their thinking. And so they, like many of their colleagues who fled to America around the same time, continued to see themselves as *Bauhäusler*—a certain kind of subject circulating in a particular set of truths about or approaches to practice and pedagogy, especially as those two were linked.

To grapple with the aftermath of the Bauhaus in America—to consider the context in which the weavers' thoughts on weaving ended up, and the purposes they came to serve—is to reconsider, first of all, where those discussions have been. Recall that the Bauhaus weavers, in their practice and in their essays on their craft, absorbed the languages of other media. In their wall hangings, for example, the weavers adopted the formal principles of expressionist painting; in their workshop's prototypes for architectural textiles, they assumed the functionalist vocabulary of the Neues Bauen; for their fabrics found in Neue Sachlichkeit photographs and glossy magazines, they considered the limits of optical and tactile perception; and within patent documents, one weaver sought intellectual property protection for her textile inventions. In the first three instances, weaving's identity came out of a *struggle* between different material disciplines associated more or less with the arts—this craft simultaneously took on and rejected the lexicons of painting, architecture, and photography. In the fourth instance, the medial relation was that of a *slippage* between two properly linguistic discourses: the discursive identity of the medium, now found within a *Patentshrift*, had moved over smoothly into an object of legal rhetoric. Either way, each instantiation of weaving was on some level only ever a mediation of other media. And so all media involved in this process (not just weaving, but also painting, architecture, etc.) were in turn shown to be specific only insofar as they had a textual apparatus to circumscribe themselves as such. Each medium's identity was never purely material or formal; to be understood as such, it had to pass through (be encoded by) a written text.

This is something the weavers grasped, if only intuitively, when they harnessed the terms of other media to define their own. But this question became more pronounced in the American context. For it is here that Anni Albers began to write more prolifically, as she struggled to articulate the goals and parameters of her practice. Having been the first to theorize the Bauhaus approach to weaving in 1924, subtly attentive to the specific (modernist) features of that technique, she began after 1933 to reflect on the process that encodes (or translates) practices and materials into words. Pursued over several decades after immigrating to America, her writings in English attempted to come to terms with the particular practice the weavers had developed most uniquely: their writing on weaving.

At first, in the essays written between 1937 and 1959, leading up to the initial publication of *On Designing,* Albers was interested in the problems but also the possibilities that ensued from such a translation. What gets lost, she seemed to ask, in the *movement* between these media, these different languages? The question would come down to her insistence on avoiding the intellectualization and professionalization of her discipline in a theory or anything that obfuscated experiential practice.[2] And this, even as she sought to advocate in teaching a fundamental approach to the material—a "starting at point zero"—a general ethos for action.[3] The act of writing thus provided Albers with a possibility for articulating her goal of bringing material practice to the fore of education, but it was also here that she had to negotiate the impasse brought on by a certain incommensurability: that between (physical) practice at a loom and writing, or "touching" material and touching on its ideas.[4]

Shifting gears in *On Weaving*, this former Bauhaus student began to speculate that textile structures, found in woven artifacts, were underpinned by certain principles—ones whose fundamentals and methods might be relevant beyond the terrain of textiles proper, textile things.[5] (See Plate 9.) While returning to a discussion of their ontic identity, she asked after their potential, as media, through which to grasp or work through various related problems. Thus she writes in the book's preface: "Tangential subjects come into view. The thoughts, however, can, I believe, be traced back to the event of a thread."[6] The intertwining of threads specific to textiles hence becomes a philosophical lens or, more precisely, a philosophical net. So, for example, Otti Berger's thoughts on the haptic identity of textiles, discussed in chapter 3, are repurposed toward what could be described as a tactile, textile philosophy. Albers redresses what she identifies in her post-Bauhaus moment as an insistence on "progress" that advances some areas ("reading and writing" or vision) only to produce regression elsewhere (a "tactile sensibility").[7]

Doubling down on the word *medium*, in this concluding chapter I will ask after the various ways this term manifests in Albers's writing over several decades, and the way she navigates its multivalent significance to her practice. Just as the school in Germany had been internally riven—a complex of multiple, contradictory forces and truths about color or architectural function, materiality or technology, as we have seen in the previous chapters—so, too, were Albers's thoughts on this term. What she does is to harness two competing directions within the use of *medium* in the postwar landscape. On the one hand, she considers the medium as *grounded in the material*—say, paint and canvas or thread; and on the other, she picks up a notion of medium as a vehicle of *communication*, a technical apparatus that transmits messages or ideas.[8] (In other words, she participates both in the development of high modernist art criticism and in the emergence of media and communication studies.) Anni Albers thus inserts herself in the aporia between these two quite different understandings of that term.

Mediation, or the Problems of Translation

At Black Mountain College, the Albers couple became the backbone of the school's art curriculum. Josef taught a version of the preliminary course he had developed while at the Bauhaus; Anni taught weaving technique and the fundamentals of fabric design, always encouraging her students to come at the material without a preconceived, formal plan. It was there, between the years of 1933 and 1949, that Anni perfected her English and where she began to cohere her thoughts—on design, craft, and art more broadly, and on weaving in particular—in articles for various magazines or manuscripts for public lectures. It was also there that she began to think about and confront the problems of translating singular practices into written concepts.

A particular anecdote about this moment stands out. In an interview recorded in 1995, she notes with frustration how common it was that Josef's hired classroom translator (before he had a sufficient grasp of English to teach on his own) did not approve of his approach and politics and would often interject incorrectly translated sentences. Such mistakes by the translator were, Anni thought, a conscious attempt to "distort what he was saying."[9] But on another level, it surely occurred to her, it was simply that Josef's ideas—his particular use of cultural linguistic idioms, Bauhaus concepts, and his nuanced approach to seeing color relations— were not part of the translator's worldview; she was not one of the *Bauhäusler*, and so she was unable to render those ideas in English. Translation had hit a complex of walls, at once linguistic, cultural, and material.

Anni Albers was also beginning to confront the difficulties of translation in another sphere: in her attempt to bring the practice of structuring and combining threads on a loom into text. Hence in her first essay in English from 1937, "Work with Material," she ultimately fixates on the maxim of listening. It is important, she argues, to recognize the limitations or "veto of the material."[10] For "more than an active process," what is needed "is a listening for [its] dictation." (The good designer should allow the material, for a moment, to become active, rendering her the receiver of its identity.) But here, the first set of paradoxes begin to be introduced:

while imploring (her student) designers to listen to materials that somehow "speak" or "dictate" their use, Albers also suggests that those materials were in some sense *ineffable*—an "original state" of "stuff" that had to be accessed physically without "information" clouding the relationship.[11] (Materials both can and cannot communicate.)

And yet at the same time any transfer from practice to text (or speech) necessarily worked against such directness; it mediated, in advance any direct relationship to stuff. Hence she would write two years later:

Layer after layer of civilized life seems to have veiled our directness of seeing. We often look for an underlying meaning of things while the thing itself is the meaning. Intellectual interpretation may hinder our intuitive insight. Here education should undo the damage and bring us back to receptive simplicity. It is obvious that a solely intellectual approach to art is insufficient and that we may have to try to redevelop those sensibilities which can lead to immediate perception.[12]

The translation of practice into text or a pedagogical approach is an act of "intellectual interpretation," the weaver seems to realize, that works against direct access to things; and yet simultaneously she also seeks out possibilities to "redevelop those sensibilities." Thus Albers calls on education by 1947 not so much to "restore" the "*direct* experience of the medium" but to "restore the *experience of the direct experience of the medium*"—a condition mediated in advance by an educational mode of restoring.[13] The translation from one effect into another has already happened, in "layer after layer of civilized life"; a designer or weaver can only hope to reengage "immediate perception" through practice, another kind of mediation of the material.

Still, according to her friend Nicholas Fox Weber, Albers found some parity between the practices of weaving and writing. It was never that one was fully on the side of ineffable materiality whereas the other was about information and communication. And she understood that "threads" had in many cultures long functioned as "transmitters of meaning."[14] She even came to approach the act of writing as she would her work at the loom, her method for one bearing "a stunning resemblance to the process" of the other:

Using her manual typewriter, she would write her text on ordinary 8½ -by-11-inch sheets of paper and then tape the pages together as if to create a scroll. She felt that only in this way could she achieve the flow continuity of the completed essay; at least initially, she did not want the barrier imposed by the need to turn the page.[15]

In writing essays, she built sentences on continuous stretches of paper, analogous to the layering of weft, the building of a scroll-like swath of fabric on the loom. So in some sense she saw these two media to be both specific and functionally analogous and was determined, according to Weber, to understand and articulate the parallel "rhythms" of each. She sought to fully grasp the craft of manipulating words in order to translate the potential of the former, weaving's meaning as a practice, its idioms and its "code."[16] Writing (or typing) would become another medium through which she understood her woven practice—this becoming perfectly metaphorized in her studies for fabric patterns on a typewriter. It was in the back-and-forth (the mediation) between these two media—the two languages as they touched on one another—that she grappled with the problems of translation, or the complicated relationship between communication and materiality within her practice.

Reflecting on this relationship in a short lecture she gave in 1982, she would conclude that the material functions within weaving "as metaphor."[17] Focusing on the struggle to "include others in that [inner] life that is invisible and intangible"—to express or communicate one's experience of the world—Albers narrated how she eventually "learned to listen to [threads] and to speak their language . . . the process of handling them." Her point was not that material is analogous to language as an abstract substance or group of signs, but that, like the activity of putting thoughts on paper, working with material (or listening to it) works to mediate the ineffable. As metaphor, material operates as a "means of communication," or, rather, it enables a movement from one space to another.[18] In this system, any experience of material is never quite direct. It is only accessed metaphorically—as an experience of an experience.

The comparison between Albers's approach to textiles and ideas about language has been made more than once. According to Brenda Danilowitz, Albers's *Ancient Writing* (1936), a pictorial work woven shortly after her initial visit to Mexico, demonstrates how she understood that like the "cryptic glyphs carved into boulders at and steles found at pre-Hispanic archaeological sites . . . the designs in ancient Peruvian textiles were an eloquent substitute for written language."[19] Historian Virginia Gardner Troy makes a slightly different point in a chapter on Albers's tapestry work from the 1950s and '60s, which looks at *Two* (1952), *Pictographic* (1953), *Haiku* (1961), and *Code* (1962). While aware of the way that threads were some of the earliest transmitters of meaning, Albers was "not interested in deciphering or copying particular written languages; rather she explored the *idea* of marks and signs as language distributed across a surface in a way that recalls the structure of a text."[20] She doesn't seek to convey information or "carry discrete information about the world."[21] Instead, through the "act of 'drawing' with thread," and by considering "the semantic implications of elementary geometric forms" found, for instance, in ancient Precolumbian weaves, Albers sought to evoke "linguistic characters and systems through the rectilinear arrangement of ideographic signs."[22]

On this matter, the small tapestry titled *Code* is worth looking at further (see Plate 10). (And not just because of its curious title, which invokes several directions in the postwar landscape of the fifties and sixties all at once: for example, the interest in deciphering the codes of pictographs found at Precolumbian archaeological sites; or the development of codes in the emergence of computer software in the 1950s; or the spread of semiotics and the fixation on languages as conventions or codes.) In this work, graphical marks made of floating black weft interpolate a matrix of beige hemp, white cotton, and metallic threads, giving the appearance of electrical conduits. At times raised above the surface of the grid and then burrowing below, these lines and dots are not entirely integral to the weave's structure, and yet they are intimate with that ground. They are floated into the weave—that is, brought in at the middle but never reaching the edges of the tapestry; unlike the ground threads, these strands aren't relied on structurally. Following the path of the weft while doubly marking this movement, the black lines wind downward on a broken route from the top to bottom of this vertical, scroll-like field. What is formed is a graphical pseudo-symbolic layer that suggests the transmission of a message, perhaps a series of unreadable sentence or word fragments, or a representation of Morse code's alphabet of dots and dashes. But more than reference the idea of language as such, these signs appears to trace, reflexively, the function of the weave. Troy sees this as an example of Albers's fundamentally modernist "self-referential" approach to weaving.[23] And indeed, the tapestry seems to communicate nothing but its own code; rather than communicate other information, external to its form, the black lines of code appear only to transmit the operation of weaving weft through warp, the tapestry's own methods or procedures.

Yet going further, one might note that Anni-the-cryptographer does not just provide a vehicle for this woven message but also blocks it, encrypts it. We only have access to the surface, the textile artifact. The floating of black lines through a densely entwined weave seems to present the material (literally) only to hide, at the same time, the method through which this fabric was made. Indeed, what is a code after all? In a Saussurian model, at the simplest level it would be that internally coherent system or set of conventions (say, English) that allow signifiers to signify, meaning to happen. It may also be a device—say, a computer algorithm—that ensures that a signal, in its movement from one point to another, will yield a certain message. A code might be used in the transmission of data so that they can be parsed and then interpreted or understood. So it is not just the abstract rules governing a language (say, the game of chess); it is that which allows a system to function. But a code is also that which—as in an algorithm in computing, for instance— may allow some pieces of information to get through only to block others. A code is based as much on a principle of transparency as it is on obfuscation.[24]

So if a code is that which enables or blocks the relay of messages, how can one represent it as such? How does one represent the functioning of a code? If weaving is like a code, Albers suggests, it both can and cannot in and of itself be translated. Even as they are there in the seemingly self-evident in the raw fact of the material, the graphic lines found winding through *Code,* as both weft and nonweft (as both code structure and communicative sign for *code*) can and cannot translate weaving's processes and operations. For no matter how hard we try to locate that process, to follow "the event of a thread," that piece of fabric or tapestry hides the particular method of entwining—its various layers of media-tion—in the evidence of its textured surface.[25] And this was some-thing the weaver knew quite well. For it is about this time that she began to unravel the threads and analyze ancient Peruvian artifacts to understand how such complex structures were made.[26] And it was in 1952 that she submitted her theory to the archaeological community regarding the execution of exceptionally wide pieces of fabric on a simple back-strap loom in Precolumbian Peru using a method of tubular weaving.[27]

To understand further, it helps to turn to the last page of *On Designing*, in which Albers provides a set of "Diagrams of Construc-tions" and a short textual explanation of an esoteric area of weav-ing known as draft notation.[28] For here she discusses what could more properly be understood as a code. What is a weave draft or system of draft notation? Basically, it is a road map to a desired fabric, like a musical score or diagram: it is a flat, graphic pattern based in a grid that can be read.[29] As Albers explains, in this "short-hand, spaces between vertical lines on the graph paper denote warp threads, spaces between horizontal lines weft threads. A filled in square indicates a lifted thread at this point of intersection."[30] From a semiotic perspective, one might say that the system of notation is at once semi-symbolic and semi-iconic. (Its system is at once arbi-trary and motivated.) But actually, if the draft notation provides an image that bears a resemblance to the threads in use, it is only very abstractly related to the actual cloth, the referent. The draft notation is something like an image of practice; it tells us not how the textile will *look* so much as how the loom's warp is threaded or spaced through heddles—that is, the technical operation through which it is made. While the weave draft is not essential to the act of weaving, this little diagram articulates the layer or process that intervenes between production and product, process and artifact. So this is not a diagram of the object but, rather, of the medium—the in-between. It is something of an algorithmic code-as-image.

Following the draft notation, three-dimensional weaves are born out of the flat geometric codes. But they are also transformed in the physical process of work at the loom. Any single draft might yield multiple, very different results, depending on the texture of threads chosen or the colors combined:

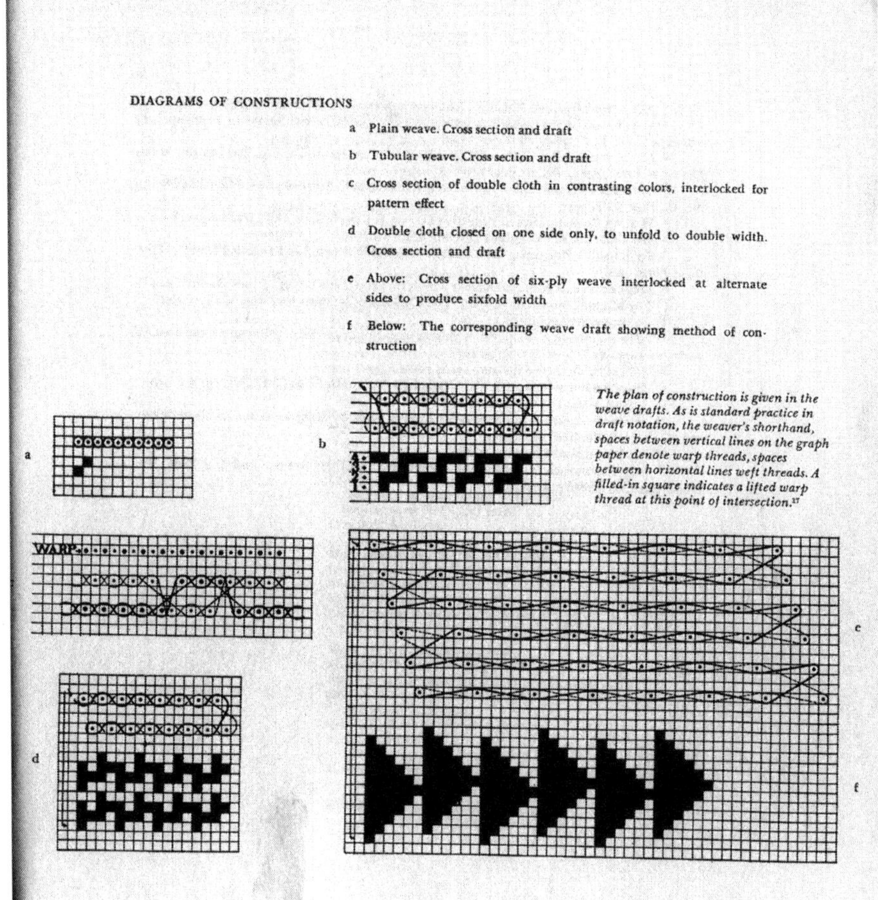

Page from Anni Albers, *Anni Albers: On Designing* (Middletown, Conn.: Wesleyan University Press, 1979). "Diagrams of Constructions."

The structure of a fabric or its weave—that is, the fastening of its elements of threads to each other—is as much a determining factor in its function as is the choice of the raw material. In fact, the interrelation between the two, the subtle play between them in supporting, impeding, or modifying each other's characteristics, is the essence of weaving.[31]

Even when codified, the fabric is also born from the "subtle play" or "interrelation" between material and structure. Thus the system of the draft notation, like any language, can never be fully exhausted through the utterance of threads—some being more "obedient" or "resistant," others more "charming" or "dull." A woven textile (a piece of fabric) is never just the direct consequence of a given plan. The practice of weaving, Albers suggests, is also bound to the particular "event of a thread"—which, in its "submissiveness," somewhat paradoxically limits or "dictates" what can and cannot be accomplished with it. Any access to the metaphors of the material is only won through work at the loom.

And so in the investigation of the problems of translation, from one language to others—from weaving to linguistic and other codes, to a tapestry, to weave drafts, and back again—we begin to understand Albers's quite expanded understanding of *medium*. As we'll see, if she defines it at all, then it would be a technique or operation (say, in the gerund form, weav*ing*), whose "potentialities and . . . limitations" are never quite determined by the object alone (the verbal noun, *a weaving*).[32]

Medium

It seems important to step back and consider how the words *medium* and *media* entered Anni Albers's texts for the first time in November 1939, six years after she left Germany for America.[33] While the Bauhaus weavers had written on weaving using words like *Stoffgebiet* or *Gestaltungsgebiet* or *Handwerk*, it was not until her deployment of the English language that this word came into Anni's repertoire, and that her writing on weaving started to consider the topic of media in the wider sense. Her first two texts in English, written in 1937 and 1938, rely on a balance of *craft* and *material* when referring to weaving and media broadly. Then in the 1939 essay, Anni uses the word *medium* and moreover seeks to define her understanding of this term:

Recognizing in matter its potentialities and its limitations may also help us clarify the ideas of the medium in art when it is immaterial. This idea of the medium in art is often misunderstood. A distinction is necessary, to any artistic end, between the medium serving a purpose outside itself and the medium in its own right as for instance words used for reporting vs. words used in poetry. Some media have to be released from their representative meaning to make them fit for artistic purpose. Words and gestures, as an example, are binary in that sense. As they are often not clearly recognized in their specific capacity as elements of form, they are often chosen as means by those who feel some vague urge for expression. They seem to be materials familiar to us through their daily use. But as media of art they have to be newly mastered just as any other material has to be.[34]

Albers seeks to define this "often misunderstood" concept by turning, first of all, to the example of words—a case in which "the medium . . . is immaterial." She moves back and forth between the words *material* and *medium* in this essay, at once distinguishing them and rendering them synonymous. But it is telling that Albers turns to the example of language to define *medium*, which must be distinguished by its ends—one "serving a purpose outside itself" and the other in "its own right." The two options are linked but not necessarily the same. These may be divided between reporting and poetry, where the understanding of the limitations of the material (the word) may develop into a new form, as "media released from their representative meaning." On the one hand, a medium is a vehicle for communicating something external to itself; on the other, it is about grappling with the material. Significantly, then, the definition of *medium* is at once singular and split; it functions or transmits information transparently, as in daily use, or it is "mastered" and made strange. Whereas all material, she argues, "dictates" certain structures or "limitations" that the artist or poet must recognize, insights gained from direct "work with a substance" provide the only viable method to grasp its parameters and work with it productively. Or, rather, the medium is less a thing than a specific kind of action taken toward the material, a process of "recognizing in matter its potentialities and limitations."

Whether it was the move from German to English—the act of translating her thoughts from one language to another—that prompted Anni to begin using the word *medium*, or whether it was her cognizance of the discourse quickly consolidating around this concept in America at this time that compelled her to begin thinking through this concept, is unclear. Either way, considerations of media and their limits, and their ability (or not) to be translated, were not Albers's alone. The word *medium*, that "barbarous term," as Rosalind Krauss recalls invoking Foucault's terminology, grew over a few decades to become the veritable "object" of a discursive field.[35] Two intellectual milieus were born out of debates around this single term. On the one hand, there was the development of high modernist art criticism in the writings of Clement Greenberg, a doubling down on the materiality of artistic objects, the empirical fact of flatness for painting.[36] On the other, there was the newly emergent field of media studies in the writings of Marshall McLuhan, who by 1962, in *The Gutenberg Galaxy: The Making of Typographic Man,* postulated that media exert effects on the way humans perceive and understand the world, which in turn affect social organization. (This would also form the basis of his axiom "the medium is the message," further elaborated in his 1964 book *Understanding Media: The Extensions of Man.*)[37] The two conceptions of medium, which consolidated by the mid-1960s, were at odds with one another.[38] While Greenberg insisted on the material identity of the medium, McLuhan focused on its perceptual and social effects; and where the former ultimately located purity, the latter described the inherent hybridity of media—each new medium (say, television) remediating as "content" earlier media forms (film and broadcast radio).

Nevertheless, these two authors were more in sync than it might appear. In each, it could be argued, the problems of translation were paramount. While Greenberg railed against the infestation of painting by literature and dimensionality, he also in some sense insisted that a medium communicate—if not something outside, then itself, its own message as a two-dimensional abstract surface. The medium's "specificity" as flat must be translated for the viewer through some form of abstraction. McLuhan, meanwhile, found that "all media are active metaphors in their power to translate experience into new forms." (Or media are effective as conduits of messages insofar as they "translate" perceptual experiences into new social forms.) So even if McLuhan found in such translation a remediation of earlier media, it is also an inherent condition of any medium that it reflexively presents its particular act of functioning—the book, for example, communicates its message (or effects) as an "extension of the eye."[39] Indeed, there is much in common between McLuhan's notion of "hot media" (like print) based on heightened, focused sense perception, and Greenberg's emphasis on "the optical" in modernist painting, which "can be traveled through, literally or figuratively, only with the eye."[40]

Albers's approach to the link between medium and translation was quite a bit different. First of all, she focused more readily on questions pertaining to practice, not identities or substrates, as Greenberg and McLuhan did. And the material never stood on its own, as an empirical thing (say, a flat surface) that would require a single approach to it over another (abstraction). While the material may "dictate" its limits, through the medium's practice, the weaver may recognize and pursue multiple possibilities. And if the medium, according to Albers, has "effects" on human experience, they are not intrinsic to the sensorial space of its substrate alone. Such effects are not so definitively determined, for another (less desired) form can just as well be "imposed on the material by the [textile] designer," whereby the curtain's pattern would cry out, "Here I am, look at me," and thus "invade the privacy of the consumer."[41] These effects are not inherent to the material, for they can be harnessed differently in the process of designing. Only in an attentive practice can one recognize the material's "limitations and potentialities" and find better avenues for its form. Neither the medium's identity nor its effects are a given. Any access to the material is neither inevitable nor transparent in a singular form but only arrived at over time. "It takes a long time to get to point zero," she exhorted.[42] Thus the problems of translation come in, initially, at the moment the practitioner interfaces with the material, attempts to "learn of its subtleties," and works with it. And subsequently, with much difficulty, she attempts to relay that experience into words. The problems of translating a medium happen across two vectors.

Although Anni and Josef Albers rarely exchanged their drafts and were, according to Weber, rather competitive with one another, they nevertheless shared a fundamental approach to the question of practice.[43] For example, in 1948 Josef would write of his Variants series:

In my paintings I adhere to what in other arts is considered a matter of course. Namely, that *performance* is prepared by rehearsal, that exercises precede recital, or plans, execution. It is still a good habit in music or dance and the theater, in architecture or typography. It also remains a good procedure in poetry or sculpture.[44]

Keeping up this discussion in a final section of his notes to *Interaction of Color*, first published in 1963, he wrote: "On the whole, variants demonstrate . . . a healthy belief that there is no final solution in form; thus form demands unending performance and invites *constant reconsideration*—visually as well as verbally."[45] This thing that is painting must account for the variability of its practice.

Indeed, the notion of performance, or the emphasis on process over empirical "data," is a central theme throughout Josef Albers's writing. By conceiving of the interaction of color as a condition of "relativity," Albers emphasized what he calls the actual experience of color over its factual dimension (as in "data on wave length"). He pointed out that we cannot know a color, because we only ever perceive it undergoing shifts in accordance with the dynamics of its environment. Colors are effects of relationships—as when we see "opaque colors as transparent or perceive opacity as translucence" or "3 colors as 4 or as 2," their "boundaries doubled or vibrating or just vanishing."[46] The color of coffee looks different in a cup than in a "silex glass" or on film, the three contexts providing different levels of reflection, refraction, and translucency.[47] In our perception, color floats in a sea of interaction and interdependence, wherein colors "influence and change each other forth and back."[48] Using the metaphor of theater, Albers imagined color as actors within a theatrical setting, who, as participants in a "cast" may be arranged differently, in different dynamics: one may recede while another is foregrounded—only then to move to the rear of yet another on the stage.[49] Hence it is crucial that the "actual fact" of color is dependent on action; it is a temporally provisional identity:

"Action" is the noun for the verb "to act." Acting in visual presentation is to change by giving up, by losing identity. When we act, we change appearance and behavior, we act as someone else. . . . When an actor is able to appear as Henry VIII, so that we overlook or forget who he factually is, and when he also can be expected to play Henry IX or Henry X, then he is a real actor, able to give up his own identity and present someone else's appearance and personality. Color acts in a similar way.[50]

Rather than a formal fact, a self-evident material, painting is only ever an *action,* a means of studying the most mutable perceptual effects of color. To teach color theoretically is impossible. One can only provide the means by which students can begin to experience its mutability. In contrast to the formalist Greenberg, who determined the medium as an absolute clarity, a pre-given topos, Albers sought in his practice a condition of temporality—the experience of color and the practice of arranging color in various patterns and rhythms. Performing the activity of painting (for Josef, preferably with a palette knife, spreading paint straight out of the tube—not once but over and over) was in some sense no different from arranging colored pieces of paper on another substrate.[51] In both materials (paper and paint), Josef studied color to "prove that color is the most relative medium in art." Indeed, it is neither paper nor paint that is the medium (a flat substrate or material substance); rather, color is that through which Albers, in his practice, perceived. Color is the vehicle through which Josef acted, and reenacted or, rather, demonstrated its mutability. Further, color was at once the medium and the method that determined his method. Because it interacts in a certain way that is temporal, color requires a temporal practice—a life spent performing and reperforming (or "rehearsing") the same scene again and again, switching out the characters. Hence more than a thousand iterations of "Homage to the Square," more than several hundred "Variants" yielded not objects but relations, exemplars of continuous deferral.

Rather like Josef's understanding of color and paint*ing*, Anni Albers proposed in her two books an understanding of design*ing* and weav*ing* that exploits the question of action—the fact that the medium is, at least in English, a gerund and a verbal noun.[52]

The Medium of Learning: Against "Professionalization"

So why might this understanding of "medium" be important to Anni (and Josef)? What are the stakes, at the end of the day?

Even as she appeared to focus on the problems of design—and titled her first book *On Designing*—the questions of "craft" emerges again and again as a means through which to think about design's specific media, as a way of approaching processes and materials. Still, she made sure to clarify to her reader that working through material or taking up the problems of craft is not some retrograde act, a romanticization of some past existence whereby all sense of the present (and the future) is ignored. If Albers promoted the seemingly Luddite practice of hand weaving, it was because she believed it could provide opportunities for the future of industry—insofar as industry could learn from the work of weavers in "laboratories" about better ways to design the material or handle it with machines. But it also provided a space in which the terms of practice (or skill) could be nuanced, less abstracted according to methods of "professionalization." In a post-Bauhaus context of design that had seemed to eclipse craft once and for all as the true heir of the Bauhaus project, Anni (and Josef) sought to rend methods of practice from within—to make "theory" experiential rather than preconceived. So in the essays that make up her first book, Albers seeks to explore the limits of theory by pushing process to the fore. What emerges is a conception of medium as a space for active learning.

Sometime between 1938 and 1959, Anni Albers-the-teacher began to rethink her tenure in the weaving workshop and the wider implications of that experience for her philosophy of education.[53] In an essay first published in the catalog accompanying the first Bauhaus exhibition at the Museum of Modern Art in New York, and later reworked for the first edition of her collection of essays, *On Designing*, Albers describes the development of thought in the Bauhaus's weaving workshop, a particular classroom.[54]

Both essays narrate a movement framed by the "chaotic" aftermath of World War I, suggesting that their experimentation was an attempt to find clarity amid that "void" left by its devastation. By disregarding traditional methods, the students set out in their (self-)education to "lay a foundation for a work which was oriented toward the future."[55] First by "playing with material amateurishly" and "unburdened by any consideration of practical application," the weavers developed what Albers calls an "unprejudiced attitude toward the materials." This formed the base from which, only later, a "purpose aside from the purely artistic one" began to come into consideration.[56] "It was a curious revolution," she wrote in the 1938 version, "when the students of weaving became concerned with practical purpose."[57] Hence, through a "joint effort" of thought, the innovation of the workshop came into relief, with a rethinking of textiles and their relationship to their environment: "Light-reflecting and sound-absorbing materials were developed."[58]

There is a slight shift in the second version, however, and the differences are revealing. Focused more heavily on the societal impetus for practice in the 1959 essay, Albers now notes how another factor, beyond experimentation and utility, was introduced: "The importance of recognizing new problems arising with changing times, of foreseeing a development" or imagining "future" needs in textiles became central to the development of the weavers' thought. "A desire to take part actively in contemporary life by contributing the forms of objects was much alive in our minds," she wrote. Thus functionalism in the weaving workshop was not a dead end of utility, according to her narrative, but a way of developing new capacities for understanding and rethinking the role of textiles in the modern world. The processes of experimenting, building foundations, and even thinking through function were laden with all of the ethical choices that circumscribed the political environment of the Weimar Republic; but they were not enough. Hence Albers introduces the thought of Alfred North Whitehead with a quote not seen in the 1938 version, to interject yet another take on the weaving workshop's development: "The habit of foreseeing is elicited by the habit of understanding. To a large extent, understanding can be acquired by a conscious effort and it can be taught. Thus the training of Foresight is by the medium of Understanding. Foresight is the product of Insight."[59] Albers concludes: "Only the imaginative mind can bring about the transformation of such rational recognition [of need] into a material form." What is interesting in the slight expansion of the text and the introduction of a prominent early-twentieth-century British philosopher circulates around the relationship of thought to practice.[60] The point was not to intellectualize the process but, rather, to open manual practice and experimentation with the material (or the "medium of Understanding," according to Whitehead) to thought beyond itself—not just utility in the abstract, but to economy and society.

This was not the first time Albers had turned to Whitehead's writing to buttress her argument regarding the social consequences of practice. That was in 1947, in her essay "Design: Anonymous and Timeless." Following a set of statements about the modern division of the previously "all-comprising work of the craftsman" among separate fields—scientists, technologists, and engineers—Albers notes how the problem ultimately comes down to specialization. In an education system that "substitutes information for experience," designing, according to Albers,

has become more and more an intellectual performance, the organization of the constituent parts into a coalition, parts whose function is comprehended but can no longer be immediately experienced. Designing today is indirect forming. It deals no longer directly with the medium but vicariously: graphically and verbally.[61]

Importantly, she suggests, "specialization" is to be distinguished from "specific" practices or work with certain materials (like the craft of weaving on a handloom). While the latter emerges as a specific action and experience of a process, the former dissects the process in a mode oriented toward information production.[62] And so here she cites Whitehead:

Effective knowledge is professionalized knowledge, supported by a restricted acquaintance with subjects useful to it. This situation has its dangers. It produces minds in a groove. Each profession makes progress; but it is profession in its own groove. Now to be mentally in a groove is to live in contemplating a given set of abstractions. The groove prevents straying across country, and the abstraction abstracts from something to which no further attention is paid. But there is no groove for abstractions which is adequate to the comprehension of human life.[63]

This excerpt comes from the final chapter, "Requisites for Social Progress," of Whitehead's *Science and the Modern World,* where he summarizes the stakes of his historical overview of the thought underpinning scientific developments since the seventeenth century. Ultimately, he argues, what is most troublesome in the progress of science is not just that it becomes applied to technology in the nineteenth century but that education models have begun to "professionalize" this application. As he notes in his chapter on the nineteenth century, in the wake of the Industrial Revolution the Germans "realized the methods by which the deeper veins in the mine of science could be reached. They abolished haphazard methods of scholarship. In their technological schools and universities progress did not have to wait for the occasional genius, or the occasional lucky thought."[64] Indeed, "the greatest invention of

the nineteenth century was the invention of the method of invention . . . the method itself; that is the real novelty."[65] His point is
that neither technology nor industry in and of themselves is the
problem but, rather, how methods of invention came to divide all
kinds of practice from within.

It surely appealed to Albers when, in a long paragraph found at
the center of this text, Whitehead thus proposed an alternative theory of education. While the student should "concentrate within a
limited, disciplinary field," and its "chief gravity" may lie within the
intellect, and its "chief tool" may be the printed book, there must
also be "the appreciation of the variety of value," by which he means
the drawing out of "habits of aesthetic apprehension."[66] According to Whitehead, "'art' in the general sense . . . is any selection by
which the concrete facts are so arranged as to elicit attention to particular values which are realisable by them. . . . The habit of art is
the habit of enjoying vivid values." But, he continues, "in this sense
art concerns more than sunsets. A factory, with its machinery, its
community of operatives . . . its designers, and stockholders," also
pertains.[67] What has become the habit of viewing the factory, in
the science of political economy after Adam Smith, has abstracted
this "organism" into parts, by fixing attention on a set of abstract
terms or pieces of information and theory.[68] What an artistic education can achieve is a way of nuancing the terms of the field, so
as to find variegated values and a deregularized organism—ways
that might allow the relationships within it to operate differently.
An aesthetic approach would enable all kinds of organisms—from
forests to factories to societies—to persist without an abstract cutting and dividing (into "properties") from within.[69] Thus Albers's
turning to Whitehead in some sense enabled her to push an understanding of weaving away from the Bauhaus language of "laws"
and "properties" first evoked by Stölzl in 1926 and culminating in
Berger's patent texts. (Albers was, after all, never interested in the
question of intellectual property.)[70]

Out of her consideration of Whitehead's philosophy, Albers
redefines her approach to practice as a maker and a teacher (the
two going hand in hand). In her articulation of weaving, throughout the forties and fifties her interest in the medium is not in its
identity but the "flux" of materiality that the practice affords.
Thus Albers's *medium specificity*, if we can call it that, is not about

self-reflexivity—a *l'art pour l'art,* an echo chamber in which the "pure" ontological identity of the medium is voiced back to itself. Rather, it is a space in which to act, to make decisions (decide which avenue to follow) based on what is and isn't possible within a limited terrain of possibilities. While medium specificity becomes for Greenberg (by 1960) a religion, which ultimately renders that medium in a "groove," for Albers the practice of "listening" to the specificity of materials is an ethic. The principles of this ethic do not so much precede the process of weaving as much as they emerge in their countless variability within it. And this goes back to the space of pedagogy and learning. The point is not to define the material or medium for its own sake, but to enable a student to arrive at an experience of practice. She felt her role was to "teach not from the top down, but from the bottom up."[71]

In fact, Albers first developed her thoughts on education in "Art—A Constant," a year after her first draft of the essay on the weaving workshop, and six years after she began teaching at Black Mountain. While "education today" so far "only mediates and sets directions," she noted, it has the "potential," more than philosophy or religion, to develop a "sense of balance" that is "uninhibited by dogmatic requirements."[72] The space of learning is a field in which "we feel free to ask for new and revealing answers from it, answers involving ethics, morals, aesthetics."[73] Thus the first step, in Albers's mind, was to "listen" to the material rather than force one's authorial agenda on it. In such an activity, the medium is no readymade stamp, and designing doesn't have to be "form imposed on the material." Designing rather becomes a method of engaging with material—a space of action—like weaving. Both, again, in the gerund form.

While it would be foolish to make too much of the word *medium* in Whitehead's use of the phrase "medium of Understanding" in *Adventure of Ideas,* the choice by Albers to cite it in her 1959 essay on the weaving workshop is indeed significant. For as she seeks to redefine this term in later texts, the "medium of Understanding" becomes that method of thinking through the material conditions of the modern world, in order to gain "Foresight." To examine the "habits of thought" that place "implicit trust in the principle of efficiency," she proposes that practice can help to "reexamine even our automatic reasoning."[74] The medium becomes a space of learning, a continuously refounded education. Such a practice might even demonstrate a new way of approaching the world—in particular, the temporality of "today's technique of communication."[75] Indeed, in the context of post-Bauhaus America, where the proliferation of this mode is central to every aspect of life, Albers's reflections are noteworthy. For this technique, she writes,

stresses the moment, i.e., the temporary, it accelerates the process of the rise and fall of ideas. We see different beliefs in quick succession or simultaneity, contradicting each other, overlapping each other, complementing each other. Faced with such devastating multiplicity, we are often forced to submit to indecision or to opinions, easily changeable, not worth being called opinions.[76]

If a rethinking of *medium* and education is important for Albers, it is because it has the capacity to challenge the more problematic "habits of thought."

An "Ancient Craft," a New Medium

One such habit of thought within postwar America and post-Bauhaus circles was a general faith in technological progress. For example, there was the work of Gyorgy Kepes, who followed Moholy-Nagy from Berlin to the New Bauhaus in Chicago and whose book *The Language of Vision* sought to educate its readers in new methods of "optical communication"—or what he called the "universal" language of vision—in order to adapt them to advancements in science and technology.[77] Kepes was also a figure who, in his work at MIT's Center for Advanced Visual Studies, or for his Vision + Value Series of thematically edited volumes (1965–66), brought together designers, architects, and artists with scientists, media theorists (like McLuhan), and cyberneticians (like Norbert Wiener or Heinz von Foerster).[78]

Anni and Josef Albers were familiar with Kepes's first attempt to forge interdisciplinary connections, *The New Landscape in Art and Science* (1956), which Kepes called a "picture book arranged . . . to help the reader *see*," and "to bring attention to a newly emerged aspect of nature, hitherto invisible but now revealed by science and technology."[79] One might even imagine that Anni was sympathetic to (perhaps inspired by) Kepes's experimental method in book design as he sought to render the pictures "the content" (or "interrelated structure that alone tells a connected story") and the comments and documents alongside them "the illustrations."[80] A similar method underpins the design of her *On Weaving*—the latter half of which comprises plates of weave draft diagrams, illustrations of looms, and photographs of textiles, which together tell a very compelling story on their own. But while Kepes's 1956 volume is motivated to bring out the "sensible richness" of the natural environment, he has utter faith that "step by step, science has been giving us . . . vastly expanding armory. Through bold scientific generalization and precise observation, phenomena which once seems unconnected have been put into a unified order."[81] Optical media like microscopes and telescopes, as the images in Kepes's volume suggest, show us that everything is interconnected and progressing. And the development of radar and electronic computers in the postwar cybernetic environment is, quite simply, a good thing.[82]

Indeed, though Anni and Gyorgy did exchange their books, and they were close with many of the same members of the post-Bauhaus cohort—including Bucky Fuller, whom she befriended at Black Mountain, who wrote a glowing review of *On Designing*, and who also published in the Kepes's volumes—these two practitioner-writers were at loggerheads ideologically.[83] While Kepes was a technological progressivist, convinced that the eradication of "routine tasks" would make men "freer," Albers was a tempered Luddite interested in developing some sense of disciplinary practice. And while the former foregrounded a "visual sensibility" to the environment, the latter was determined, as the penultimate chapter of *On Weaving* makes clear, to resuscitate a "Tactile Sensibility." A lopsided orientation toward vision, she would suggest, presupposes too much focus on the eye (or a centering on the "I" of the designer), whereas touch is about accessing relationships, thinking through one's quite physical relationship to the material and how by extension that material might affect others in its path. To understand where Kepes was coming from is to get a sense of what Albers was up against.

So what are we to make of Anni Albers's *On Weaving*, the final text she wrote on her Bauhaus medium before abandoning it altogether? (She moved on to printmaking in the late 1960s, with which she "felt free to go into curves and into lacing"—forms that were not as easily achieved on the loom's grid.)[84] On the one hand, the book reads as a synthetic treatise—a final conclusive statement that brings together and coheres all of the modernist discoveries she and her Bauhaus weaving workshop colleagues made while in practice on the loom. Its statements about the "essence" of weaving seem to provide the fullest expression of modernist thought. Yet it should also be recognized that Albers engages here in a multi-ply examination of her medium—focusing on its "visual and structural side" through text but also copious diagrams and photographs of textile artifacts, various types of looms, and drafting notations. In these pages, weaving's specificity is fleshed out less as a defined object than as an interrelated set of actions related to constructing surfaces out of distinct parts, and methods of dealing with tactile effects that are not limited to that thing we call fabric. Indeed, by considering "textile problems," she hopes to show how her thoughts might help illuminate other "tangential subjects": "Starting from a defined and specialized field [one can] arrive at a realization of ever-extending relationships."[85] Albers's engagement with a specialized medium, in other words, is about developing a new "line of thought" or "attitudes and convictions" vis-à-vis designing and media more broadly.[86]

To understand the book's complex approach to the matter of technological history, an extended reading of one section may be useful. Perusing diagrams connected to a chapter on "Early Techniques in Thread Interlacing," one finds examples of knotted nets, knotless nets, various methods in twining, gauze or leno weaves, and braiding. Although the book is concerned primarily with weaving techniques and structures produced on looms and is, in the final count, speaking to modern designers in the midst of a postindustrial landscape, Albers spends some time discussing the historical relationship of weaving to these earlier-developed methods—from Neolithic Europe, Ancient Coptic, and Precolumbian cultures.[87] Turning the page, there is a diagram for a loom from Santa Ana Hueytlalpan, Mexico. Here, any sense of Bauhaus coordinates get out of whack, for this fabric's grid is not rectilinear—made by the perpendicular joining of warp (the vertical threads held in tension) and weft (horizontal threads threaded through them). Rather, a *curve* has been introduced to the fabric's grid through a switch in the function of the threads—a literal turning or recoding of the woven operation. This diagram of a particular, very rudimentary loom thus completely alters any assumptions around weaving—so closely tied to the grid, based on a binary logic of plusses and minuses (warp and weft—two different classes of thread). Here, the logic is no longer that of division but of rejoining—the terms neither unified nor split, but some combination thereof. Then on the following page is the result of a similar technique as developed in northern Chile—a "shaped shirt" in which a piece of fabric had been molded *on an apparatus,* without the intervention of cutting and that much sewing after the fact. Seeing this shirt above a Coptic knit shawl, one finds that the technique makes sense in a new way: not as an ancient artifact but as a product related to the present, with the production of stockings, for instance, or seamless gloves and underwear through knitting machines. The juxtaposition is significant, as Albers notes in the final two paragraphs of the corresponding text:

Today, this problem of shaping, usually linked to clothing, is effectively solved by the process of knitting, which is moving more and more to the foreground. Our nylons, our underwear ... [anything that requires elasticity, have moved] away from the horizontal-vertical construction of woven materials. These usually demand laborious tailoring or complicated draping to give them shape. Furthermore, our new synthetic materials can now be molded in some cases and are moving us further toward fabrics shaped *in the process of production* rather than afterwards.

Thus, with the long glance backward we can discern the rise of the technique of weaving [to generate large swaths of fabric with mechanical apparatuses in industrial textile mills of the eighteenth and nineteenth century], and with a long glance forward we may see it perhaps dimming in its dominance.[88]

The mechanical progress of the loom toward efficiency had hindered weaving's ability to evolve new structures; the modern, industrial system, in other words, was no longer progress when flexible methods were required. New systems of flexible manufacturing, Albers foresaw in 1965, would soon take over, especially with textile production merging into computing. (Technological progress, as found in "steps toward mechanization," she understood, would

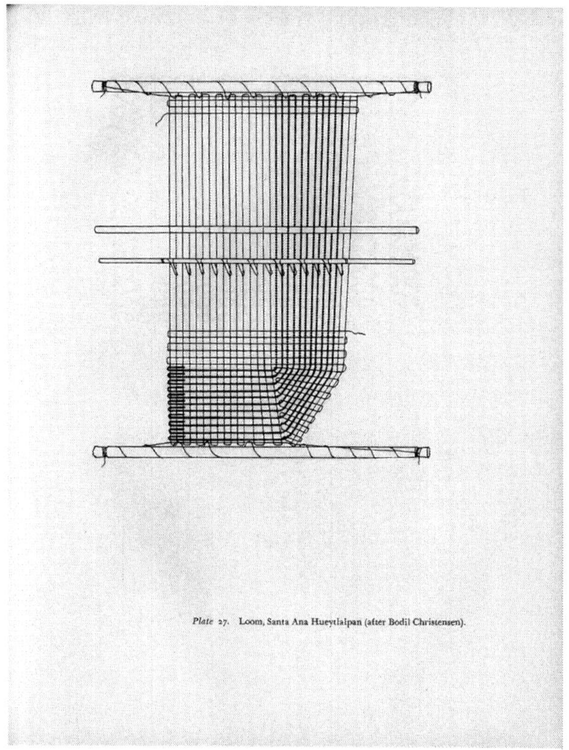

Page from Anni Albers, *Anni Albers: On Weaving* (Middletown, Conn.: Wesleyan University Press, 1965). "Plate 27. Loom, Santa Ana Hueytlalpan (after Bodil Christensen)."

always be met with "limits" and hence diminishment, but could also move backward, toward earlier forms.)

Amid the restructuring and historical sweeps of time found in Albers's book, a question emerges: what is to be made of the (seemingly) ahistorical collisions found among her text and choice of images—the book's loops between past, present, and future? The question, it seems, emerges precisely from the medium that she sets out to define—that is, modern industrial textiles and their modes of manufacture, necessarily linked to a vast history and geography by way of the means of colonialism and anthropological purloining. Any discussion of this medium, Albers suggests, cannot fit neatly into a social-historical method that insists on defining "moments" and cultures discretely. But neither can the method

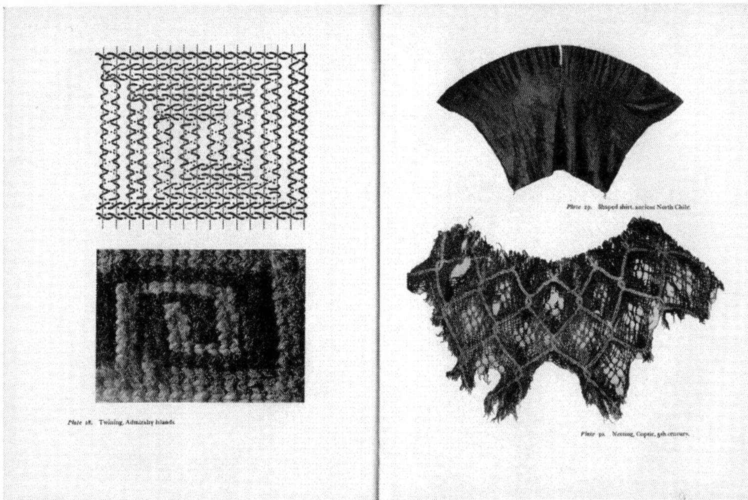

Page spread from Anni Albers, *Anni Albers: On Weaving* (Middletown, Conn.: Wesleyan University Press, 1965). "Plate 28. Twining, Admiralty Islands. Plate 29. Shaped shirt, ancient North Chile. Plate 30. Netting, Coptic, fifth century."

depend on ontological arguments of *medium specificity*. If textiles cut across ancient Mesoamerican and contemporary modes of variable manufacture, it is not because they simply predate, like some Ur-image, the computational logic of 0s and 1s (as someone like Sadie Plant might suggest regarding the relationship of Babbage's to Jacquard's apparatuses).[89] Rather, it is that, as media, textiles are so adaptable to historical shifts, new uses and means. (Indeed, we would be better off to use the plural form *media* instead of "*medium*" here.) For Albers, understanding textiles requires a kind of methodological reticulation, a netting of the past, present, and future.[90]

Indeed, if textile media are also bound to a long *durée*—from possibly Paleolithic worlds to the present—any understanding of their specificity must account for what Ernst Bloch has called the "*Ungleichzeitigkeit* (or 'nonsynchronous development') of cultural and social life."[91] It is perhaps why Albers dedicates her book to her "great teachers, the weavers of ancient Peru," even as she seeks to transform approaches to industrial modes of manufacture in 1960s America. Any moment in history is never locked in time; rather, it is part of a dialectical mesh, in which a coexistence of various

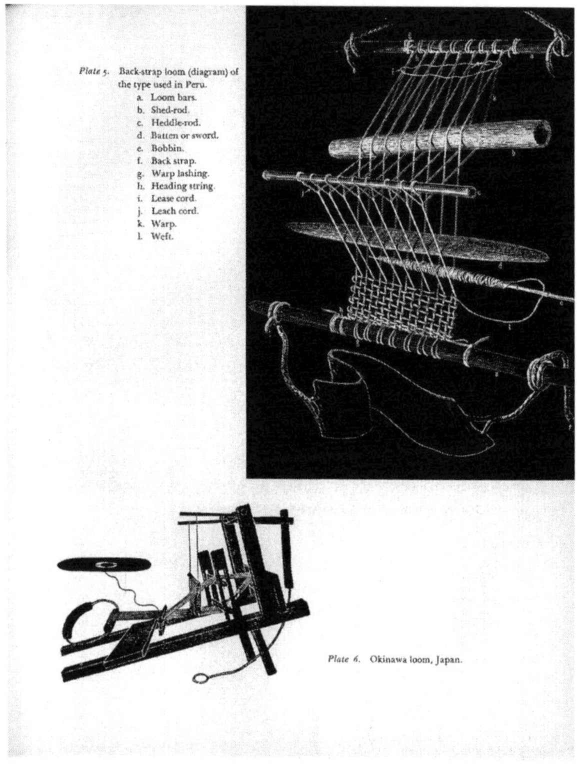

Page from Anni Albers, *Anni Albers: On Weaving* (Middletown, Conn.: Wesleyan University Press, 1965). "Plate 5. Back-strap loom (diagram) of the type used in Peru. . . . Plate 6. Okinawa Loom, Japan."

modes of production has a tendency to become, as Fredric Jameson would say, "visibly antagonistic." It is troublesome to classify texts or other objects of cultural life too simply, according to an "appropriate mode of production," for any such object or technique emerges in a space that is "crisscrossed and intersected by a variety of impulses from contradictory modes of production all at once"— economic modes aligned, for instance, with the back-strap loom, medieval hand loom, or the modern factory floor.[92]

Thus despite (or perhaps because of) its modernist, synthetic goal, *On Weaving* insists on the timelessness of this "ancient craft," and this means a kind of collapsing of past, present, and future. But that collapse also works against a unidirectional history of loom technology, which would only see progress in a hastening of the process of manufacture. Take, for instance, Albers's chapter on the loom: she does not present the loom as some neutral phenomenon but, rather, as a tool whose parts and shape have been determined by specific economic modes and values. The goal of efficiency in modern Europe has led to its present shape, and modern textiles have moved in favor of the basic weave, in which a perfectly binary 1:1 relationship reigns supreme. But the making rectilinear of the warp thread through this instrument, with the invention of heddles (that raise and lower warp in perfectly sequenced intervals) and warp beams (that perfectly space the warp), is also that which has been instrumental in denying other possibilities. While the "technical advance of the heddle prepared the way" for the mechanization of the loom and has "contributed to greater speed of execution," it has also meant that more radical structural possibilities are now far less easily attained.[93] In other words, the fact that *On Weaving* celebrates the work of ancient Incan weavers for producing some of the most sophisticated expressions of weaving's structural thought—what one contemporary artist, Florian Pumhösel, refers to as a kind of "anti-primitivist" impulse in Albers's writing—is also that which allows her to make a dent in her post-Bauhaus colleagues' technologically progressive linear time.[94] History, in some sense, is reticulated according to a textile method.

Albers's book, in fact, might be best understood as an attempt to reset the ground for understanding what is *specific* to textile media—especially modern textiles—that is, the hybrid vocabulary necessary to understanding those media that interlace threads. But also, more important, the questions that this plurality consistently evokes. If *On Weaving* asks questions about and tries to define a specific medium, or textile media, that object also forms the method by which she can ask about "textile problems" in other fields. The medium dilates beyond itself. Hence we begin to understand the statement made in her book's introductory note, which bears worth repeating: "My concern here was to comment on some textile principles underlying some evident facts. By taking up textile fundamentals and methods, I hoped to include in my audience not only weavers but also those whose work in other fields encompasses textile problems."

Indeed, if the medium of weaving that Albers discusses in her final treatise begins to take on a new shape and point to new

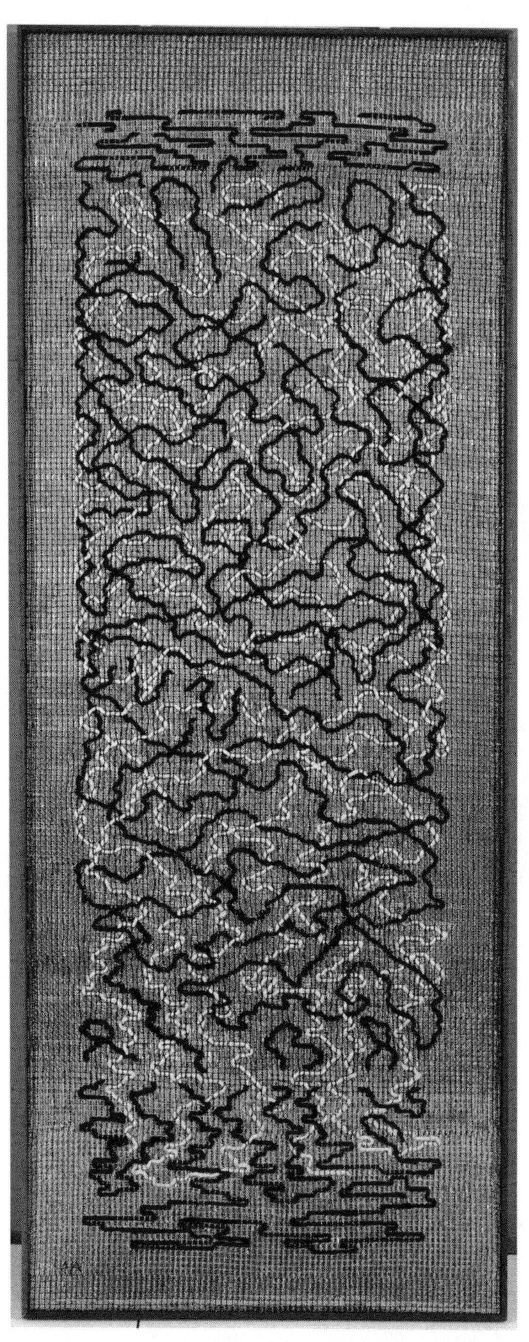

Anni Albers, *Epitaph,*
1968. Cotton, jute,
and metallic ribbon.
Copyright 2013
The Josef and Anni
Albers Foundation /
Artists Rights Society
(ARS), New York.

methods, this may be for several reasons. For just as Albers's book was being written, its object was being replaced not just within the textile industry but also within this medium's domain of the so-called fine arts. Tapestry as the traditional area of nonutilitarian, artistic practice using threads would soon be replaced by something called "fiber art." Following on artist-weaver Lenore Tawney's removal of the warp beam from the loom to bring curves into the fabric—as in her *Dark River* (1962), which is reproduced as plate 107 of *On Weaving*—a variety of off-loom techniques came into use in the late 1960s. Various methods of knotting and felting would quickly take over and the field of tapestry would begin to resemble something more three-dimensional like sculpture—or, rather, like those postminimalist objects that defied categorical boundaries and introduced the viewer to phenomenological experience.[95] In 1968, having recognized the loss (or reshaping) of this modernist medium, Albers would complete her final tapestry, the title of which metaphorized the apparent death of the loom's grid, *Epitaph*. Not long after this, Mildred Constantine and Jack Lenor Larsen would begin to curate their seminal exhibitions at the Museum of Modern Art in New York and by 1972 would declare the field had moved on, once and for all, "Beyond Craft" into a new realm of the "Art Fabric."[96] In this sense, Anni's writing of *On Weaving* harnesses (and redefines) the question of "medium specificity," just as this concept was becoming obsolete, on the brink of the "postmedium" age brought in by minimalism and new media.

Coda: On the Matter of Method

In the midst of Y2K anxiety, sometime between 1997 and 2000, Rosalind Krauss began to rethink the concept of medium.[97] Prompted by a concern over developments that had led from the conceptualists' investigation of the "generic category Art" in the 1960s to the proliferation of installation art (the "post-medium condition") in the 1990s, this *October* editor found herself redrawn to the Greenbergian language of medium specificity, even as it seemed completely obsolete.[98] Of course, after the lessons of Jean-Luc Nancy and Stanley Cavell, Krauss had learned to frame the question a bit differently.[99] Considering the work of artists James

Coleman, Marcel Broodthaers, and William Kentridge, she asked not after specific materials and forms but after repeated processes embedded in artistic strategies—the structures netted between "technical supports" and the artist's systematic employment of them. Krauss resuscitated the concept of medium specificity by reframing it as a "recursive structure—a structure some of the elements of which will produce the rules that generate the structure itself," which is, importantly, "something made rather than something given."[100] And so, less ontically than structurally motivated, Krauss developed a new method for understanding what was medium specific about Coleman's particular, incongruous use of slide-tape (projected images and voice-over) and Kentridge's use of drawing and film. In Kentridge, for instance, the medium was to be found in the procedure of walking back and forth from drawing surface to filmic camera—the film registering like a palimpsest this process of drawing, erasing, and pushing a button—a recursive act, a new language. As these two artists had each in their own way "invented a medium," Krauss invented a method for understanding them.

With Krauss's new understanding of medium in mind, I am compelled to ask one final question: could we align her method with that of Albers's, or with my reading of the weaving workshop's texts throughout this book? Does a discussion of this verbal noun, *weaving*, ultimately benefit from Krauss's understanding of the medium as a recursive procedure and language? The medium is in some sense similarly expanded. But the historian's and the weaver's approaches to this concept are also quite different, and here's why. First of all, in Krauss's method, each newly invented medium is rather tethered to a certain artist, whose particular body and method of working with various techniques are ultimately specific to that particular artist's praxis, a proper name: Coleman, Kentridge, or Christian Marclay. By contrast, textile media as specific materials, structures, and techniques more frequently run amok in the land of anonymity. Moreover, weaving is not just a set of processes: it is also, as I've indicated, a certain mediation of the semiautonomous zones of form and history. Textiles are so *overtly* bound up in the modes of production that define precapitalist and capitalist societies, and the gendered problematics that circumscribe labor, that they are rarely called "art." Krauss may be interested in expanding the medium's parameters, and even recognizing, for instance, how Kentridge's medium helps him make connections between mines and capitalists in South Africa, but she is still a structural formalist at heart. In Krauss's method, the notion of medium has come a long way since the mid-twentieth-century treatises of Greenberg, whereby it seemed so simple, so self-evident, but it remains nevertheless still rather formal for Krauss—that is, rather unified under a singular practice. And perhaps most significantly, to avoid confusion with the word *media*, she insists that the plural of artistic *medium* must be *mediums*, each being a specific art, not a culture industry–infiltrated field that is bothered by the problems of communication.[101]

Since in the end one has to choose sides (on this matter of *mediums* and *media*), it seems more helpful to turn to the hybrid realm of media studies and its methods. For the thing about (Bauhaus) weaving that is *most* particular, as we have seen, is that its very specificity lies in its ability to absorb so many other disciplines or, alternatively, shed light on "textile problems" across other fields. And as Albers's investigations into "material as metaphor" clarify, the medium occupies, for her, the aporia between materiality and communication—or "touching" and "touching on." So following on statements made by German media theorist Josef Vogl, I would summarize this and the previous chapters by saying that "no such thing as a medium exists in any permanent sense."[102] What does exist is a medium "event"—"a complex formation comprising material, discursive, practical, and theoretical elements."[103] Bauhaus weaving is (was) an event that stretched out and absorbed the limits of other media in its path.

Still one important detail is worth mentioning to show how weaving might also throw a wrench in Vogl's overarching (Kittlerian-Foucaultian) philosophy of media.[104] For if media are "self-referential, world creating organs," Vogl writes, they are also

events in a particular and double sense: the events are communicated through media, but the very act of communication simultaneously communicates the specific event-character of media *themselves.* Media make things readable, audible, visible, perceptible, but in doing so they also have a tendency to erase themselves and their constitutive sensory function, making themselves imperceptible and "anesthetic."[105]

Vogl calls this condition of media—most evident in a medium's initial moment of invention—a "double becoming," a mode of presencing that simultaneously erases itself. By contrast, in the most literal sense, weaving has no definable moment of invention. It's simply been around too long, in too many different geographical contexts and in too many different forms. There is no singular event, for it always adapts and readapts. As discussed by the Bauhaus weaving workshop weavers and later expanded by Anni Albers, its continual *reinvention* (in pictorial wall hangings, functional prototypes, optical-tactile things, patented objects and so on) was subtended by its ever-present gerund form. Moreover, the medium of weaving, unlike, say, Galileo's telescope or photography, can never quite erase itself to yield anesthetic objects of intellectual inquiry (like the shape of the universe). What the medium of weaving and other forms of thread interlacing make visible, or rather tangible, in the end is their material stuff, their physicality as evidence of a practice—however inaccessible that practice is in the space of the cloth. And yet textiles do, simultaneously, stretch the limits of perception: as we wear or sit on them, we tend to forget they exist. This is a rather different version of the "double becoming."

NOTES

Introduction

1. Anni Albers, *Anni Albers: On Designing* (Middleton, Conn.: Wesleyan University Press, 1971). The initial publication of *Anni Albers: On Designing* was by Pelango Press in 1959.
2. Anni Albers, "Tactile Sensibility," *Anni Albers: On Weaving* (Middletown, Conn.: Wesleyan University Press, 1965), 64.
3. Albers, "Introductory Note," *On Weaving*, 13.
4. Walter Gropius, "Program of the State Bauhaus in Weimar" (1919), in Hans M. Wingler, *The Bauhaus: Weimar, Dessau, Berlin, Chicago*, ed. Joseph Stein, trans. Wolfgang Jabs and Basil Gilbert (Cambridge, Mass.: MIT Press, 1976), 32.
5. Elaine S. Hochman's political history of the school, *Bauhaus: Crucible of Modernism* (New York: Fromm International, 1997), explains how Gropius's attempt to unify the Bauhaus under a single ideological framework throughout the first several years was an impossible task. The conflicted political and disastrous economic fabric of the Weimar Republic, as well as the school's need to appeal for funding to different patrons, from both the Left and the Right, ultimately formed an institution whose ideological goals were never coherent. Thus the Bauhaus as a discursive and practical field is almost impossible to define.
6. Gropius, "Program of the State Bauhaus," 32.
7. Gunta Stölzl, "Weaving at the Bauhaus," in *Gunta Stölzl: Bauhaus Master*, ed. Monika Stadler and Yael Aloni (Ostfildern, Germany: Hatje Cantz Verlag, 1926; and New York: Museum of Modern Art, 2009), 85–87. Another translation of this essay can be found in Wingler, *The Bauhaus*, 116. Throughout this book, I will use Stadler and Aloni's translation of Stölzl's text, unless otherwise noted. Originally printed as Gunta Stölzl, "Weberei am Bauhaus," *Offset Buch- und Werbekunst* 7: Bauhaus special issue (1926): 405–406.
8. Walter Gropius, "Bauhaus Dessau—Principles of Bauhaus Production" (1926), in Wingler, *The Bauhaus*, 109–110.
9. It is important to mention here, as I discuss throughout the book, that the apparent break from romanticism and expressionism to technology and functionalism after the 1923 exhibition was never so definitive.
10. Gropius, "Bauhaus Dessau—Principles of Bauhaus Production,"

109; Stölzl, "Weaving at the Bauhaus," in Stadler and Aloni, *Gunta Stölzl*, 85.

11. Stölzl, "Weaving at the Bauhaus," in Stadler and Aloni, *Gunta Stölzl*, 83. The translation of "Bild aus Wolle" is slightly revised here and throughout the book: Stadler and Aloni translate *Bild* as "painting," but I prefer the translation of *Bild* as "picture," as in "picture made of wool," found in Wingler, *The Bauhaus*, 116.

12. Ibid., 83. Throughout this book, I use the German spelling "Wassily," as this was used at the Bauhaus.

13. Annelise Fleischmann (Anni Albers), "Bauhausweberei," *Junge Menschen* 5, no. 8 (November 1924), 188. All citations from this text are my translation.

14. Ibid.

15. Certainly architect Gottfried Semper's extensive treatise on textiles in volume 1 of his *Stil* (1855) represents the first sustained attempt to analyze and describe different methods of fabric production, different materials and methods of linking threads (knitting, felt, crochet, etc.), or the relationship of textiles to architecture. And the Bauhaus weavers likely knew this text, given Semper's importance to German design movements. But Semper's *Stil* was more concerned with premodern techniques, whereas the Bauhaus weavers saw their medium firmly grounded within the demands of industry and modern life. Semper, *Style in the Technical and Tectonic Arts; or, Practical Aesthetics*, trans. Harry Francis Mallgrave and Michael Robinson (Los Angeles: Getty Research Institute, 2004).

16. William Morris, "Textiles," in *Arts and Crafts Essays by Members of the Arts and Crafts Exhibition Society* (1893), available online at *http://en.wikisource.org/wiki/Arts_and_Crafts_Essays*, accessed July 15, 2010. On this webpage one can also find short essays on other crafts, including embroidery, lace, metalwork, and wood. See also Linda Parry, *Textiles of the Arts and Crafts Movement* (London: Thames and Hudson, 1988); and Oliver Fairclough, *Textiles by William Morris and Morris & Co., 1861–1940* (London: Thames and Hudson, 1981).

17. See Varvara Stepanova, "From Clothing to Pattern and Fabric" (1929), in Alexander Lavrentiev, *Varvara Stepanova: The Complete Work*, ed. John E. Bowlt, trans. Wendy Salmond (Cambridge, Mass.: MIT Press, 1988), 180. See also Alexandra Exter, "In Search of New Cloth" (1923), in *Amazons of the Avant-Garde*, ed. John E. Bowlt and Matthew Drutt (New York: Solomon R. Guggenheim Foundation, 2000), 299–301; and Christina Kiaer's "The Constructivist Flapper Dress," in *Imagine No Possessions: The Socialist Objects of Russian Constructivism* (Cambridge, Mass.: MIT Press, 2005), 88–141. This chapter by Kiaer discusses Varvara Stepanova and Liubov Popova's work for the First State Cotton-Printing Factory beginning in 1923 as well as Stepanova's writing on clothing, fashion, and composition.

18. Stepanova, "From Clothing to Pattern and Fabric," 180. According to Alexander Lavrentiev, Stepanova "felt . . . the artist should design the fabric 'from within,' starting with the rules governing its weaving so as to attain

not just new decorative surfaces, but also fabrics with new physical properties" (82), but it's not clear from her published writings that Stepanova was at all concerned with the techniques and structures of weaving (as opposed to printed patterns). Notably, before they were textile designers for the First State Cotton-Printing Factory in Moscow in 1923, both Stepanova and Popova had been members of the Working Group of Objective Analysis, a group concerned with the specific conditions of a medium. On the question of "medium specificity" there, see Gough, *The Artist as Producer: Russian Constructivism in Revolution* (Berkeley: University of California Press, 2005), 32–33. It is strange that Stepanova did not concern herself more fully with the properties of woven cloth, as she did, for instance, analyze clothing, fabric patterning, "construction," composition, color, and every other aspect of the textile industry. This may be because by 1923 the earlier concerns with "medium specificity" in the Russian avant-garde had shifted almost entirely to the role of art in the economy and production.

19. One might say this was the case in the English-speaking context until more recently, when, for the 2009 Bauhaus exhibition at MoMA, large wall hangings were prominently displayed throughout the galleries, suggesting the significant role of the weaving workshop in the school's program. See *Bauhaus 1919–1933: Workshops for Modernity*, exhibition catalog, ed. Barry Bergdoll and Leah Dickerman (New York: Museum of Modern Art, 2009).

20. Sigrid Wortmann Weltge, *Bauhaus Textiles: Women Artists and the Weaving Workshop* (London: Thames and Hudson, 1993). This book was also printed under a different title, *Women's Work: Textile Art from the Bauhaus* (San Francisco: Chronicle Books, 1993). The first major study of the Bauhaus weaving workshop was a master's thesis by Ingrid Radewalt, "Bauhaustextilien 1919–1933." (Universität Hamburg, 1986).

21. See *Das Bauhaus Webt: Die Textilwerkstatt am Bauhaus*, exhibition catalog, ed. Magdalena Droste and Manfred Ludewig (Berlin: G + H Verlag, 1998); *Gunta Stölzl: Weberei am Bauhaus und aus eigener Werkstatt*, exhibition catalog, ed. Magdalena Droste (Berlin: Bauhaus-Archiv, 1987); *Gunta Stölzl. Meisterin am Bauhaus Dessau. Textilien, Textilentwürfe und freie Arbeiten 1915–1983*, exhibition catalog (Dessau: Stiftung Bauhaus Dessau and Verlag Gerd Hatje, 1997). These volumes include collected essays by art historians and reprints of some archival documents.

22. Anja Baumhoff, *The Gendered World of the Bauhaus: The Politics of Power at the Weimar Republic's Premier Art Institute, 1919–1932* (Frankfurt: Peter Lang GmbH, 2001).

23. Virginia Gardner Troy, *Anni Albers and Ancient American Textiles: From Bauhaus to Black Mountain* (London and Burlington, Vt.: Ashgate Publishing, 2002).

24. Albers, "Weaving at the Bauhaus," *On Designing*, 38.

25. See Weber's and Danilowitz's discussion of Albers's writing practice in the "Foreword" and "Introduction" to Anni Albers, *Selected Writings on Design*, ed. Brenda Danilowitz (Hanover and London: University Press of New England, 2000).

26. Especially important to the recent surge in craft history and theory is Glenn Adamson's *Thinking through Craft* (Oxford: Berg Publishers, 2007). The *Journal of Modern Craft*, which Adamson also coedits, is another strong point in this development. In the realm of art history, notable contributions include Elissa Auther's *String, Felt, Thread: The Hierarchy of Art and Craft* (Minneapolis: University of Minnesota Press, 2010), Rozika Parker's *The Subversive Stitch: Embroidery and the Making of the Feminine* (London: I. B. Tauris, 2010), and Julia Bryan-Wilson's forthcoming book *Crisis Craft* on the use of craft in politically engaged art since the 1970s. The establishment of *Textile: Journal of Cloth and Culture*, initiated in 2003, has contributed enormously to the scholarly and theoretical study of cloth from historical and contemporary contexts around the globe and has been crucial in forming an international voice for research on technological textiles and how textiles relate to other fields, like architecture or literature.

27. See, for example, the work and writings of technological textile designer Joanna Berzowska at *http://www.berzowska.com*. For a catalog covering recent industrial and electronic textile developments, see Matilda McQuaid, *Extreme Textiles: Designing for High Performance* (New York: Smithsonian Cooper-Hewitt Design, National Design Museum, and Princeton Architectural Press, 2005).

28. *Textile Research Journal*, whose audience is primarily industry specialists, publishes articles on research and development in textile fabrication and material technology.

29. Philosophically oriented discussions of textiles exist, but they focus less on the practice or craft than on the metaphorical status of weaving or cloth in philosophy and culture. See Arthur Danto's discussion of weaving as a "conceptual scheme" for Greek political theory: "Weaving as Metaphor and Model for Political Thought" in *Sheila Hicks: Weaving as Metaphor*, ed. Nina-Stritzler-Levine (New York: Bard Graduate Center; New Haven: Yale University Press, 2006), 22-36. See also Pennina Barnett, "Folds, Fragments, Surfaces: Towards a Poetics of Cloth," in *Textures of Memory: The Poetics of Cloth* (Nottingham: Angel Row Gallery, 1999), 25-34; and Claire Pajaczkowska, "On Stuff and Nonsense: The Complexity of Cloth," *Textile: The Journal of Cloth and Culture* 3, no. 3 (2005): 220-249.

30. See, for example, Paul Mathieu, "Toward a Unified Theory of Crafts: The Reconciliation of Differences," *Studio Potter* 29, no. 1 (Dec 2000): 72–75; and Howard Risatti, *A Theory of Craft: Function and Aesthetic Expression* (Chapel Hill: University of North Carolina Press, 2007). Mathieu's essay argues that what differentiates craft centers on the concept of "containment." Whereas art is contained (by a frame), craft objects contain. Although this argument is useful, it considers craft as a category, a noun, or object, but it deals less with an understanding of the practice.

31. Adamson, *Thinking through Craft*, 1.

32. Rafael Cardosa gives an excellent discussion of the division between intellectual and manual labor in art, design, and craft in his essay "Craft versus

Design: Moving beyond a Tired Dichotomy" (2008), in *The Craft Reader*, ed. Glenn Adamson (Oxford: Berg, 2010), 321–32.

33. It should be noted that the division between intellectual and manual labor may be far less strong in many other cultures.

34. Pye's writing is cited in Adamson, *Thinking through Craft*, 70–78. As Adamson shows, textual activity existed around craft throughout the twentieth century, but it was most often at the margins of art criticism and theory.

35. Ibid., 4, 7.

36. Ibid., 4.

37. Ibid., 11. Adamson cites Adorno's 1965 speech "Functionalism Today," delivered to the German Werkbund concerning handicraft and art, and Adorno's *Aesthetic Theory*. Derrida's notion of the *parergon* or supplement in *The Truth in Painting* is used by Adamson to understand how craft works as a kind of frame, as that which is next to but also obfuscated by the work of art at its center.

38. Ibid., 13.

39. Glenn Adamson, *The Invention of Craft* (London: Bloomsbury, 2013).

40. R. Buckminster Fuller, cited on the back cover of the third paperback edition of Albers's *On Designing* (1979).

41. It should be noted that the first glimpses of a theory of medium are evident in Leonardo da Vinci's *Treatise on Painting* (New York: Dover Publications, 2005), which sought to distinguish painting as a visual art, different from poetry and bearing its own particular "rules" regarding the depiction of space, light, shadow, form, and color. Leonardo's *paragone* also distinguished it from sculpture, which he defined as a "mechanical art," not "liberal" or of the mind, like painting.

42. Moshe Barasch, *Modern Theories of Art, 1: From Winckelmann to Baudelaire* (New York: New York University Press, 1990), 147. On the topic of this contradiction in nineteenth-century art theory, see especially Barasch's chapter "Unity and Diversity of Visual Arts."

43. Lessing, cited in Barasch, *Modern Theories of Art*, 1, 157. The longer quote cited from Lessing's sixteenth chapter is: "If it be true that painting, in its imitations, makes use of entirely different means and signs from those which poetry employs; the former employing figures and colors in space, the latter articulate sounds in time . . . it follows that painting and poetry represent objects of a different nature." Barasch argues that Lessing's distinguishing between "artificial" and "natural" signs parallels what semioticians would later call symbolic and iconic signs (154).

44. Barasch, *Modern Theories of Art*, 1,174.

45. Hegel, cited in Barasch, *Modern Theories of Art*, 1, 196. Architecture corresponds with Ancient Egypt and is symbolic, or "has an 'external' reason, whereas sculpture is identified with Ancient Greece and performs the perfect unity of matter and spirit. Finally, painting (along with music and poetry) is the Romantic form that accomplishes 'the outward appearance of the self-concentrated inner life,' or the mind itself."

46. Wassily Kandinsky, "Cologne Lecture," in *Kandinsky: Complete Writings on Art*, ed. Kenneth C. Lindsay and Peter Vergo (New York: De Capo Press, 1994), 399.

47. See Leah Dickerman, "Vasily Kandinsky, without Words," in *Inventing Abstraction 1910–1925: How a Radical Idea Changed Modern Art*, exhibition catalog, ed. Leah Dickerman and Matthew Affron (New York: Museum of Modern Art, 2012), 52.

48. Kandinsky, "Abstract Synthesis on the Stage" (1923), in Lindsay and Vergo, *Kandinsky: Complete Writings on Art*, 506.

49. Clement Greenberg, "Modernist Painting" (1960), in *Clement Greenberg: The Collected Essays and Criticism*, vol. 4, ed. John O'Brian (Chicago: University of Chicago Press, 1993), 86.

50. Elissa Auther discusses Greenberg's disparaging attitude toward "handicrafts" as "decoration" in *String Felt Thread*, xvi–xviii. It is important to note that Greenberg was also troubled to define architecture as a medium because of its functionality.

51. Immanuel Kant, *Kant's Critique of Judgement*, trans. J. H. Bernard (London: Macmillan, 1914), §43, 184. "*Art* differs from *handicraft*; the first is called *free*, the other may be called mercenary. We regard the first as if it could only prove purposive as play, i.e. as occupation that is pleasant in itself. But the second is regarded as if it could only be compulsorily imposed on one as work, i.e. as occupation which is unpleasant (a trouble) in itself and which is only attractive on account of its effect (e.g. the wage)"; emphasis in the original.

52. In the concluding chapter, I will look at the way the term *medium* evolves in America in the 1960s, just as Anni Albers publishes her final book, *On Weaving*, in 1965. This term was later addressed and redefined by Rosalind Krauss as she considers the "post-medium condition" in a number of articles and books written since 1997. See, for example, her most recent book on the topic, *Under Blue Cup* (Cambridge, Mass.: MIT Press, 2011).

53. Otti Berger, "Stoffe im Raum," *ReD* (Prague) 3, no. 5 (1930): 143–45. This essay and others by Berger are discussed in chapter 3.

54. Adamson, *Thinking through Craft*, 2.

55. Albers, "The Pliable Plane: Textiles in Architecture," *On Designing*, 19.

56. Watenphul was given permission by Gropius to participate in all workshops, so the weaving workshop was not the sole locus of his activities. During the history of the workshop, only two other male students were members: Friedrich Wilhelm Bogler, from 1923–1924, and Max Enderlin, from 1928–1932. Enderlin was simultaneously a member of the metal workshop.

57. Oskar Schlemmer, cited in Weltge, *Bauhaus Textiles*, 41.

58. This anecdote regarding Muche's aversion to weaving is recounted by Weltge, *Bauhaus Textiles*, 59.

59. A text from 1928 by German art historian Hans Hildebrandt also reiterates the idea that weaving work was essentially feminine. Hildebrandt, *Die Frau als Künstlerin: Mit 337 Abbildungen nach Frauenarbeiten Bildender Kunst von*

den Frühesten Zeiten bis zur Gegenwart (Berlin: Rudolf Mosse Buchverlag, 1928).

60. Weaving's status in Western art since the Renaissance as an "applied art" is demonstrated in the fact that tapestries were most often copies of cartoons (drawn by artists like Raphael) and produced by craft guilds.

61. I am deploying Luce Irigaray's theory of "woman" as both a "linguistic absence" in discourse and as a term that reveals the asymmetry of the sexes. See Irigaray, *This Sex Which Is Not One*, trans. Gillian C. Gill (Ithaca, N.Y.: Cornell University Press, 1985).

62. Indeed, other arts, like painting, have held feminine associations: Michelangelo, for instance, implied that the detailed oil paintings of northern Europe appealed to the instincts of women, nuns, and aristocrats. See, for instance, Jeffrey F. Hamburger's "To Make Women Weep: Ugly Art as 'Feminine' and the Origins of Modern Aesthetics," *RES: Anthropology and Aesthetics* 31, The Abject (Spring 1997), 9–33.

63. According to Mitchell Schwarzer, Karl Bötticher's theoretical formulation of "tectonics" in the mid–nineteenth century was an attempt to define the "Art" of architecture when it was otherwise seen in Romantic discourse as "mere mechanics" or lacking an "idea." See Schwarzer, "Ontology and Representation in Karl Bötticher's Theory of Tectonics," *Journal of the Society of Architectural Historians* 52, no. 3 (September 1993): 267–80.

64. Adolf Loos, "Ornament and Crime" (1910), in *The Industrial Design Reader*, ed. Carma Gorman (New York: Allworth Press, 2003). Anja Baumhoff also refers to Loos's essay for her entry "The Role of Arts and Crafts at the Bauhaus," in *Bauhaus*, ed. Jeannine Fiedler and Peter Feierabend (Cologne: Könemann Verlagsgesellschaft mbH, 1999), 479. See also Mark Wigley's *White Walls, Designer Dresses: The Fashioning of Modern Architecture* (Cambridge, Mass.: MIT Press, 1995), in which he discusses gender anxiety in modernist definitions of architecture, ornament, and style.

65. The labor strikes of 1903–1904 in the textile industry town of Crimmitschau, which established unions in Germany, were significant demonstrations organized by women. For a further discussion of these strikes, see Kathleen Canning, *Languages of Labor and Gender: Female Factory Work in Germany, 1850–1914* (Ithaca, N.Y.: Cornell University Press, 1996). I consider Canning's text further in chapter 4.

66. Karl Marx references the specificity of female labor in *Capital* most explicitly in a section of chapter 15 on the "effects of machine production on the worker." Marx, *Capital: A Critique of Political Economy, Volume 1*, trans. Ben Fowkes (London: Penguin Classics, 1990), 517.

67. The "surplus women" problem peaked in 1925 following the war, with many women required to remain single and join the workforce (typically in the textile industry), which created anxieties among male workers about the security of their jobs. See Detlev J. K. Peukert, *The Weimar Republic: The Crisis of Classical Modernity*, trans. Richard Deveson (New York: Hill & Wang, 1993), 86–87.

68. Frederic J. Schwartz, *Blind Spots: Critical Theory and the History of Art in Twentieth-Century Germany* (New Haven, Conn.: Yale University Press, 2005), 76.

69. Adrian Sudhalter, "Walter Gropius and László Moholy-Nagy. Bauhaus Book Series. 1925–30," in Bergdoll and Dickerman, *Bauhaus 1919–1933*, 196.

70. Included among the series' authors were Theo van Doesburg, Kasemir Malevich, and Piet Mondrian in addition to the Bauhaus figures Gropius, Moholy-Nagy, Klee, Kandinsky, and Oskar Schlemmer.

71. Sudhalter, "Walter Gropius and László Moholy-Nagy," 98.

72. Along these lines, it is important to keep in mind that a different geographical and cultural context, such as that of Latin America, would frame and produce a material practice differently. Evidence of this can be seen in how female practitioners in a different context conceived of weaving as a communicative tool for the spiritual and cultural rites of a community. See Janet Catherine Berlo, "'Beyond Bricolage': Women and Aesthetic Strategies in Latin American Textiles," in *Textile Traditions of Mesoamerica and the Andes*, ed. Margot Blum Schevill, Janet Catherine Berlo, and Edward B. Dwyer (New York: Garland, 1991).

73. Michel Foucault, *Power/Knowledge: Selected Interviews and Other Writings, 1972–1977*, ed. Colin Gordon (New York: Pantheon, 1980), 194.

1. Pictures Made of Wool

1. Adolf Hölzel is an important figure for early German abstraction, as he helped found the New Dachau school of painting in 1888 and developed a method of abstraction suited to an exploration of "basic" units (shapes and colors). He influenced both Johannes Itten and Oskar Schlemmer, his students in Stuttgart, and also Kandinsky, who learned his methods while studying painting at the academy in Munich. Hölzel attributed his fundamental approach to color and form to the French painter Georges Seurat's scientific approach to painting, but he also sought to develop a formal language that would at once express "inner feelings" and "objective" impressions of the external world.

2. The designation *expressionist* for either Muche or Itten is up for debate: Georg Muche is not usually referred to as an expressionist, for he only began showing in 1918, toward the end of that movement in Germany, though his earliest exhibitions of abstract, cubist-style paintings placed him in contact with the Munich-based expressionist circle. As for Itten, his painting, which was similarly inspired by the angular, geometrical lines of cubism, is considered a post–WWI "Weimar expressionist," but he was always more of a pedagogue than an active painter.

3. Renaissance tapestry technique would wrap each warp thread (typically linen) completely in the finer weft threads (wool and/or silk), rendering the foundational warp invisible beneath the strands that form the picture. Jungnik's work employs a different method, similar to the seventeenth-

century French Gobelin, which deploys weft and warp (figure and ground) in equal measure to produce the visible surface of the image.

4. This quote comes from Wilhelm Worringer's *Abstraction and Empathy* (1907), trans. Michael Bullock (Chicago: Ivan R. Dee, 1997). For Worringer, the value of abstraction lies in the "suppression of representation of space," in which "all endeavor was therefore directed toward the single form set free from space," 22. Worringer's text was foundational to certain strands of expressionist theory, specifically the writings of Paul Fechter and Kandinsky, and that of the Bauhaus. Its publication in 1908 (a year after he completed his thesis by the same title) inaugurated a critical focus on "immaterial abstraction" over and above naturalism. According to the art historian's system, "primitive" and modern art are informed by a drive to "abstraction," whereas Classical and Renaissance work, with its movement toward naturalism and the representation of space, are characterized by "empathy." Gothic art, in particular the architecture and plastic arts of German Gothic ornament, stands as the ideal synthesis of the two terms. Worringer assumes that a psychology, or "feeling about the world," informs the evolution of styles and can be classified according to two generally distinct categories, abstraction and empathy. Worringer's argument in terms of the "human drive toward abstraction" is a complex one and cannot be gone into further here but is well explicated by Geoffrey C. W. Waite in "Worringer's *Abstraction and Empathy*: Remarks on Its Reception and on the Rhetoric of Its Criticism," in *Invisible Cathedrals: The Expressionist Art History of Wilhelm Worringer*, ed. Neil H. Donahue (University Park: Pennsylvania State University Press, 1995), 13–40.

5. Anja Baumhoff, "The Role of Arts and Crafts at the Bauhaus," in *Bauhaus*, ed. Jeannine Fiedler and Peter Feierabend (Cologne: Könemann Verlagsgesellschaft, 2000), 478–79.

6. Referring to the architect Adolf Loos's quintessentially modernist essay "Ornament and Crime," which denigrated the applied arts as "ornamental," "feminine," and "degenerate," Baumhoff writes: "The feminine, the ornamental, the craft-oriented and the fashionable seemed inevitably interrelated and thus had to be reformed together if modernism was to prevail" (479).

7. See the editors' introduction to the reprint of this volume in *Kandinsky: Complete Writings*, 534. They note that a preliminary version of this text can be found in the three essays that Kandinsky contributed to the 1923 Bauhaus exhibition catalog: "The Basic Elements of Form," "Color Course and Seminar," "Abstract Synthesis on a Stage," in Lindsay and Vergo, *Kandinsky: Complete Writings*, 498–507. A logical development of what he wrote in *On the Spiritual in Art*, these texts also looked forward, summarizing the ever-more scientific approach to form and color theory that he undertook in his courses at the Bauhaus and in his connection to the mural workshop and later collaboration with the stage workshop.

8. Wassily Kandinsky, *Point and Line to Plane: A Contribution to the Analysis of*

Pictorial Elements (1926), in Lindsay and Vergo, *Kandinsky: Complete Writings*, 527–699, 637.

9. The book is titled *The ABCs of [triangle square circle]: The Bauhaus and Design Theory,* ed. Ellen Lupton and J. Abbott Miller (New York: Cooper Union for the Advancement of Science and Art, 1993). Even the manifestation of the title, where a formal triangle, circle, and square are used instead of words, suggests that the Bauhaus's design theory was simple, straightforward, and concretely rational.

10. G. F. Hartlaub, "Art and the New Gnosis" (1917), in *German Expressionism: Documents from the End of the Wilhelmine Empire to the Rise of National Socialism,* ed. Rose-Carol Washton Long (New York: G.K. Hall, 1993), 91–94. Long notes that "Hartlaub's article is one of the clearest examples of the point of view connecting expressionism with occultism and mysticism." See also Shearer West's chapter "The Spiritual in Art," in *The Visual Arts in Germany 1890–1937: Utopia and Despair* (New Brunswick, N.J.: Rutgers University Press, 2001).

11. See Foucault, *Power/Knowledge: Selected Interviews and Other Writings 1972–1977,* ed. Colin Gordon (New York: Pantheon Books, 1980), 69.

12. It seems important to make the point that I do not seek to establish a neat homology or structural parallel between the physical matter of weaving and certain modes of production (textile factory labor and related class struggles). As Fredric Jameson argues, it is important to recognize that these zones are "relatively autonomous" and only relate through mediation. See Jameson, "On Interpretation," *The Political Unconscious: Narrative as a Socially Symbolic Act* (Ithaca, N.Y.: Cornell University Press, 1981), esp. 43–46.

13. In *Der Expressionismus,* Paul Fechter acknowledged such a possibility when he wrote: "By itself, the call: 'abandon nature!' was fully justified. But its combination with the call: 'back to the picture!' was *contaminated* to the core, and thus inevitably led to the ills of decorativeness in painting." Fechter, "Die Späten Gegenbewegung" (1914), in Long, *German Expressionism,* 82; emphasis mine.

14. The Deutscher Werkbund included such architects as Hermann Muthesius and Peter Behrens, as well as industrial manufacturers, and was closely bound to the nationalist goals of Wilhelmine Germany. Gropius was a member of this group, and its rhetoric, found in the writing of Muthesius primarily, largely informed his initial 1916 proposal to the Weimar state for the school.

15. Walter Gropius, "Recommendations for the Founding of an Educational Institution as an Artistic Counseling Service for Industry, the Trades, and the Crafts" (1916), in Wingler, *The Bauhaus,* 23–24.

16. Marcel Franciscono, *Walter Gropius and the Creation of the Bauhaus in Weimar: The Ideals and Artistic Theories of the Founding Years* (Urbana: University of Illinois Press, 1971). Franciscono examines the architect's writings and ideas prior to and after WWI, finding in all of them traces of spiritual utopianism and machine progressivism. The apparent historical break of 1923—seen by many historians as a return to his original, Werkbund-like

1916 proposal to the Thuringian government—is for Franciscono a false division.

17. The political capital and methods of the *Wandervogel* movement were ultimately appropriated by the Nazis in the development of the Hitler Youth. See Hermann Gieseke, *Vom Wandervogel bis zur Hitlerjugend: Jugendarbeit zwischen Politik und Pädagogik* (München: Juventa Verlag, 1981).

18. See Elaine S. Hochman, *Bauhaus: Crucible of Modernism* (New York: Fromm International, 1997).

19. See also Walter Laqueur, *Weimar: A Cultural History: 1918–1933* (New York: Perigee, 1980).

20. Hochman writes of the RGA: Its "program advocated a bewildering array of ideas, endorsing among other issues the radical reform of education, workers' rights, the inviolability of life, and sexual freedom. In addition to this confused agenda, the program's ecstatic mood could not disguise the fact that such terms as *brotherhood* and *Geist* were easier to talk about than act upon." Hochman, *Bauhaus*, 53.

21. Ibid., 51.

22. For more on Bruno Taut's expressionist architecture, see Rosemarie Haag Bletter's dissertation "Bruno Taut and Paul Scheerbart's Vision: Utopian Aspects of German Expressionist Architecture" (PhD diss., Columbia University, 1973); and Iain Boyd Whyte, *Bruno Taut and the Architecture of Activism* (Cambridge: Cambridge University Press, 1982).

23. Taut, cited in Whyte, *Bruno Taut*, 175–76, 181. Whyte quotes Taut's letter to architects to join the group: "Let us consciously be 'imaginary architects'!" The Gläserne Kette group exhibited at the Arbeitsrat für Kunst's April 1919 exhibit, the "Ausstellung für unbekannten Architekten." See also Iain Boyd Whyte, *The Crystal Chain Letters: Architectural Fantasies by Bruno Taut and His Circle* (Cambridge, Mass.: MIT Press, 1985).

24. Hochman, *Bauhaus*, 65.

25. Documents signed by Feininger, Itten, Georg Muche, and Oskar Schlemmer express this sentiment. Thür. Hauptstaatarchiv, Weimar, Best.: Bauhaus, Nr. 120.

26. Baumhoff, *Gendered World of the Bauhaus*, 19.

27. See note 64 in the introduction concerning this issue.

28. Baumhoff, *Gendered World of the Bauhaus*, 19.

29. Itten arrived at the school along with other students of Hölzel's from Stuttgart's academy: Ida Kerkovius, Hölzel's former assistant, who later joined the weaving workshop, and the painter Oskar Schlemmer, who soon acted as form master for the mural painting workshop, and later as master of the theater workshop.

30. Mazdaznan came into European discourse in the late nineteenth century when a certain Otoman Zar-Adusht Ha'nish was sent by Tibetan leaders to America and then to Europe to preach world peace. Friedrich Nietzsche subsequently wrote on Zarathustra, one of the religion's prophets.

31. Norbert M. Schmitz, "Johannes Itten," in *Bauhaus*, ed. Fiedler and Feierabend, 241. Schmitz opens his essay with the following statement: "To

give an account of Johannes Itten inevitably also entails speaking about a repressed irrationalism in modernism, for his art was first and foremost a form of esoteric propaganda."

32. Johannes Itten, *Design and Form: The Basic Course at the Bauhaus* (London: Thames and Hudson, 1965), 11.

33. Franciscono, *Walter Gropius and the Creation of the Bauhaus in Weimar*, 180–81.

34. Johannes Itten, diary entry for October 20, 1916, in *Johannes Itten: Werke und Schriften*, 51. Cited and translated in *Bauhaus*, ed. Fiedler and Feierabend, 366.

35. It should be said that Itten's retrospective account of his teaching at the Bauhaus from 1919 to 1923 was subject to revisionism. No doubt influenced by subsequent developments in art education, it bears, for example, traces of Kandinsky's 1926 text *From Point to Line to Plane* (1926).

36. Itten, *Design and Form*, 79.

37. Ibid., 129–30.

38. Stölzl's notebook is titled "Analysen der Alten Meister Johannes Itten," Bauhaus-Archiv Berlin, Gunta Stölzl Files, Folder 3; translation mine. Original German: "In der Form ist Bewegung, unendlich Bewegung. Sie ist der Aufgang der Welt. . . . wir [sie] noch nicht erkennen, wir [sie] fühlen."

39. Each of these texts was popularly read at the early Bauhaus. Anni Albers refers to Worringer as a major source for her work when she entered the school in 1924.

40. See, for example, Ludwig Rubiner's edited volume *Kameraden der Menschheit. Dichtungen zur Weltrevolution*, which can be found at http://www.uni-due.de/lyriktheorie/scans/1919_1rubiner.pdf; accessed October 19, 2012. Many of the journals in which Rubin published, including the anarchist journal *Der Kampf: Zeitschrift für gesunden Menschenverstand*, and *Der lose Vogel*, occupied a space between poetry and radical left-wing anarchist politics. Nevertheless, as with much art of this moment, the apparent political rift between expressionism (as Leftist) and the Right is complicated. Georg Lukács, for example, analyzed Worringer's writing, with its praise of the German Gothic, as a problematic attempt to shore up "autochtonous" German culture ultimately supportive of Nazi ideology.

41. Herbert Kühn, "Expressionism and Socialism" (1919), in Long, *German Expressionism*, 178.

42. Fechter, "Die Späten Gegenbewegung," in Long, *German Expressionism*, 82.

43. Thür. Hauptstaatarchiv, Weimar, Best.: Bauhaus, Nr. 52.

44. Kandinsky references the work of "Mrs. H. P. Blavatsky," who began the Theosophical Society. Kandinsky, *On the Spiritual in Art*, in Lindsay and Vergo, *Kandinsky: Complete Writings*, 143–45.

45. Ibid., 128. Although Kandinsky is critical of market-driven tendencies in art, he is equally critical of socialist materialism and "Marx's Capital," which he marks as too "positivist" (140).

46. Ibid., 135; emphasis in original. While the translators of the Lindsay and Vergo edition use the word *portrayal*, the original German text uses the verb

wiederzugeben, which may translate as "to reproduce": "Die Gegenstände, die wiederzugeben sie für ihr einziges Ziel halt, bleiben unverändert dieselben." Kandinsky, *Über das Geistege in der Kunst* (Bern-Bümpilz: Benteli Verlag, 1963), 32. I emphasize the word *wiederzugeben* since it relates to his general argument against technique, or means, in this passage.

47. Ibid., 165, 160.
48. Ibid., 167–68.
49. Ibid., 177, 170.
50. Ibid., 175.
51. Ibid., 173.
52. Ibid., 176.
53. It should be noted that the adverb "hermetically," often used with "sealed" in scientific discourse to denote the closure of an absolute space or vacuum, also has an etymology that suggests a relationship to mysticism, spirituality, and alchemy. See definition for "hermetically" in *The Oxford English Dictionary*, online edition, http://www.oed.com. One example of usage from 1883 by H. Drummond (in *Law in the Spiritual World*, ed. 2) seems especially relevant: "The passage from the Natural World to the Spiritual World is hermetically sealed on the Natural Side."
54. Jean-Joseph Goux, "The Unrepresentable," *Symbolic Economies*, trans. Jennifer Curtiss Gage (Ithaca, N.Y.: Cornell University Press, 1990), 178.
55. Ibid., 182.
56. Ibid., 183.
57. Dickerman, "Vasily Kandinsky, without Words," in Dickerman and Affron, *Inventing Abstraction 1910–1925*, 51.
58. Ibid., 52.
59. Kandinsky, "Painting as Pure Art" (1913), in Lindsay and Vergo, *Kandinsky: Complete Writings on Art*, 349.
60. In their "Introduction" to *Kandinsky: Complete Writings*, the editors Lindsay and Vergo reference Kandinsky's complex relationship to writing. Even as he wrote prolifically, he eschewed "catalogue clutchers" (those who rely on the painting's label to understand it) and insisted that "the central meaning of each art defies translation" (11–12). Yet the editors acknowledge the perception of artists as self-promoters: "Particularly open to mistrust are artists who write. Is such an artist using the recorded word to foster his own posterity? . . . Are his paintings little more than a justification of his theory?" (11). One might say that the editors are as anxious as Kandinsky on this topic.
61. Kandinsky, *On the Spiritual in Art*, in Lindsay and Vergo, *Kandinsky: Complete Writings on Art*, 189–91.
62. Ibid., 192–93.
63. Itten, like Kandinsky, drew a lot from the lectures and writings of Rudolf Steiner. Itten also references Oswald Spengler's *Decline of the West* when speaking of the material conditions of modernity as justification for his move toward Mazdaznan spiritual philosophy.
64. Itten, *Design and Form*, 147.

65. Johannes Itten, letter to Anna Höllerling, entries for December 1919, in *Johannes Itten: Werke und Schriften*, catalogue raisonné by Anneliese Itten, ed. Willy Rotzler (Zurich: Orell Füssli Verlag, 1978); translation mine.

66. By *recursively*, I mean it here as understood by Rosalind Krauss: "Modernist theory held this self-definition to be a *recursive* structure—a structure some of the elements of which will produce the rules that generate the structure itself." Krauss, *Under Blue Cup*, 4.

67. Karl Marx, "Theses on Feuerbach" (1845), trans. Cyril Smith, http://www.marxists.org/archive/marx/works/1845/theses/index.htm (accessed June 12, 2013).

68. Karl Marx, "Estranged Labour," in *Economic and Philosophic Manuscripts of 1844*, trans. Martin Mulligan, http://www.marxists.org/archive/marx/works/1844/manuscripts/preface.htm (accessed June 12, 2013).

69. In German, the noun *Stoff* denotes "matter" and "substance," but also "fabric, material, cloth."

70. It was often difficult to acquire wool, silk, or cotton in Germany from 1919 to 1923, thus Germany increasingly used and developed viscose-based threads like *Kunstwolle* (artificial wool) and *Kunstseide* (artificial silk) as substitutes. Maria Makela examines these developments in "Artificial Silk Girls: Cloth and Culture in Weimar Berlin," which was given at the conference Berlin's Culturescape in the 20th Century, September 22, 2006, University of Regina, Regina, Saskatchewan.

71. Karl Marx, "The Chapter on Capital," in *Grundrisse* (Outlines of the Critique of Political Economy), trans. Martin Nicolaus, http://www.marxists.org/archive/marx/works/1857/grundrisse/index.htm, 296 (accessed June 6, 2013).

72. See Marx's lengthy citations of Wilhelm Schulz on textile mills, for example, in the first chapter, "Wages of Labour," of *Economic and Philosophic Manuscripts*.

73. See a report given by female textile workers from 1930, titled "My Workday, My Weekend," in *The Weimar Republic Sourcebook*, ed. Anton Kaes, Martin Jay, Edward Dimendberg (Berkeley: University of California Press, 1995).

74. Gerhart Hauptmann, "The Weavers," in *Plays: Before Daybreak, The Weavers, The Beaver Coat*, ed. Reinhold Grimm and Carolina Molina y Veidia (New York: Continuum, 1994), 91–166.

75. For a discussion of Weber's method and relationship to the political environment in which his work developed, see Randall Halle, "The Historical and Biographical Context of Max Weber's Methodology," in *From Kant to Weber: Freedom and Culture in Classical German Social Theory*, ed. Thomas M. Powers and Paul Kamolnick (Malabar, Fla.: Krieger, 1999).

76. Max Weber, *General Economic History*, trans. Frank H. Knight (New York: Greenberg, 1927), 303.

77. Ibid., 168.

78. Ibid., 159.

79. Ibid., 26.

80. Ibid., 117. Weber writes: "The 'medicine man' is the earliest profession. In

general every highly skilled occupation was originally regarded as influenced by magic. The smiths especially were everywhere viewed as characterized by supernatural qualities because a part of their art appears mysterious and they themselves make a mystery of it." For further discussion of the "artist as magician," see Ernst Kris and Otto Kurz, *Legend, Myth, and Magic in the Image of the Artist,* trans. Alastair Laing (New Haven, Conn.: Yale University Press, 1979); and Catherine M. Soussloff, *The Absolute Artist: The Historiography of a Concept* (Minneapolis: University of Minnesota Press, 1997).

81. As to "men's work," with respect to "weaving there are indeed characteristic exceptions. In Egypt, Herodotus was rightly impressed by the fact that men (servile) worked at the looms, a development which took place generally where the loom was very heavy to manipulate or the men were demilitarized." Ibid., 116.

82. Weber, *General Economic History,* 26–27.

83. There exists very little writing on Muche in English. One short monograph in German covers his work from 1912 to 1927, a year after he stopped heading the weaving workshop. *Georg Muche: Das Künstlerische Werk 1912–1927* (Berlin: Bauhaus-Archiv, Museum für Gestaltung; Gebr. Mann Verlag, 1980).

84. Georg Muche, "Vorschläge zur wirtschafflichen Organisation der Weberei" (1923), Thür. Hauptstaatarchiv, Weimar, Best.: Bauhaus, Nr. 178.

85. Document in Thür. Hauptstaatarchiv, Weimar, Best.: Bauhaus, Nr. 58.

86. Kandinsky, "Cologne Lecture" (1914), in Lindsay and Vergo, *Kandinsky: Complete Writings,* 399.

87. Semper's texts are cited as an origin to the ideas that later developed at the Bauhaus, specifically the concern for technique in education. See Wingler's brief discussion of Semper's relevance to the Bauhaus in Wingler, *The Bauhaus,* 18. See Semper's "Science, Industry, and Art" (1852) in Wingler, *The Bauhaus,* 18, which is an excerpt from Gottfried Semper, *Wissenschaft, Industrie, und Kunst* (Brunswick, Germany: Vieweg, 1852).

88. Aloïs Riegl, *The Problem of Style: Foundations for a History of Ornament,* trans. Evelyn Kain (Princeton, N.J.: Princeton University Press, 1992), 33.

89. Gottfried Semper, *Style in the Technical and Tectonic Arts; or, Practical Aesthetics,* trans. Harry Francis Mallgrave and Michael Robinson (Los Angeles: Getty Research Institute, 2004), 113.

90. Riegl, *Problem of Style,* 6.

91. Loos, "Ornament and Crime," in Gorman, *Industrial Design Reader,* 78–79.

92. Kracauer, "The Mass Ornament," 76.

93. Kracauer elsewhere points to photography's strength as one of being able to suggest, through a "contiguous relationship," the "remnants of an organic nature." Kracauer seeks an organic world that would not fragment social beings, such as the Tiller Girls or the "film diva," into parts. The figure of the film diva opens Kracauer's discussion in his essay on "Photography," in *The Mass Ornament.*

94. See Kracauer's essay "Women's Work," in *Weimar Republic Sourcebook,* ed.

Anton Kaes et al., in which he points to the problematic myth of white-collar working women, developed through Weimar-period films, which lauds their freedom and success and denies the reality of their lived conditions.

95. The complexity of the situation with respect to gender and technique cannot be overemphasized. Precisely at the moment when "femininity" pervaded much of the concern about the body and labor in a technical society, "feminine values," meaning domestic values, were being identified as an alternative to "technification." Writing on women's movements in Weimar, Ute Frevert writes: "Since 'masculine culture' found itself in a crisis characterized by de-individualisation, alienation from nature, technification and objectification, there was all the more reason to inject into society feminine values and orientations and so nurture motherly and humane behaviour at all levels." Ute Frevert, *Women in German History: From Bourgeois Emancipation to Sexual Liberation*, trans. Stuart McKinnon-Evans (Oxford: Berg, 1989), 171.

96. Max Beckmann, "Thoughts on Timely and Untimely Art" (1912), in Long, *German Expressionism*, 99.

97. Michel Foucault, *Archaeology of Knowledge*, trans. Alan Sheridan (New York: Pantheon, 1972), 28.

98. Anni Albers, "Weaving Workshop," in *Bauhaus 1919–1928* (reprint), ed. Herbert Bayer, Walter Gropius, Ise Gropius (Boston: Charles T. Branford, 1952), 57. Albers refers in a caption to the image of this work as a "woven cover," not a wall hanging. Originally published in 1938.

2. Toward a Modernist Theory of Weaving

1. Gropius's lecture "Art and Technology—A New Unity" was given during the "Bauhaus week" from August 15 to 19, during the opening week of the 1923 exhibition. See Frank Whitford, *Bauhaus* (New York: Thames & Hudson, 1988), 139.

2. Walter Gropius, cited in Anna Rowland, "Business Management at the Weimar Bauhaus," *Journal of Design History* 1, no. 3/4 (1988): 153–75, 164. The arguments made in this chapter are especially indebted to Rowland's groundbreaking research and thesis that the Bauhaus in Weimar after 1923 was not simply a romantic ivory tower of education but, rather, a school engaged heavily in the marketing of its craft products.

3. See Barry Bergdoll's discussion of the Sommerfeld House in his essay "Bauhaus Multiplied: Paradoxes of Architecture and Design in and after the Bauhaus," in *Bauhaus 1919–1933*, ed. Bergdoll and Dickerman, 43–44. Citing Gropius's essay on wood, which claimed it to be the perfect material for the purposes of modern building, Bergdoll discusses how the house incorporated fixtures from all of the workshops (except pottery) and was meant as a replicable model geared toward the postwar housing shortage in Germany.

4. Gropius's modular housing designs are reproduced in Adolf Meyer, *Ein Versuchshaus des Bauhauses in Weimar. Haus am Horn. Bauhausbücher* 3 (Munich: Albert Langen Verlag, 1925).

5. See Robin Schuldenfrei, "The Irreproducibility of the Bauhaus Object," in *Bauhaus Construct: Fashioning Identity, Discourse, and Modernism*, ed. Jeffrey Saletnik and Robin Schuldenfrei (London: Routledge, 2010), 37–60. Schuldenfrei points out that until Gropius left the Bauhaus in 1928 and the Swiss architect Hannes Meyer took over as director, calling for "people's needs instead of luxury needs," most of the objects from the metal and woodworking workshops were expensive, one-of-a-kind items (tea sets and lamps) for a specialty audience interested in the "look" of a technologically progressive, "modern" design (37–38). Schuldenfrei does not discuss the case of Bauhaus textiles, however, which is a bit more complicated, given that the weaving workshop was by 1924 already producing fabric sold by the meter and as such was better positioned to "industrialize" a bit earlier than the metal or wood workshops.

6. Rosemarie Haag Bletter points out that Behne wrote *Der moderne Zweckbau* in November 1923 (and indicated as much on the page following the copyright) but delayed publication until 1926 because Gropius asked him to do so. Bletter, "Introduction," in Adolf Behne, *The Modern Functional Building*, trans. Michael Robinson (Santa Monica, Calif.: Getty Research Institute), 1.

7. Rowland, "Business Management at the Weimar Bauhaus," 159. Rowland writes: "In a memorandum of July 11, 1924, it was noted that the weaving workshop had already begun to sell prototypes to outside manufacturers, at first earning 20 percent in license fees. The weavers were in the business of conceptualizing the function of weaving work. In October 1924, another memo reported that the vast majority of textiles were sold by representatives."

8. The students were undoubtedly aware of the debate ten years earlier at the Deutscher Werkbund between Hermann Muthesius and Henry van de Velde regarding the *Typ* (prototype) and the individual artist's specific style, respectively identified with each architect. See Frederic J. Schwartz's analysis of this debate in his *The Werkbund: Design Theory and Mass Culture before the First World War* (New Haven, Conn.: Yale University Press, 1996).

9. This is a translation of the title of Schmidt-Nonné's article, originally published as "Das Gebiet der Frau im Bauhaus," *Vivos Voco: Zeitschrift für Neues Deutschum* 5, no. 8/9 (1926).

10. Rowland discusses the degree to which many of the orders for textiles after the 1923 exhibition came from a female clientele who asked for "slight variations on the pattern offered. For example, a typical order would look like this: N493 Lilac stripes instead of red stripes." Rowland, "Business Management at the Weimar Bauhaus," 157.

11. The subtitle for *Junge Menschen* magazine is "Monatshefte für Politik, Kunst, Literatur und Leben aus dem Geiste der jungen Generation."

12. Walter Gropius, cited in Rowland, "Business Management at the Weimar Bauhaus," 165. Writing to Lilly Reich, who was organizing the exhibition, Gropius declared: "We intend to abandon the applied arts stand point which we have had up until now, and to aim our products more and more at serial production. Therefore, I would ask you to plan the display in such a way that the effect is not the normal, pretty arts and crafts arrangement, i.e., a higgledy-piggledy scattering of the individual products according to a purely visual point of view. I would rather that each product was separated from the others according to type and displayed in rows: 10 lamps in a row, all the fabrics next to one another, etc. That is in my opinion a more serious and more effective display method."

13. Albers, "Bauhausweberei," 188.

14. This is discussed further in chapter 1.

15. At a visit to Krefeld's textile school in 1924, the two older students learned traditional methods in dyeing and then taught them to the others. Interestingly, the Krefeld faculty found their interest in dyeing to be quaint.

16. Rowland, "Business Management at the Weimar Bauhaus," 155.

17. Ibid., 161.

18. Anna Rowland refers to the 1923 exhibition and 1924 fair as a barometer for the "state of flux" in the Bauhaus ideology. "The debate about display styles is interesting because it illustrates the Bauhaus's state of flux at this stage, poised between a craft and an industrial orientation." Ibid., 165.

19. Barry Bergdoll's "Semperian reading" of Gropius's attitude toward the "experimental worksite" of the Sommerfeld House might apply to Albers's essay. Like Semper, Albers maintained a "search for the new in primeval methods." Commenting on the form of the building, which resembled a log cabin, Bergdoll notes: "One might easily develop a Semperian reading of Gropius's attitude to the search for the new within the primeval." Bergdoll, "Bauhaus Multiplied," in Bergdoll and Dickerman, *Bauhaus 1919–1933*, 43.

20. Rowland discusses the two viewpoints on business held by Gropius and Lange. While the former pushed to industrialize the workshops, Lange more pragmatically tried to ensure that the handicraft work was simply well done and palatable to a market of distributors who sold expensive applied-arts products.

21. A similar point is made by Gropius in an essay from 1926: "Where Artists and Technicians Meet," in *Form and Function: A Source Book for the History of Architecture and Design 1890–1939*, ed. Tim Benton, Charlotte Benton, Dennis Sharp (London: Crosby Lockwood Staples, 1975), 147–48. Original publication: "Wo Berühren sich die Schaffensgebiete des Technikers und Künstlers," *Die Form* 1, no. 6 (March 1926): 117–21. He writes: "It is precisely the most clear-cut and obvious ideas which take the longest to be realized. They are radical, that is to say, rooted, in origin which allows them to be effective not in a narrow, easily comprehensible sphere of influence, but instead in all spheres of life" (147).

22. Albers, "Bauhausweberei," 188.

23. Ulrike Müller, *Bauhaus Women: Art, Handicraft, Design* (Paris: Flammarion, 2009), 56–61. Müller discusses Gertrud Arndt's reluctant entrance into the weaving workshop but focuses on her photographic self-portraits, for which she remains better known.

24. Bauhaus-Archiv Berlin, Polytex-Textil collection, Inv. Nr. 332, 480, 481, 1066—1073/2. See chapter 4 for a further discussion of the achromatic textiles.

25. Gunta Stölzl's notebooks from Paul Klee's form-theory courses, for instance, hold many pages demonstrating this relationship. See Bauhaus-Archiv Berlin, Gunta Stölzl files, folder 1. The degree of Klee's influence on the weavers' textile practice has been discussed by Virginia Gardner Troy and Jenny Anger, particularly for the period the painter was the workshop's form master between 1927 and 1929. See Troy, *Anni Albers and Ancient American Textiles*; and Jenny Anger, *Paul Klee and the Decorative in Modern Art* (Cambridge: Cambridge University Press, 2004). Troy discusses the profundity of Klee's influence in the workshop beginning in 1923, when he arrived at the school (80–89). But the influence was not a one-way street. Both Troy and Anger discuss how Klee's thinking was similarly influenced by the horizontal-vertical grid structure of weaving.

26. Quoted in Müller, *Bauhaus Women*, 57.

27. Benita Koch-Otte, for instance, later commented on the different ways the form masters influenced her teaching and work: "If I were to say what Klee's teaching has meant to me, I don't know how to summarize it with words, whereas Itten's method was very direct. Klee reaches much deeper layers, layers unknown, bringing the unconscious and unknown in us to sound; you listen to it. This carries through one's entire life." *Farblehre und Weberei. Benita Koch-Otte: Bauhaus, Burg Gebichenstein, Weberei Bethel*, exhibition catalog (Bethel, Germany: Werkstatt Lydda, 1972), 13; translation mine.

28. For a discussion of the difference between "things" and "objects," see Bill Brown's "Thing Theory," *Critical Inquiry* 28, no. 1 (Autumn 2001), 1–22, 5.

29. Although Koch-Otte never taught at the Bauhaus, she used its theories for her own development of a pedagogical method while teaching at the school in Burg-Giebichenstein between 1925 and 1933. Berger's "Bindungslehre," which she developed between 1929 and 1930 while teaching in Stockholm for six months and then back at the Bauhaus, is another example of an instruction manual serving as a catalyst for theory. Bauhaus-Archiv Berlin, Otti Berger textile collection, Inv. Nr. 2001/49.

30. For an exemplary description of the use and importance of pattern books in the American textile industry, see Florence M. Montgomery, *Textiles in America, 1650--1870: A Dictionary Based on Original Documents, Prints and Paintings, Commercial Records, American Merchant's Papers, Shopkeepers' Advertisements, and Pattern Books with Original Swatches of Cloth* (New York: W. W. Norton, 2007).

31. Bauhaus-Archiv Berlin, Gunta Stölzl textile collection, Inv. Nr 2993/1–35.

32. Stölzl, cited in Baumhoff, *Gendered World of the Bauhaus,* 104.

33. Oskar Schlemmer, "The Stage and the Bauhaus," quoted in Wingler, *The Bauhaus,* 117.

34. See Kai Konstanty Gutschow's dissertation for a comprehensive bibliography of Behne's texts, which were published throughout German culture in magazines, newspapers, and journals. "Adolf Behne and the Development of Modern Architecture in Germany, 1910–1914" (Columbia University, 2005).

35. Bletter, "Introduction," in Behne, *The Modern Functional Building,* 4. Bletter points out that Behne's criticism was especially instrumental in developing and applying the concepts "*Sachlichkeit* (objectivity, functionalism) and *Zweck* (purpose, function)" to architecture.

36. Bletter addresses the difficult relationship between Behne and Gropius: "The three-year delay in *Internationale Architektur*'s publication reveals much about the competitive nature of early Modernism" (ibid., 1). Gropius asked Behne to help prepare the 1923 exhibition, for which there would be an accompanying book published by the *Bauhausbücher* series. In exchange for his assistance, Behne requested that Gropius delay the publication date because its content and scope were so similar to Behne's *Der moderne Zweckbau.* Gropius refused to comply, and when the Bauhaus books series got off the ground it further delayed Behne's publication; the Dutch architect J. J. P. Oud, whose work Behne hoped to use, said he would prefer to have his work published in Gropius's series. Because of the break with Gropius, Behne faced a number of obstacles in getting the book to print.

37. For a concise analysis of the term *function* in architectural discourse, see Larry L. Ligo, *The Concept of Function in Twentieth-Century Architectural Criticism* (Ann Arbor, Mich.: UMI Research Press, 1984). Ligo identifies five primary categories of function that pervade German and American architectural criticism: "Structural articulation," which includes the building's and its material's functions; "physical function," which includes environmental functions, like traffic patterns; "psychological function" that a building might invoke in its viewer; "social function," which "refers to the concretization of social institutions"; and finally "cultural/existential function," 5. For a dismissal of functionalism's relevance to modern architecture, see Stanford Anderson, "The Fiction of Function," *Assemblage* 2 (February 1987): 21. Anderson's argument and the concept of functionalism are also discussed in Bletter, "Introduction," 14.

38. Hilde Heynen, *Architecture and Modernity* (Cambridge, Mass.: MIT Press, 2001), 48.

39. Ibid., 49.

40. This is also the year that Ernst May's *Siedlung* project in Frankfurt took off and his magazine, *Das neue Frankfurt,* entered publication.

41. Bletter, "Introduction," in Behne, *The Modern Functional Building,* 11–13. Bletter is referencing Henry Russell Hitchcock and Philip Johnson, *The International Style: Architecture since 1922* (New York: Norton, 1932).

42. According to the prologue of *Der moderne Zweckbau,* primitive forms of

architecture were seen by builders as something of a "tool" (*Werkzeug*), a device for protecting inhabitants from the elements or enemies. But they also integrated an element of play, of design. Primitive architects always had a way of treating architecture not just as a *Werkzeug* but also as a *Spielzeug*, as a space of formal play. Architecture of the Baroque or Neoclassical eras, by contrast, shifted emphasis from this balance toward a singular focus on the building's form, its facade. The new movement in architecture was about finding equilibrium.

43. For a fuller discussion of *Sachlichkeit* in Behne's later writing, which increasingly took over from the term *Zweck*, see Frederic J. Schwartz, "Form Follows Fetish: Adolf Behne and the Problem of 'Sachlichkeit,'" *Oxford Art Journal* 21, no. 2 (1998): 47–77. According to Schwartz, Behne became especially focused on the question of *Sache* at its root in three later texts written between 1926 and 1928: *Neues Wohnen—Neues Bauen*; *Max Taut: Bauen und Pläne*; and *Eine Stunde Archtektur*. Schwartz notes that *Sachlichkeit* is a difficult word to render into English. The adjective *sachlich* could be translated literally as "material," "practical," or "objective," but it also implies a "matter-of-factness" or "practicality" and "suitability" of a *Sache* as an "instrument for human use" (48, 50).

44. Messel's Wertheim Building, "the prototypical department store," moved in the direction of "the house," but its use of windows on the upper level had neither "significance for advertising purposes" nor for light, and in this sense "was not entirely *sachlich*." Behne, *Modern Functional Building*, 96.

45. For further discussion of Behrens's AEG turbine factory, see Stanford Anderson, *Peter Behrens and a New Architecture for the Twentieth Century* (Cambridge, Mass.: MIT Press, 2000).

46. Behne, *Modern Functional Building*, 106–109.

47. Ibid., 111. Van de Velde's work, according to Behne, "is important for the further development of functional architecture."

48. Ibid., 111, 121.

49. Ibid., 113.

50. Ibid., 129.

51. Ibid., 137.

52. Ibid., 137–38.

53. Bletter nevertheless points out that Behne "describes the pitfalls of both these positions" (functionalism and rationalism). Bletter, "Introduction," 44.

54. Behne, *Modern Functional Building*, 109.

55. Ibid., 146.

56. Gropius, "Grundsätze der Bauhausproduktion," *Neue Arbeiten der Bauhauswerkstätten. Bauhausbücher 7* (Munich: Albert Langen Verlag, 1925), 5–8.

57. Walter Gropius, "Bauhaus Dessau—Principles of Bauhaus Production" (March 1926), included in Wingler, *The Bauhaus*, 109–10.

58. Ibid., 110.

59. Ibid.

60. Behne rarely addresses the question of practice, though he describes the

differences among various kinds of architects according to their assessment of the machine: "When the functionalist refers to the machine, he sees it as a moving tool, the perfect approximation to an organism. When the utilitarian refers to the machine, he sees it as an economic principle of saving work, power, and time. When the rationalist refers to the machine, he sees it as the representative and patron of standardization and typification." Behne, *Modern Functionalist Building*, 130.

61. Gropius, "Principles of Bauhaus Production," 110.

62. Gropius, "Where Artists and Technicians Meet," included in Benton, *Form and Function*, 147.

63. Ibid.

64. Stölzl, "Weaving at the Bauhaus," in Stadler and Aloni, *Gunta Stölzl*, 86.

65. Ingrid Radewalt has explained that Muche thought it was necessary for the weaving workshop to be reconceived in Dessau, and new tools had to be purchased. Radewalt, "Bauhaustextilien 1919–1933," 26.

66. The tense relationship between Georg Muche and the weaving workshop is discussed further in chapter 1.

67. It should be noted that despite his contempt Muche was nevertheless a strong advocate for the weaving workshop and its students' financial interests. Rowland notes a disagreement between Lange and Muche over the sale of goods from the weaving workshop in particular: Muche insisted on different pay rates for the weavers. Muche, as it turns out, proposed to have all the weaving workshop's goods bought by the school, whereas Lange proposed to give each weaver only "10 percent of the pure profit on the sale of his/her work." Rowland, "Business Management at the Weimar Bauhaus," 156.

68. Anja Baumhoff describes this situation in *Gendered World of the Bauhaus*, 93.

69. Gropius, cited in Baumhoff, *Gendered World of the Bauhaus*, 93.

70. Monika Stadler and Yael Aloni note that Stölzl did not use the feminine *Meisterin*, which indicated that Stölzl was asserting her identity as "master, plain and simple," *Gunta Stölz*, 13.

71. Stölzl was named technical master in April 1925. In June 1926 she took over Georg Muche's role as the workshop's primary master.

72. Stölzl, "Weaving at the Bauhaus," in Stadler and Aloni, *Gunta Stölzl*, 85. The German reveals some differences from the English translation, so I have slightly altered the quotation in the text, using brackets to indicate any changes from the Aloni and Stadler translation: "Auf allen Gestaltungsgebieten zeigt sich heute ein Bestreben nach Gesetzmäßigkeit und Ordnung. So haben auch wir in der Weberei uns zur Aufgabe gemacht, die Grundelemente unseres besonderen Stoffgebietes zu untersuchen. Während z.b. in den Anfängen der Bauhausarbeit von bildmäßigen Prinzipien ausgegangen wurde, ein Gewebe sozusagen ein Bild aus Wolle war, sind wir uns heute darüber klar, daß ein Gewebe immer ein dienender Gegenstand ist, der von seinem Verwendungszweck und in gleichem Maße von den Gegebenheiten seiner Herstellung bestimmt wird."

73. Ibid., 87.

74. Ibid.

75. Stölzl, "Utility Textiles of the Bauhaus Weaving Workshop" (1931), in Wingler, *The Bauhaus,* 174; emphasis mine.

76. Ibid. The English translation of this text in Wingler uses the word *bond* in place of *Bindung.* Typically *Bindung* would translate as "weave" with respect to textiles, and "bond" with respect to chemicals like glue. *Bond* nevertheless seems an appropriate word given its usage in architecture to refer to masonry.

77. Bauhaus-Archiv, Gunta Stölzl textile collection, Inv. Nr. 489.

78. For a further discussion of the question of "adaptability" in Bauhaus textiles, see Magdalena Droste, "Anpassung und Eigensinn: Die Weberai Werkstatt des Bauhauses," in Droste and Ludewig, *Das Bauhaus Webt,* 18. It should be noted, however, that this relative invisibility in photographs would change again in 1929, when photography became an official part of the curriculum under Walter Peterhans, and beautiful close-ups of fabrics made their way into Bauhaus brochures, advertisements, and the *bauhauszeitschrift.* See chapter 3 for further discussion of this development.

79. A great example of this is a fabric of cellophane and chenille designed by Anni Albers, discussed later in the chapter. Designed for the auditorium walls of a school in Bernau by Hannes Meyer (1929), the fabric would later be marketed by Design Within Reach as a multipurpose fabric, including upholstery.

80. Stölzl, "Weaving at the Bauhaus," 86; emphasis mine.

81. Ibid., 87; emphasis mine.

82. Helene Nonné-Schmidt, "Woman's Place at the Bauhaus" (1926), in Wingler, *The Bauhaus,* 116–17. Note that Wingler puts her maiden name, Nonné, before Schmidt. The Wingler edition's translation of the original title, "Das Gebiet der Frau im Bauhaus," is "Woman's Place at the Bauhaus" rather than "The Woman's Field in the Bauhaus," which I suggest here. There is a difference between "place" and "field" that is worth specifying. Wingler's translation implies an essential place for the weavers rather than the area in which the weavers practiced and explored their medium, or field.

83. This is similar to what Aleksandr Rodchenko projected for his hanging *Spatial Constructions* (1920). Cut from a single piece of plywood, the *Constructions* could be arranged into a three-dimensional form with the use of wire. And after display in an exhibition, they could be collapsed and stored or easily transported. See Christina Lodder, *Russian Constructivism* (New Haven, Conn.: Yale University Press, 1983), 24.

84. Walter Gropius, "The Theory and Organization of the Bauhaus," in *Bauhaus 1919–1928,* 27. Originally published as "Idee und Aufbau des staatlichen Bauhauses Weimar," in *Staatliches Bauhaus in Weimar* (Munich: Bauhaus-verlag, 1923).

85. For a discussion of the way mass customization operates in new media, see, for example, Lev Manovich's discussion of variability in *The Language of New Media* (Cambridge, Mass.: MIT Press, 2001), 36–45. In fact, textiles'

variability and software's variability are similar in many ways. The "infinite possibilities" and variability that the weavers identified with their medium (i.e., soft fabrics) parallel the kind of flexibility and "scalability" of software, "in which different versions of the same media object can be generated at various sizes or level of details" (38) or modular media elements "give rise to many different versions instead of identical copies" (36). The analogy and differences between software and textiles could be drawn out further, but this would be better served as the subject of another future analysis.

86. Anni Albers's essay "The Pliable Plane: Textiles in Architecture" (1957), in *On Designing*, makes a similar argument to discuss the differences between architecture and textiles: one signals grounding and permanence whereas the other is defined by its flexibility.

87. Mark Peach, "'Der Architekt Denkt, Die Hausfrau Lenkt': German Modern Architecture and the Modern Woman," *German Studies Review* 18, no. 3 (October 1995): 441–63, 442.

88. Ibid., 454.

89. Rosemary Haag Bletter, "Expressionism and the New Objectivity," *Art Journal* 43, no. 2: Revising Modernist History: Architecture of the 1920s (Summer 1983): 108–20.

90. Bruno Taut, cited in Peach, "'Der Architekt Denkt,'" 442; translation by Peach.

91. Taut, *Die neue Wohnung*, 10–11.

92. Ibid., 5.

93. Ibid., 58–59.

94. Le Corbusier, *Towards a New Architecture* (1923), trans. Frederick Etchells (New York: Dover, 1986).

95. Taut, *Die neue Wohnung*, 64. Giedion would later repeat the equation of the housewife's domestic work with mechanics and Taylorization twenty-four years later: "The mechanization of the Housewife's work is not unlike the mechanizing of the other complex handicrafts. The alleviation of domestic drudgery proceeds along like paths: first, through mechanization of the work process; and again by its organization." Sigfried Giedion, *Mechanization Takes Command: A Contribution to Anonymous History* (1948) (New York: Norton, 1975), 5.

96. Annelise Fleischmann [Anni Albers], "Wohnökonomie," *Neue Frauenkleidung und Frauenkultur* 1 (1925): 7–8, 7. All translations of this text are mine.

97. Ibid., 7. It should be noted that Taut, like other architects of the time, also put housework in the language of "nervousness." See Wigley, *White Walls, Designer Dresses*.

98. Fleischmann [Albers], "Wohnökonomie," 7.

99. Barbara Miller Lane, *Architecture and Politics in Germany 1918–1945* (Cambridge, Mass.: Harvard University Press, 1985), 127. Lane notes how "women's magazines . . . frequently illustrated the Bauhaus buildings and the new housing projects and commented upon the virtues of the 'new dwelling.'" Lane (249, n. 8) also mentions one article from that period that responded to Taut's text: "Wohnkultur," *Frau und Gegenwart* (June 1925).

100. *Die Frau: Monatschrift für das gesamte Frauenleben unserer Zeit* was published by the Bund deutscher Frauenvereine from 1893–1944 and was edited by two prominent voices of the German movement, Helene Lange and Gertrud Bäumer. See Lydia Klante, "Die Vereinigung von Haushalt und Beruf," *Die Frau: Monatschrift für das gesamte Frauenleben unserer Zeit* 33, no. 6 (March 1926): 307–308; and Rosine Speicher-Nürnberg, "Vereinigung von Haushalt und Beruf," *Die Frau* 33, no. 8 (May 1926): 491–93.

101. See Margarete Thomas, "Zur Frage der Rationalisierung der Hauswirtschaft," *Die Frau* 34, no. 1 (October 1926): 97–101. See also Emma Kromer, "Wohnungsprobleme der Neuzeit," in *Die Kultur der Frau: Eine Lebensymphonie der Frau des XX Jahruhundert*, ed. Ada Schmidt-Beil (Berlin-Frohnau: Verlag für Kultur und Wissenschaft, 1931). Here Kromer speaks, from a perspective of five years, of the "rationellen Hauhaltführung" in the New Dwelling movement. A copy of this book is in the Bauhaus-Archiv in Berlin, suggesting the weavers may have been aware of it.

102. Gertrud Lincke, "Wohnungsbau und Hausfrauen," *Die Frau* 33, no. 11 (August 1926): 673–79. Lincke is relatively unknown, and yet in the context of *Die Frau* magazine in 1926 she was the representative voice of the Neues Bauen. Citing Le Corbusier's *Towards a New Architecture* at length in the opening paragraph of her second text, she explicated the key aspects of his theory in order to establish its usefulness to women's thinking about the home.

103. This is the title of one article, by Erna Meyer, "Hausarbeit—Kopfarbeit," *Die Frau* 35, no. 2 (November 1927): 207–10.

104. Certain fields, however, were more pertinent to certain moments and, in fact, *Die Frau* as a whole acts as a kind of index of Germany's general social and cultural concerns at this time.

105. Grete Lihotzky, "Rationalization in the Household," reprinted in Kaes et al., *Weimar Republic Sourcebook*, 462–65; originally published as "Rationalisierung im Hauhalt," *Das neue Frankfurt* 5 (1926): 120–23.

106. Ibid., 463.

107. Peukert, *The Weimar Republic*, 100. See also Vibeke Rützou Petersen, *Women and Modernity in Weimar Germany: Reality and Representation in Popular Fiction* (New York: Berghahn, 2001).

108. See Marsha Meskimmon, *We Weren't Modern Enough: Women Artists and the Limits of German Modernism* (Berkeley: University of California Press, 1999), especially her chapters on "The Mother" and "The Hausfrau."

109. Marianne Weber, "The Special Cultural Mission of Women" (1919), cited in Kaes et al., *Weimar Republic Sourcebook*, 197. For a strong discussion of the complexities of the women's movement and in particular the ideologies of women on the Right in Weimar Germany, see Raffael Scheck, *Mothers of the Nation: Right-Wing Women in Weimar Germany* (Oxford: Berg, 2004).

110. See Ute Frevert's chapter "The Weimar Republic," in *Women in German History: From Bourgeois Emancipation to Sexual Liberation*, trans. Stuart McKinnon-Evans (Oxford: Berg, 1989), 170.

111. Baumhoff, *Gendered World of the Bauhaus*, 108.
112. For a critique of the capitalization of feminism in contemporary culture, see Nina Power, *One-Dimensional Woman* (Winchester, U.K.: O Books, 2009).
113. Rowland, "Business Management at the Weimar Bauhaus," 157.

3. The Haptics of Optics

1. The tactile has been an issue for different artistic contexts throughout modernism. For a perspective on the optical and the haptic through a discussion of *Einfühlung* (empathy) in late-nineteenth- and early-twentieth-century German discourse, see Juliet Koss, "On the Limits of Empathy," *Art Bulletin*, vol. 88, no. 1 (March 2006): 139–57. See also Margaret Olin, "Validation by Touch in Kandinsky's Early Abstract Art," *Critical Inquiry*, vol. 16, no. 1 (Autumn 1989): 144–72. The question of the tactile also emerges in criticism of post-1960s installation art; Alex Potts discusses this in "'Tactility: The Interrogation of Medium in Art of the 1960s," *Art History*, vol. 27, no. 2 (April 2004): 282–304. According to Potts, the emergence of "tactility" at this time is responsible for the dissolution of the medium (meaning painting and sculpture) in contemporary art. For an analysis of the issue of tactility in contemporary photography and film, see Jean Arnaud's essay on Michael Snow, "Touching to See," *October* 114 (Fall 2005): 5–16.
2. *bauhaus zeitschrift für gestaltung* 2 (July 1931). The issue includes Gunta Stölzl, "Die Entwicklung der Bauhaus-Weberei"; Amédée Ozenfant, "Mein Besuch in der Textilwerkstatt des Bauhauses"; and Johanna Schütz-Wolff, "An die Wolle."
3. It is important to note that, for example, Greenberg's use of term *optical* as the quintessential feature of modernist painting links his argument to a number of German and Austrian contributors to art history, beginning with Lessing and Kant, whom Greenberg mentions, but also to Aloïs Riegl, Robert Vischer, and Konrad Fiedler, all of whom were deeply influential in the Bauhaus context. In other words, the question of opticality—so integral to the modernist notion of medium specificity—was initially developed through the writings of Bauhaus practitioners.
4. Otti Berger, "Weberei und Raumgestaltung" (c. 1932–1934), folder 3, Otti Berger Files, Bauhaus-Archiv Berlin, 3. All translations of Berger's texts are mine.
5. Otti Berger, "Stoffe im Raum," *ReD* (Prague) 3, no. 5 (1930): 143–45, 143.
6. This includes those authors such as Moholy-Nagy writing on photography, the art historian Hans Hildebrandt, who wrote on wall painting and relief, Walter Gropius, and architect Ludwig Hilberseimer, all of whom contributed to the *bauhaus* magazine. For a thorough discussion of Riegl's ideas and their influence on art history, see Margaret Olin, *Forms of Representation in Alois Riegl's Theory of Art* (University Park: Penn State University Press, 1992); and Margaret Iverson, *Alois Riegl: Art History and Theory* (Cambridge, Mass.: MIT Press, 1993).

7. Jacqueline E. Jung makes the comment that in Riegl's posthumously published book *Historical Grammar of the Visual Arts* he does not use the term *haptisch*. Instead, Riegl uses the word *Tastsinn*, which can be translated as either "sense of touch" or "tactile sense," suggesting that he differentiated between these terms. Jacqueline E. Jung, "Translator's Preface," in Aloïs Riegl, *Historical Grammar of the Visual Arts*, trans. Jacqueline E. Jung (New York: Zone Books, 2004), 47.

8. Aloïs Riegl, *Late Roman Art Industry*, trans. Rolf Winkes (Rome: Giorgio Bretschneider Editore, 1985).

9. For an analysis of this genealogy, see Mitchell W. Schwarzer, "The Emergence of Architectural Space: August Schmarsow's Theory of *Raumgestaltung*," *Assemblage* 15 (August 1991): 48–61.

10. Riegl, *Late Roman Art Industry*, 23.

11. Riegl, *Historical Grammar*, 187.

12. Riegl, *Late Roman Art Industry*, 22.

13. Ibid., 25.

14. *bauhaus zeitschrift für gestaltung* 1 (1928).

15. László Moholy-Nagy, *Malerei Fotografie Film*, Bauhausbücher 8 (Munich: Albert Langen Verlag, 1925); and László Moholy-Nagy, *Von Material zu Architekur*, Bauhausbücher 14 (Munich: Albert Langen Verlag, 1929). The latter text was translated into English as *The New Vision*, trans. Daphne M. Hoffman (New York: George Wittenborn, 1967). Originally published in 1947. All citations of *Von Material zu Architekur* throughout this chapter are from *The New Vision*.

16. Lászlo Moholy-Nagy, "Photography in Advertising," in *Photography in the Modern Era: European Documents and Critical Writings, 1913–1940*, ed. Christopher Phillips (New York: Metropolitan Museum of Art and Aperture, 1989), 91; emphasis in original. Originally published as "Die Photographie in der Reklame," *Photographische Korrespondenz* (Vienna), no. 9 (September 1927): 257–60.

17. László Moholy-Nagy, "Fotografie ist Lichtgestaltung," *bauhaus zeitschrift für gestaltung* 1 (1928): 2; translation mine.

18. Ibid., 2; translation mine.

19. Rosemarie Haag Bletter, "Introduction," in Behne, *Modern Functionalist Building*, 51. Bletter provides a useful discussion of the term as it came from *Sachlichkeit*, used in earlier architectural debates. See chapter 2.

20. Moholy-Nagy, "Sharp or Unsharp? A Reply to Hans Windisch" (1929), in Phillips, *Photography in the Modern Era*, 135, 134.

21. Hugo Sieker, "Absolute Realism: On the Photographs of Albert Renger-Patzsch," in Phillips, *Photography in the Modern Era*, 114.

22. Ibid., 113; emphasis in original.

23. Hans Windisch and Moholy-Nagy debate the topic of the objectivity of the lens in Moholy-Nagy, "Sharp or Unsharp," 132–39.

24. Ernö Kállai, "Painting and Photography, with Responses from Willi Baumeister, Adolf Behne, László Moholy-Nagy," trans. Harvey L. Mendelsohn,

in Phillips, *Photography in the Modern Era*, 96. Originally published as Ernst Kállai, "Malerei und Fotografie," *i10* (Amsterdam) 1, no. 4 (1927): 148–57; with responses in *i10* 1, no. 6 (1927): 227–40.

25. Ibid., 97; emphasis added.

26. *bauhaus zeitschrift* 3, no. 2 (April–May 1929).

27. Ernö Kállai and Albert Renger-Patzsch, "Postscript to Photo-Inflation / Boom Times," reprinted in Phillips, *Photography in the Modern Era*, 140–41. Originally "nachträgliches zur photo-inflation" and "hochconjunktur," *bauhaus zeitschrift* 3, no. 4 (October–December 1929): 20. Poking fun at the "boom times" in the world of photography, the authors comment on the "recipe for success," which seems a perfect description of the kind of photographs encouraged by Moholy: "Shoot from above or below . . . the trash can as the most satisfying motif. . . . Send negative prints to the press, the monster eats everything. (Motive: new, interesting visual effects.) . . . And then let chance work for you."

28. Ernst (Ernö) Kállai, "Augendemokratie u. Dergleichen," *bauhaus zeitschrift* 3, no. 2 (April–June 1929): 18. This issue also features two other, unattributed essays, including "filmrhythmus, film gestaltung" (5–11) and "malerei und film" (12–18).

29. Kállai, "Augendemokratie," 18; translation mine.

30. Ibid.

31. The most significant contributions to the discussion of facture in modern art history are in texts on Russian constructivism, in which the term most often implies a demonstration of the means of production. See in particular Maria Gough, *The Artist as Producer: Russian Constructivism in Revolution* (Berkeley: University of California Press, 2005); and Benjamin Buchloh, "From Faktura to Factography," *October* 30 (Fall 1984): 82–108. But *facture* can also refer to the quality of execution as registered on a surface, like painting. The debates here in 1927 drew on both meanings simultaneously.

32. Kállai, "Painting and Photography," in Phillips, *Photography in the Modern Era*, 96.

33. Moholy-Nagy, response to ibid., 101.

34. Moholy-Nagy, *The New Vision*, 26. Moholy-Nagy's definition of *facture* and *surface treatment* draws on the definition of *faktura* by the constructivist theorist Nikolai Tarabukin. This theory is outlined by Maria Gough: "*Faktura* means "texture" or "facture" . . . [and] refers to the overall handling or working of the material constituents of a given medium, and thus to the process of production in general: 'By *faktura*,' the critic Tarabukin writes, 'we mean the working of the material.' In this sense, *faktura* is an integral term in the Russian vanguard's broadly modernist conception of art as a mode of production rather than expression." Gough, *The Artist as Producer*, 12.

35. Moholy-Nagy, response to Kállai, "Painting and Photography," 101–102.

36. László Moholy-Nagy, "Unprecedented Photography" and "Photography in Advertising," in Phillips, *Photography in the Modern Era*, 83–85, 86–93.

37. Moholy-Nagy, "Photography in Advertising," 90.

38. Josef Albers, cited in Leah Dickerman, "Bauhaus Fundaments," in *Bauhaus*

1919–1933: Workshops for Modernity, exhibition catalog (New York: Museum of Modern Art, 2009), 15–39, 32–34.

39. Rainer Wick, *Teaching at the Bauhaus* (Ostfildern, Germany: Hatje Kantz, 2000). Wick also argues, through reference to Herbert Marcuse, that Moholy's focus on the haptic was socially and politically motivated by the "loss" of this sense in the modern age.

40. In a side note to *Von Material zu Architektur,* Moholy-Nagy expressed his concern: "How neglected our tactile education is was demonstrated to me again recently in a striking way in a conversation with the director of a training school of nurses, who spoke of the difficulties she had encountered in teaching massage." Moholy-Nagy, *The New Vision,* 24.

41. Ibid., 23.

42. The grafting of optical onto tactile properties was made perhaps more poignant when photographs of various touch panels from Moholy-Nagy's course (including Berger's and Zierath's) were found in the pages of Moholy-Nagy's *Von Material zu Architecture.* See his *Von Material zu Architektur,* 22–23, 25–29.

43. More than thirty years later, Anni Albers would again address the question of tactility in fabric. See Albers, "Tactile Sensibility," *On Weaving,* 62–65; and this book's concluding chapter.

44. The first major text on Otti Berger was a German master's thesis by Regina Lösel, later published as an essay, "Die Textildesignerin Otti Berger (1898–1944): Vom Bauhaus zur Industrie," in *Textildesign: Voysey-Endell-Berger,* vol. 3 of *Textil- Körper-Mode,* ed. Gabriele Mentges and Heide Nixdorff (Berlin: Edition Ebersbach, 2002), 215–294, 31.

45. After Stölzl was forced to leave the Bauhaus due to a political scandal that pitted several students against her, Berger and Anni Albers took over many aspects of technical instruction.

46. I discuss these developments, which happened after she left the Bauhaus in 1932, in chapter 4.

47. Otti Berger, "Stoffe im Raum," *ReD* (Prague) 3, no. 5 (1930): 143.

48. See Stölzl, "Weaving at the Bauhaus."

49. Berger, "Stoffe im Raum," 145.

50. Lösel, "Die Textildesignerin Otti Berger," 237.

51. The topic of tactility was also considered by the futurist F. T. Marinetti, who published a manifesto on "tactilism" in 1921 in Italy. See Marinetti, "Manifest," in *Experiment Theater* (Zurich: Peter Schifferli Verlag AG, 1960). Quoting Moholy-Nagy, Marinetti "was a passionate advocate of a new kind of art, to be based on tactile sensations alone, and proposed tactile ribbons, carpets, beds, rooms, stage settings, etc." Moholy-Nagy, *The New Vision,* 24. Berger may have been acquainted with Marinetti's ideas, but Berger's discussion was more sustained than Marinetti's and involved a deeper reflection on the status of cloth in modern space and vis-à-vis other media, like photography.

52. See Hajo Düchting, ed., *Farbe am Bauhaus: Synthese und Synästhesie* (Berlin: Gebr. Mann; and Dessau: Stiftung Bauhaus, 1996).

53. Clark V. Poling, *Kandinsky's Teaching at the Bauhaus: Color Theory and Analytical Drawing* (New York: Rizzoli, 1986), 49.

54. Otti Berger, "Aufzeichnungen aus dem Kandinsky-Unterricht," Bauhaus-Archiv Berlin, Otti Berger files, folder 13, 6–9. The German: "Der Wert der Farbe kann nicht nur mit dem Auge festgestellt werden sondern auch mit allen anderen Sinnen."

55. Just as Aristotle had argued in *De Anima*, Berger suggests that to feel, or to touch, is primary to sense perception in general. Aristotle's point is further elaborated by Jean Luc-Nancy in *The Muses* (Palo Alto, Calif.: Stanford University Press, 1996): "The heterogeneity of the senses is not homothetic to that of the arts. . . . The classical distribution of the five senses either does not refer to five arts or raises infinite problems of the 'minor' arts (e.g., cooking, perfumery). As for touch, which is established by a very long tradition as the paradigm or even the essence of the senses in general, it does not open onto any kind of art. (When it is said that sculpture is an art of touch, one means touch at a distance—which may well be the essence of touch, but that does not do away with what, in sculpture, exceeds touch)" (11).

56. Lösel, "Die Textildesignerin Otti Berger," 234.

57. Berger, "Weberei und Raumgestaltung," 4.

58. Droste and Ludewig, *Das Bauhaus Webt*, 261.

59. Otti Berger, "Effect through the Material," *International Textiles* 4 (Bauhaus-Archiv Berlin, Otti Berger files, folder 27), and "Umsatzsteigerung durch Geschmacksveredelung," (Increase of Sales through the Refining of Taste) *Der Konfektionär* 47, no. 95 (November 1932), 5.

60. Berger, "Weberei und Raumgestaltung," 3.

61. Berger, "Stoffe im Raum," 145.

62. Lösel, "Die Textildesignerin Otti Berger," 237; emphasis added.

63. Berger, "Stoffe im Raum," 145.

64. *Kunstseide* translates literally as "artificial silk" and can be used to refer to either viscose silk (a material made from wood that came into widespread use in Germany during the interwar years) or rayon.

65. Berger, "Weberei und Raumgestaltung," 5.

66. *Touching for Knowing: Cognitive Psychology of Manual Perception*, ed. Yvette Hatwell, Arlette Streri, and Edouard Gentaz (Amsterdam and Philadelphia: John Benjamins B.V., 2003), 2.

67. Berger, "Weberei und Raumgestaltung," 4.

68. Ibid., 5.

69. Ibid.

70. Berger, "Stoffe und neues Bauen" (c. 1932–34), Bauhaus-Archiv Berlin, Otti Berger files, folder 3, p. 2; emphasis mine.

71. Benjamin writes, "Tactile appropriation is accomplished not so much by attention as by habit. As regards architecture, habit determines to a large extent even optical reception." Walter Benjamin, "The Work of Art in the Age of Mechanical Reproduction," in Walter Benjamin, *Illuminations*, ed.

Hannah Arendt, trans. Harry Zohn (New York: Schocken, 1968), 240. For a further discussion of Benjamin and architecture with respect to this essay, see Hilde Heynen, *Architecture and Modernity* (Cambridge, Mass.: MIT Press, 2001), 107. Benjamin's essay followed Riegl's account of "modes of perception" as historical phenomena.

72. Walter Peterhans specified his alternate anti-Moholyian program for the article "Zum gegenwärtigen Stand der Fotographie," *ReD* (Prague) 3, no. 5 (1930): 138–40. The essay is reprinted and translated in Phillips, *Photography in the Modern Era*, 170–71. His concern was that experimentation of that kind would simultaneously lead to dilettantism and academicism insofar as the details of an object would be lost.

73. *bauhaus zeitschrift für gestaltung* 1 (1928) and perhaps issue 2/3 (1928) are the issues most interested in showcasing "experimental" photography. Published just as Moholy-Nagy was leaving the Bauhaus, issue 1 from 1928 was a special issue on photography that exhibited experimental work with the medium.

74. Moholy-Nagy, *Vom Material zu Architektur*, 50.

4. Weaving as Invention

1. Otti Berger's patent was initially registered on June 16, 1932, but the *Patentschrift* for German patent 594075 was not printed until November 6, 1934.

2. Busch-Reisinger archive, Harvard University, BR 52.46–48, sample book #5.

3. Some of the textile manufacturers she worked with include C. F. Baumgärtel & Sohn, Schriever, and Websky, Hartmann & Wiesen.

4. Only a few other members of the Bauhaus sought patents for their designs, produced during or just after their tenures at the Bauhaus: Walter Gropius, Ludwig Mies van der Rohe, Marcel Breuer, and Walter Peterhans. For further discussion of the issue of intellectual property around Bauhaus design, see my "The Identity of Design as Intellectual Property," in *Bauhaus Construct: Fashioning Identity, Discourse, Modernism*, ed. Jeffrey Saletnik and Robin Schuldenfrei (London: Routledge, 2009).

5. The origins of the product known in Germany as kunstliches Rosshaar date back to the late nineteenth century. But based on the kinds of synthetic fibers being developed in the 1930s, the specific fiber Berger uses may in fact be a kind of plastic material, a vinyl or Polyvinyl chloride (PVC), developed by the I. G. Farben company in Germany between 1931 and 1938, though it is unclear if this vinyl material was made into threads or only sheets. Regina Lösel, in "Die Textildesignerin Otti," refers to the thread as a type of polyamide (255).

6. Plexiglas (methyl polymethacrylate) was invented in Germany between 1927 and 1933 by the Rhom et Hass company. Different plastics and nylons, which were invented in the United States at this time, were all advertised

with a language of "flexibility," "durability," "lightness," and "ease." Berger similarly uses this language in her patent application.

7. Walter Benjamin, *The Arcades Project*, ed. Rolf Tiedemann, trans. Howard Eiland and Kevin McLaughlin (Cambridge, Mass.: Belknap Press of Harvard University Press, 1999), 216.

8. Ibid., 221, 216. Benjamin is citing an 1865 review of two novels by Honoré de Balzac and Eugène Sue by the French literary critic Paulin Limayrac. Limayrac, according to Benjamin, criticizes *Juif errant* (*Wandering Jew*) for its "denigration of the Jesuits and the unmanageable abundance of characters who do nothing but appear and disappear: 'A novel is not a place one passes through; it is a place one inhabits.'"

9. Ibid., 220–21.

10. Helmut Lethen, *Cool Conduct: The Culture of Distance in Weimar Germany*, trans. Don Reneau (Berkeley: University of California Press, 2002). According to Lethen, the concept of the persona was theorized by Karl Vossler in 1925 and again later by Karl Löwith in 1928 with his book *Das Individuum in der Rolle des Mitmenschen*. The persona is defined as the individual whose identity as a bounded being derives from his role in society and "correspondence with others" (39). Lethen's text also makes reference to the writing of Benjamin, Kracauer, Brecht, Ernst Jünger, Carl Schmitt, and Helmuth Plessner.

11. Ibid., 33. Lethen is citing Bertolt Brecht, *Ozeanflug* (1929), in *Gesammelte Werke*, vol. 2 (Frankfurt am Main, 1967), 584.

12. Ibid., 27.

13. Ibid., 190–91.

14. Albert Sigrist, cited in Lethen, *Cool Conduct*, 191.

15. Benjamin, *The Arcades Project*, 221.

16. Otti Berger, Patent #476,966, "Improvements in or Relating to Textile Fabrics Made of Ramie Fibers," London, December 1937.

17. Ibid.

18. According to a letter from Berger's attorney Hans Heimann to the English patent office, the product known as "Lamé plume" was manufactured by the company Erste deutsche Ramie-Gesellschaft in Emmendingen, Germany. Heimann, letter to English Patent office, Re: "Gewebe (Lamé-Plume)," October 28, 1936, Bauhaus-Archiv Berlin, Otti Berger files, folder 20.

19. Plessner is quoted in Lethen, *Cool Conduct*, 57. To understand the cool persona, Lethen's book is especially concerned with analyzing the "codes of conduct" that Plessner constructs. Plessner emphasizes "the anonymity of the public sphere in which life, in all of its shadings of otherness and familiarity, can fluctuate" (ibid., 54).

20. The history of design registration is strongly connected to textile history. The first law to deal with the copyright of industrial designs in England, for instance, was the Designing and Printing Act of 1787, which specifically "gave a very limited copyright protection to those who engaged in the 'arts of designing and printing on linens, cottons, calicos and muslin' and gave proprietors the sole right of printing and reprinting them" for a specified

period of time. English Modern design law is founded even further on the Copyright of Design Act of 1839, which furthered the scope of design beyond textiles but also "considerably increased the protection afforded to fabrics by extending the law to fabrics composed of wool, silk or hair and to mixed fabrics made up of any two of the following materials: linen, cotton, wool, silk or hair." UK Patent Office, "Design History in UK," http://www.ipo.gov.uk, accessed May 3, 2013.

21. Walter Benjamin, "The Author as Producer," in *Reflections*, ed. Peter Demetz (New York: Schocken Books, 1986), 220-238. Benjamin originally wrote this text as an address to be given at the Institute for the Study of Fascism in 1934, though it is not clear he actually gave the lecture.

22. All in all, though Berger applied to patent three of her designs, only the first Möbelstoff-Doppelgewebe received both a patent and *Gebrauchsmuster* (prototype model) status in Germany. But even that object was held under increased scrutiny by the German patent office when Berger applied for renewal after two years. Given a less profitable prototype status, Gewebe (Lamé-plume) was rejected as a patent in Germany. It was later patented in England in 1938. The third, Gewebe für Möbel und Wandbekleidung, was also rejected as a patent.

23. The English representative, cited in letter from Heimann to Berger, November 2, 1936, Bauhaus-Archiv Berlin, Otti Berger files, folder 20.

24. The English representative, cited in letter from Heimann to Berger, December 9, 1937. Bauhaus-Archiv Berlin, Otti Berger files, folder 20.

25. Otti Berger, BR58.166, Busch-Reisinger archive.

26. Bauhaus-Archiv Berlin, Otti Berger files, folder 3. Somewhat paradoxically, more than a decade later Anni Albers would use a similar personification of cloth to make her argument for anonymity in design: "The tablecloth that calls, 'Here I am, look at me,' is invading the privacy of the consumer. The curtains that cry, 'We are beautiful, your attention please,' but whisper 'though not very practical, we will need much of your time to keep us in shape,' are badly designed." Albers, "Design: Anonymous and Timeless," in *On Designing*, 7. I will explore this text by Albers further in the conclusion.

27. Berger, cited in Lösel, "Die Textildesignerin Otti Berger," 244.

28. Ibid.

29. Ibid.

30. Dr. Else Meißner, "Kunstschutz auf Textilemuster," *Die Form* 2, no. 3 (March 1927): 92–94. Basing her argument on painterly questions of composition, she examines questions of copyright according to its artistic value. However, Meißner never examines the question of textile design protection from the vantage of structure, purpose, or procedure, as would have been relevant to Berger's patented inventions.

31. Part of the reason for misattribution within and outside the Bauhaus-Archiv is likely due to a general lack of specialized knowledge about textiles. Anja Baumhoff makes this observation: "The image and the status of the women weavers and their success depended on the appreciation of their work, yet the technical sophistication of the woven fabric was only visible to spe-

cialists, seldom to the untrained eye." Baumhoff, *The Gendered World of the Bauhaus*, 84.

32. Magdalena Droste, *Gunta Stölzl*, 226. Droste notes that "textiles intended for use and commodity sale existed during the entire span of the Bauhaus. . . . Many of these fabrics were anonymous, which was encouraged in the area of prototype development. As such, one cannot clearly attribute many [of the workshop's] fabric designs" (my translation).

33. Droste and Ludewig, *Das Bauhaus Webt*, 232. The prototypes are in Bauhaus-Archiv Berlin, Polytex-Textil collection.

34. Most discussions of the chair do not acknowledge the significance of the fabric for the overall function of the design. See Christopher Wilk, *Marcel Breuer: Furniture and Interiors* (New York: Museum of Modern Art, 1981); Magdalena Droste, *Marcel Breuer* (London: Taschen, 1994); Alexander von Vegesack and Matthias Remmele, eds., *Marcel Breuer: Design and Architecture*, trans. Jeffrey Lieber, Ian Pepper, Julia Thorson (Weil am Rhein: Vitra Design Stiftung, 2003). Wilk's discussion of the club armchair mentions the use of *Eisengarn*—a material "formerly used only in military belts and boot laces"—but does not indicate that Breuer's chair used a version of the cloth woven by the weaving workshop (38).

35. According to the editors Jeannine Fiedler and Peter Feierabend of *Bauhaus*, the fabric, which is now manufactured by Tecta and called "metallized yarn," is attributed to Bauhaus weaver Grete Reichardt (632). However, an exhibit in 2004 at the Bauhaus Museum Berlin that focused on the Afrikanische Stuhl (made in collaboration with weaver Gunta Stölzl) and the evolution of Breuer's subsequent chair designs suggested that Stölzl was the designer of the Eisengarn fabric for the original tubular steel furniture.

36. Éva Forgács, *The Bauhaus Idea and Bauhaus Politics*, trans. John Bátki (Budapest: Central European University Press, 1995), 126.

37. Walter Gropius, "Breviary for Bauhaus Members (Draft)," in Wingler, *The Bauhaus*, 76.

38. Frederic Schwartz's *The Werkbund* explores the history of an antagonism between the collective and the individual. Schwartz describes the debate in the Deutscher Werkbund between Hermann Muthesius and Henry van de Velde over the merits of the Typ versus Individuality, and suggests this may be foundational to the debates later engaged at the Bauhaus. Muthesius's *Typ*, the prototype form, foregrounded function and simplicity in order to better streamline production and provide a simple identifiable form that a customer could easily associate with the Werkbund as an entity. By contrast, van de Velde's focus on individuality insisted on maintaining the look of the individual object as a reflection of each unique designer, much like the model of the artist.

39. Sigfried Giedion, *Mechanization Takes Command: A Contribution to Anonymous History* (New York: W. W. Norton, 1975). Originally published in 1948.

40. The topic has been addressed more recently by Magdalena Droste in "The Bauhaus Object between Authorship and Anonymity," in *Bauhaus Construct*,

ed. Saletnik and Schuldenfrei. See also Iain Boyd Whyte, *Bruno Taut and the Architecture of Activism* (Cambridge: Cambridge University Press, 1982), which includes a chapter on the Unbekannten Architekten (Unknown Architects) exhibition organized by the Arbeitsrat für Kunst in 1919. Whyte addresses the relationship between the collective and the unknown architect.

41. The Bauhaus logo was never legally trademarked, but it functioned similarly. The topic of the trademark and branding in early German design history is explored at length in Frederic J. Schwartz, "Commodity Signs: Peter Behrens, the AEG, and the Trademark," *Journal of Design History* 9, no. 3 (1996): 153–84, and in part III of *The Werkbund*. According to Schwartz, the German Werkbund found the trademark to be most profitable to its interests. By having "the power to set prices, go straight to the retailer, or even to become one itself," with the trademark the German Werkbund was in a better position to promote "basic" good design, in contrast to the excessive ornamentation and the fashionable flourishes that were added by marketers.

42. On this matter, Anja Baumhoff cites a student campaign by Emil Lange, who in June 1922 became the managing director of the school, and soon ran into similar problems as a master of craft. He wrote letters to Gropius pointing out what he felt were contradictions in the policy. Baumhoff writes: "Some Bauhäusler felt exploited, he said, and disliked the way in which the differences between masters, artists and students were emphasized. . . . The Bauhaus image consisting of famous masters of form and an 'an anonymous mass to be exploited' had to be changed." Baumhoff, *Gendered World of the Bauhaus*, 35–36.

43. Forgács, *The Bauhaus Idea and Bauhaus Politics*, 152. Standard Möbel had financial problems from the start, and so Breuer began to manufacture and market his designs first through Lorenz and then Thonet simultaneously. This situation is reported in further depth in Forgács's chapter, "Why Did Gropius Leave?"

44. Breuer, quoted in Wilk, *Marcel Breuer*, 40; and in Forgács, *The Bauhaus Idea and Bauhaus Politics*, 152.

45. Marcel Breuer also dealt with legal difficulties over the question of authorship and technical innovation with his tubular steel cantilever chair design, and it seems that legal issues began to pervade avant-garde design at this moment. See Otakar Macel, "Avant-Garde Design and the Law: Litigation over the Cantilever Chair," *Journal of Design History* 3, no. 2/3 (1990): 125–43.

46. See Wigley, *White Walls, Designer Dress*, 65–66. According to Wigley, Gropius's 1913 essay is basically a reiteration of Behrens's argument in his 1910 lecture "Kunst und Technik" (Art and Technology). Here Behrens deployed Aloïs Riegl's art historical arguments against Gottfried Semper's "materialism" to claim architecture was "art"—and thus deserving of a signature—not simply (anonymous) engineering.

47. Interestingly, Sigfried Giedion praised Gropius's "faith" in the concept of collectivity or teamwork. Regarding the idea of teamwork in relation to the

American TAC (The Architect's Collaborative), for which Gropius was the founding member, Giedion wrote: "The idea of *teamwork* is part of Gropius' very nature as well as of his actions. His faith in the value of teamwork—of human cooperative effort—has stood unshaken throughout his life. . . . Under the name of 'The Architect's Collaborative' his own name has become absorbed within the team . . . with partners and associates," such as Adolph Meyer or, later in America, Marcel Breuer. Sigfried Giedion, *Walter Gropius: Work and Teamwork* (New York: Reinhold, 1954), 13–14. One might say that the contradictions of modern architectural discourse were manifold in the figure of Walter Gropius.

48. Similarly, years later Breuer left an architectural partnership with Gropius when the two were at Harvard because of Breuer's feeling that Gropius's name dominated all of Breuer's designs.

49. Hannes Meyer, quoted in Forgács, *The Bauhaus Idea and Bauhaus Politics*, 163.

50. Georg Simmel, "Group Expansion and the Development of Individuality," in *On Individuality and Social Forms*, ed. Donald N. Levine, trans. Richard P. Albares (Chicago: University of Chicago Press, 1971), 252.

51. The obvious correlative example today would be the fact that companies and stores like Ikea, Moss, Design Within Reach, and Target exploit the name of designers for marketing purposes.

52. Another example would be the "wandering Jew," whose capacity to "disappear and reappear" is also a feature of his or her anonymity. This identity is referenced in Benjamin's *Arcades Project* (221).

53. Baumhoff, *Gendered World of the Bauhaus*, 83.

54. Kathleen Canning, *Languages of Labor and Gender: Female Factory Work in Germany, 1850–1914* (Ithaca, N.Y.: Cornell University Press, 1996), 2.

55. Ibid., 3. Canning is citing Robert Wilbrandt.

56. Ibid., 1.

57. Alfons Thun, cited in ibid., 36.

58. See Judith Butler, "Sexual Inversions," in *Feminist Interpretations of Michel Foucault*, ed. Susan J. Hekman (University Park: University of Pennsylvania Press, 1996).

59. Canning, *Languages of Labor and Gender*, 44. Canning is citing Thun.

60. Even after the return to so-called normal statistics in other industries following the upsurge in women workers during the war, in 1922 for every 165 men in the textile industry there were 226 women. See K. Gaebel-Berlin, "Die Frau in der industriellen Arbeit," *Die Frau Monatschrift* 33, no. 3 (December 1925): 166–69, 166.

61. In Lethen's investigation of Plessner, he comments on the role of the woman in Plessner's texts: "Banned from the world of artificiality . . . woman is still the preserver of first nature, because she is incapable of realizing an identity in the 'second fatherland' of the symbolic order." Lethen, *Cool Conduct*, 67, 47.

62. Irmgard Keun, *Das Kunstseidene Mädchen* (Frankfurt am Main: Fischer Bücherei, 1964). There are several good discussions of Keun as a female

author in Weimar culture and the impact of her novel on contemporary perceptions of women. See, for instance, Katharina von Ankum, "Gendered Urban Spaces in Irmgard Keun's *Das Kunstseidene Mädchen*," in *Women in the Metropolis: Gender and Modernity in Weimar Culture,* ed. Katharina von Ankum (Berkeley: University of California Press, 1997).

63. Lethen, *Cool Conduct,* 193.

64. For another discussion of the contrast between masculine and feminine counterparts in this context (the flaneur and the prostitute), particularly in the writing of Walter Benjamin and Georg Simmel, see Janet Wolff, "The Invisible Flaneuse: Women and the Literature of Modernity," in *The Problems of Modernity: Adorno and Benjamin,* ed. Andrew Benjamin (London: Routledge, 1989), 141–56; and Janet Wolff, "The Feminine in Modern Art: Benjamin, Simmel and the Gender of Modernity," *Theory, Culture & Society* 17, no. 6. (December 2000): 33–53.

65. Mark Peach, for instance, comments on the fact the *"neue Frau* was not necessarily identical with the *neue Mensch."* Peach, "Der Architekt Denkt," 461, n. 5.

66. See Maria Brinckmann, "Charakteristik des Schönen fur einige Textilien," and Johanna Schütz-Wolff, "Werkstoff—Technik—Form: Zum Weben von Bildteppichen," *Die Form* 1, no. 15 (December 1926); and Meißner, "Kunstschutz auf Textilemuster."

67. Richard Lisker, "Über Gewebte Stoff," *Die Form* 8, no. 3 (March 1933): 65–74; translation mine.

68. Ibid., 70.

69. See Stölzl's argument in 1931 in "Utility Textiles of the Bauhaus Weaving Workshop" (cited in Wingler, *Bauhaus,* 174). See chapter 2 for further discussion of this text.

70. Sigmund von Weech, "Handwerk und Maschine in der Weberei," *Die Form* 8, no. 3 (March 1933): 75–82, 75; translation mine.

71. Anni Albers, "Bauhausweberei," 188. See chapter 2 for further discussion of this text.

72. Otti Berger, "Umsatzsteigerung durch Geschmacksveredelung," *Der Konfektionär* 95 (30 November 1932): 5. The pages of the essay Berger published in *International Textiles* are found in the Otti Berger files at the Bauhas-Archiv Berlin.

73. Kees Gispen, *Poems in Steel: National Socialism and the Politics of Inventing from Weimar to Bonn* (New York: Berghahn, 2002), 8, 30–31.

74. Ibid., 45.

75. Ibid., 9. The author also notes that reform of the Patent Code, with origins in the Great Depression, became an important source for Nazi control of the government.

76. One might reference here Hannah Arendt's discussion of the "right to have rights" in *Origins of Totalitarianism* (New York: Houghton Mifflin Harcourt, 1973); or Giorgio Agamben's *Homo Sacer: Sovereign Power and Bare Life,* trans. Daniel Heller-Roazen (Stanford, Calif.: Stanford University Press, 1998), which explores the dialectic of biopolitical life (or national iden-

tity) and "bare life," and draws on German critical theorists important to the Weimar era—Benjamin and Carl Schmitt.

77. See Walter Gropius papers, Houghton Library, Harvard University, Cambridge, Massachusetts, container 446.

Conclusion

1. In a recorded interview with Nicholas Fox Weber in 1995, Anni Albers relays portions of the narrative that brought her and Josef to Black Mountain College in America. One of the details she recounts is how Philip Johnson later referred to her diploma project for soundproofing and light-reflective wall fabric using cellophane and chenille, which he saw on a visit to the Bauhaus in 1932, as her "passport to America." He not only secured their visas but also recommended them for positions at the college. "Anni Albers: Interview" (takes 1–3), February 1, 1995: raw footage for *Bauhaus in America* (dir. Judith Pearlman, Clio Films). A VHS copy of this footage is located in the Josef and Anni Albers Foundation Archives in Bethany, Conn.

2. Brenda Danilowitz points out that Albers's view of education would lead her to think that "theoretical knowledge can be useless knowledge and an impediment to creation." Danilowitz, "Introduction," in *Selected Writings on Design*, xi. Nicholas Fox Weber also emphasized this point in my conversation with him (June 2008).

3. Nicholas Fox Weber, "Anni Albers: Interview." Weber asks Albers about the fact that her students said they felt under her tutelage "they were starting at point zero."

4. See, for example, Jacques Derrida's discussion of the aporia of the concept of touch in Aristotle and Jean-Luc Nancy, in Derrida, *On Touching—Jean-Luc Nancy*, trans. Christine Irizarry (Stanford, Calif.: Stanford University Press, 2005).

5. Anni Albers, "Introductory Note," *On Weaving*, 13.

6. Anni Albers, "Preface," *On Weaving*, 15.

7. Anni Albers, "Tactile Sensibility," *On Weaving*, 62.

8. For a discussion of the "philological preconditions" of the concept of media, as based in "the ancient arts of rhetoric, logic, and dialectic," see John Guillory, "Genesis of the Media Concept," *Critical Inquiry* 36, no. 2 (Winter 2010): 321-362.

9. Anni Albers, "Anni Albers: Interview." She even goes so far as to say that she suspected the translator was "related to a Nazi." While it may only be evidence of the Albers's postwar paranoia, this association interestingly foregrounds how underlying ideological differences would render translation so difficult.

10. Anni Albers, "Work with Material," *On Designing*, 53.

11. Ibid., 50–51.

12. Anni Albers, "Art—A Constant," *On Designing*, 45–46. Although Albers seems to reference the language of Martin Heidegger here, it's not clear she ever read his work. This statement is surprisingly similar to an essay

by Heidegger, originally delivered as a lecture in Germany in 1950. Martin Heidegger, "The Thing," in *The Craft Reader*, ed. Glenn Adamson, 404–408.

13. Albers, "Design: Anonymous and Timeless," *On Designing*, 6.

14. Anni Albers, "Tapestry," *On Weaving*, 68. Albers writes: "Along with cave paintings, threads were among the earliest transmitters of meaning."

15. Nicholas Fox Weber, "Foreword," in Anni Albers, *Selected Writings on Design*, ed. Brenda Danilowitz (Hanover, N.H.: University Press of New England, 2000), vii.

16. Ibid., 69.

17. Anni Albers's "Material as Metaphor" was written for a panel at the College Art Association's annual conference in 1982. The typescript of the text has been printed in *Selected Writings*, 73–75.

18. In *Understanding Media: The Extensions of Man* (Cambridge, Mass.: MIT Press, 1994), Marshall McLuhan notes: "The word 'metaphor' is from the Greek *meta* plus *pherein*, to carry across or transport" (89).

19. See Brenda Danilowitz, "'We Are Not Alone,'" in *Anni and Josef Albers: Latin American Journeys*, exhibition catalog, ed. Brenda Danilowitz and Heinz Liesbrock (Ostfildern: Hatje Cantz Verlag, 2007), 23.

20. Virginia Gardner Troy, *Anni Albers and Ancient American Textiles*, 148; emphasis in original.

21. Ibid., 153.

22. Ibid., 147, 155. Troy suggests that Albers had "surely seen the royal Inca *tocapu* tunic at Dumbarton Oaks" in Washington, D.C., by the time she wove *Pictographic* (155).

23. Ibid., 153. Troy writes: "Like much of modernism, and like many Andean textiles, her work was self-referential." In her chapter 7, Troy cites Albers's combined experience at the Bauhaus, her viewing of a De Stijl exhibition in 1951 at the Museum of Modern Art in New York, and her interest in Andean textiles as influencing her modernist approach to the pictorial weavings.

24. On the contradictory operations of transparency and obfuscation in software code, see Alexander Galloway, *The Interface Effect* (Cambridge: Polity Press, 2012), 69.

25. Or, as Galloway says of the "occult logic" of numbers (the numerical coding of data): "They are hidden at exactly the moment when they express themselves." Ibid., 66.

26. Anni Albers collected and apparently unraveled and studied several textile artifacts from ancient Peru—like the "sampler" currently found at the Josef and Anni Albers Foundation and reproduced in *On Weaving*, plate 80.

27. According to her essay, most theories focused on the potential of an alternative loom type, whereas Albers speculates that the use of a tubular weave construction (similar to double weave, though the layers are unconnected) is what enabled these ancient weavers to create these wide pieces of cloth. See "A Structural Process in Weaving: A Suggestion Applied to a Weaving Problem of a Remote Past and Applicable Today," in *On Designing*, 65-78.

28. In *On Weaving*, several years later, Anni will dedicate an entire chapter and

many pages of her book to a discussion of draft notation and the reproduction of weave drafts for different kinds of woven structures.

29. Important to understand the weave draft's grid is that weaves are typically divided into three basic structures: plain, twill, and satin. (We'll ignore leno or gauze/open weaves, for the moment.) Out of these basic structures, new structures can be formed and recombined to create new designs for cloth.

30. *On Designing,* 79.

31. Anni Albers, *On Weaving,* 38.

32. Anni Albers, "Art—A Constant," *On Designing,* 46.

33. Ibid., 41–48. Although Albers provides the date of 1939, Brenda Danilowitz notes in the bibliography of *Anni Albers: Selected Writings on Design* (77) that this essay wasn't published until 1959, when it appeared in the first edition of *On Designing,* published by Pellango Press.

34. Albers, "Art—A Constant," *On Designing,* 46; emphasis mine.

35. Rosalind Krauss, *Under Blue Cup* (Cambridge, Mass.: MIT Press, 2011), 25.

36. Interestingly, the same year that Albers wrote "Art—A Constant" in which she first used the word *medium,* Greenberg set this term into play in one of the first of his canonical essays on art, "Avant-garde and Kitsch" (1939), in Clement Greenberg, *The Collected Essays and Criticism,* vol. 1, ed. John O'Brian (Chicago: University of Chicago Press, 1988), 5–22.

37. See Marshall McLuhan, *The Gutenberg Galaxy: The Making of Typographic Man* (Toronto: University of Toronto Press, 1962; and *Understanding Media: The Extensions of Man* (Cambridge, Mass.: MIT Press, 1994). In the latter, the quoted axiom is typically interpreted to be some kind of literal argument that the medium's physical form is equivalent to the medium's content, but it is a bit more complicated. McLuhan writes on the first page of the book's first chapter: "In a culture like ours, long accustomed to splitting and dividing all things as a means of control, it is sometimes a bit of a shock to be reminded that, in operational and practical fact, the medium is the message. This is merely to say that the personal and social consequences of any medium—that is, of any extension of ourselves—result from the new scale that is introduced into our affairs by each extension of ourselves, or by any new technology." McLuhan goes on to make much of the relationship between communication and metaphor. In fact, this book may best be read as a series of metaphors about media and their role in society than an analytical set of truths.

38. The exemplary texts would be Greenberg's "Modernist Painting" (1960, revised 1965), and McLuhan's *Understanding Media.*

39. Marshall McLuhan and Quentin Fiore, *The Medium Is the Massage: An Inventory of Effects* (Berkeley, Calif.: Gingko Press, 1996), 34–37. Originally published in 1967.

40. Greenberg, "Modernist Painting," 90. It is useful to compare this essay with McLuhan's chapter "Media Hot and Cold," in *Understanding Media.*

41. Albers, "Design: Anonymous and Timeless," *On Designing,* 7.

42. Cited in "Anni Albers: Interview."

43. Interview with Nicholas Fox Weber by author, June 10, 2008.

44. Josef Albers, "On My Variants," reprinted in *Anni and Josef Albers: Latin American Journeys,* 147.
45. Josef Albers, *Interaction of Color: Text of the Original Edition with Selected Plates* (New Haven, Conn.: Yale University Press, 1971), 74; emphasis mine.
46. Ibid., 73.
47. Ibid., 45.
48. Ibid., 72–73.
49. Ibid., 44.
50. Ibid., 73.
51. Jeffrey Saletnik has also argued that Josef Albers's approach to painting is based in a pedagogical philosophy of active engagement, which may explain why Greenberg was so dismissive of and didn't understand the artist's work. See Saletnik, "Pedagogic Objects: Josef Albers, Greenbergian Modernism, and the Bauhaus in America," in *Bauhaus Construct,* ed. Saletnik and Schuldenfrei, 83–102.
52. Importantly, I am not suggesting that Anni's husband directly influenced her on this point. It is more likely that the couple worked in parallel and arrived at similar ideas around the same time. Any supposed influence would have been a two-way street.
53. For a related discussion of the pedagogy and practice of Josef Albers at Black Mountain College, see Adamson, *Thinking through Craft,* 81–87. Adamson draws a comparison between Josef Albers and the educational philosophy of John Dewey, who was especially important in the founding of that school, though as Adamson concedes, Albers did not "believe in him much" (Albers, cited in ibid., 84). Interestingly, Adamson does not consider contemporaneous texts by Anni Albers in *Thinking through Craft,* though she was arguably a more prolific writer on this subject.
54. Albers, "Weaving Workshop," in Bayer et al., *Bauhaus 1919–1928,* 56-59, 140–45; and Albers, "Weaving at the Bauhaus," *On Designing.* The latter essay provides the precise months and years of the two versions at the end: "September, 1938 (Revised July, 1959)."
55. Albers, "Weaving at the Bauhaus," 38.
56. Ibid., 39.
57. Albers, "Weaving Workshop," 141.
58. Albers, "Weaving at the Bauhaus," 39–40.
59. Alfred North Whitehead, cited in ibid., 39. This quote comes from Whitehead's *Adventures of Ideas* (London: Cambridge University Press, 1933, 1942), 95.
60. Sometime after moving to the United States, Albers became an avid reader of Whitehead's work and later cited him as an influence (see Weber, "Foreword," in *Anni Albers: Selected Writings,* viii), though it seems she read from his oeuvre somewhat selectively.
61. Albers, "Design: Anonymous and Timeless," 6.
62. To further understand the relationship between specificity or specific skills and their abstraction under professionalized modes of specialization, it helps to invoke Marx on the difference between labor under guild and

capitalist modes of production: "In guild and craft labour, where capital itself still has a limited form, and is still entirely immersed in a particular substance, hence is not yet capital as such, labour, too, appears as still immersed in its particular specificity: not in the totality and abstraction of labour as such, in which it confronts capital. . . . On the other side [under capital] . . . labour loses all the characteristics of art; as its particular skill becomes something more and more abstract and irrelevant, and as it becomes more and more a purely abstract activity, a purely mechanical activity, hence indifferent to its particular form; a merely formal activity, or, what is the same, a merely material [*stofflich*] activity, activity pure and simple." Marx, *Grundrisse*, 296.

63. Whitehead, cited in Albers, "Design: Anonymous and Timeless," 5. Quote from Alfred North Whitehead, *Science and the Modern World, Lowell Lectures, 1925* (New York: Macmillan, 1960), 282–83.

64. Whitehead, *Science and the Modern World*, 142. Whitehead continues: "This discipline of knowledge applies beyond technology to pure science, and beyond science to general scholarship. It represents the change from amateurs to professionals."

65. Ibid., 141.

66. Ibid., 286–87.

67. Ibid., 287.

68. Ibid., 288.

69. Threaded throughout Whitehead's *Science and the Modern World* and contemporaneous texts about a philosophy of education are hints of his incipient "process philosophy," which he would elaborate four years later in *Process and Reality: An Essay in Cosmology* (New York: Free Press, 1978). Originally published in 1929.

70. When asked whether Anni Albers's ever sought intellectual property protection for her work, Nicolas Fox Weber said, "She didn't care much for issues of copyright. She found it uninteresting." Author's interview with Weber, June 10, 2008.

71. Albers, "Anni Albers: Interview."

72. Albers, "Art—A Constant," 45.

73. Ibid.

74. Ibid., 44.

75. Ibid.

76. Ibid. Although Albers dates "Art—A Constant" to November 1939, it was not published until the first edition of *On Designing* in 1959, and so it is possible this discussion of "today's technique of communication" was also informed by the increasingly rapid technological developments of the 1950s.

77. Gyorgy Kepes, *The Language of Vision* (Chicago: Paul Theobold, 1967), 12–13. Originally published in 1944.

78. For an excellent discussion of Kepes's influence within the postwar field of design, especially as it integrated the "organicist" and "networked" logic of the industrial-military complex, see Reinhold Martin, "Organicism's Other," *Grey Room* 4 (Summer 2001): 34–51.

79. Gyorgy Kepes, "Preface," *The New Landscape in Art and Science,* ed. Kepes (Chicago: Paul Theobold, 1956, 1967), 17. Kepes references C. S. Peirce on the principles of logic as a "guide" for his method. Interestingly, the quote he cites is suggestive of Anni Albers's interest in the methodological possibilities based on the "event of the thread." Here is Peirce, cited in Kepes, 17: "Its reasoning should . . . form . . . a cable whose fibers may be ever so slender, provided they are sufficiently numerous and intimately connected."

80. Ibid.

81. Gyorgy Kepes, "Introduction," *The New Landscape,* 19.

82. Ibid., 19. Kepes continues: "Knowledge gained by [scientific advancements] has given the additional resources of nuclear energy, new materials, new techniques and means of transportation and communication. We now possess machines that can react and, after a fashion, think. . . . Precise and flexible control of machinery and appliances is now possible without human intervention, as instruments connected by complicated electrical circuits carry out the appropriate thought-processes. The widespread applications of these, from automatic doors to radar and electronic computers, suggest that men will need progressively less of their physical and nervous energy for routine tasks and will be left freer for more creative work" (19–20).

83. The Josef and Anni Albers Foundation archive has a letter from Gyorgy Kepes to Anni Albers, dated January 28, 1960, thanking her for sending her book. A letter from Josef Albers to Kepes, dated January 22, 1957, congratulates him on his book (to which Josef contributed images of his work) and thanks him for a copy. An excerpt of R. Buckminster Fuller's review of *On Designing* can be found on the back cover of the third (1979) printing of that book; a copy of that review is also located in the Albers Foundation archive. Fuller contributed the essay "Conceptuality of Fundamental Structures" to *Structure in Art and Science,* ed. Gyorgy Kepes, Vision + Value Series (New York: George Braziller, 1965).

84. Albers, "Anni Albers: Interview."

85. Albers, "Preface," *On Weaving,* 15.

86. Albers, "Designing as Visual Organization," *On Weaving,* 78.

87. For further discussion of Anni Albers's interest in the Meso- and South American archaeological field, see Troy, *Anni Albers and Ancient American Textiles*; and Danilowitz, "'We Are Not Alone.'" In *On Weaving,* Albers cites the research of archaeologist and textile specialist Junius Bird, who was then curator of South American artifacts at the American Museum of Natural History in New York.

88. Albers, "Early Techniques of Thread Interlacing," *On Weaving,* 57–58.

89. See Sadie Plant, *Zeroes + Ones: Digital Women and the New Technoculture* (New York: Doubleday, 1997).

90. In this sense, *On Weaving* is similar to George Kubler's *The Shape of Time: Remarks on the History of Things* (New Haven, Conn.: Yale University Press, 1962). Kubler's book is perhaps the most prominent methodological challenge to conceptions of history and formalism in that era (he argues against

"biological" metaphors and linear time using metaphors borrowed from astronomy and cybernetics). Although there is no record in the Josef and Anni Albers Foundation archive of Anni having read or owned Kubler's book, she was certainly familiar with his work, having attended his course on Mesoamerican textiles in 1952. She later published her final essay for the course as "A Structural Process in Weaving: A Suggestion Applied to a Weaving Problem of a Remote Past and Applicable Today," in *On Designing*, 65–78.

91. Bloch is cited in Fredric Jameson, *The Political Unconscious: Narrative as a Socially Symbolic Act* (Ithaca, N.Y.: Cornell University Press, 1981), 97.

92. Ibid., 95. See Albers, *On Weaving*, plate 9. The caption reads: "A modern weaving room. One man (in corner of photograph) is supervising the weaving of the looms shown here—in some cases as many as one hundred looms."

93. Albers, "The Loom," *On Weaving*, 25, 22.

94. Florian Pumhösel, "Textiles and Abstract Pictures," presented at Textiles: Open Letter; A Haptic Space: Praxis and Discourse, conference held at the Academy of Fine Arts, Vienna, December 14, 2012.

95. See Auther, *String Felt Thread*, especially her second chapter, "Process Art, Postminimalism, and Materiality," where she discusses the formal and structural resemblance of fiber art in the 1960s and early '70s to the postminimalist work of Eva Hesse and Robert Morris.

96. See Mildred Constantine and Jack Lenor Larsen, *Wall Hangings*, exhibition catalog (New York: Museum of Modern Art, 1969); and *Beyond Craft: The Art Fabric* (New York: Van Nostrand Reinhold, 1972).

97. See the following essays and book by Rosalind Krauss: "'. . . And Then Turn Away?' An Essay on James Coleman," *October* 81 (Summer 1997); "Reinventing the Medium," *Critical Inquiry* 25, no. 2 (Winter 1999); "'The Rock': William Kentridge's Drawings for Projection," *October* 92 (Spring 2000); "*A Voyage on the North Sea": Art in the Age of the Post-medium Condition* (London: Thames & Hudson, 2000).

98. Krauss, "*A Voyage on the North Sea*," 10, 5.

99. Specifically, she cites Stanley Cavell, *The World Viewed* (Cambridge, Mass.: Harvard University Press, 1979); and Jean-Luc Nancy *The Muses*, trans. Peggy Kamuf (Stanford, Calif.: Stanford University Press, 1996). Krauss considers Cavell's redefinition of the medium of film as a matter of "rules" and "conventions," which he names "automatism." Krauss, "*A Voyage on the North Sea*," 5.

100. Krauss initially provides this definition in the preface to "*A Voyage on the North Sea*," (6–7), in reference to the words of Maurice Denis on painting. She repeats this wording in several places, including *Under Blue Cup*, 4.

101. Krauss, "*A Voyage on the North Sea*," 57, n. 4.

102. Josef Vogl, "Becoming Media: Galileo's Telescope," *Grey Room* 29 (Winter 2008): 14–25, 23.

103. Ibid., 23.

104. Eva Horn's "Editor's Introduction: There Are No Media," *Grey Room* 29 (Winter 2008), explains how new work in German media theory, like Vogl's, is largely indebted to the Foucaultian-discursive approach of Friedrich Kittler.

105. Vogl, "Becoming Media," 16.

T'ai Smith is assistant professor of art history at the University of British Columbia, Vancouver.